# AGAINST CYBERCRIME

This book advances a theoretically informed realist criminology of computer crime. Looking beyond current strategies of online crime control, this book argues for a new sort of policy that addresses the root causes of computer crime and criminality, reduces the harms experienced by the victims of such crimes, and does not unduly contribute to state and corporate power and surveillance.

Drawing both on the proponents of realist criminology and on those who have leveled critiques of the approach, Steinmetz illustrates the contours of a realist criminology of computer crime by considering definitions of harm with online crime, the idiosyncrasies of online locality and community, the social relations of computer crime, the tension between piecemeal reform and structural changes, and other matters. Furthermore, Steinmetz surveys the methodological dimensions of computer crime research, offers a critique of positivist "computational criminology," and posits an agenda for computer crime policy.

*Against Cybercrime* is an essential reading for all those engaged with cybercrime, realist criminology, criminological theory, and social harm online.

**Kevin F. Steinmetz** is Professor at the Department of Sociology, Anthropology, and Social Work, Kansas State University, USA.

## New Directions in Critical Criminology

Editor: Walter S. DeKeseredy, *West Virginia University, USA*

This series presents new cutting-edge critical criminological empirical, theoretical, and policy work on a broad range of social problems, including drug policy, rural crime and social control, policing and the media, ecocide, intersectionality, and the gendered nature of crime. It aims to highlight the most up-to-date authoritative essays written by new and established scholars in the field. Rather than offering a survey of the literature, each book takes a strong position on topics of major concern to those interested in seeking new ways of thinking critically about crime.

**Literary Theory and Criminology**
*Rafe McGregor*

**Against Cybercrime**
Toward a Realist Criminology of Computer Crime
*Kevin F. Steinmetz*

For more information about this series, please visit: www.routledge.com/New-Directions-in-Critical-Criminology/book-series/NDCC

# AGAINST CYBERCRIME

## Toward a Realist Criminology of Computer Crime

*Kevin F. Steinmetz*

Routledge
Taylor & Francis Group

LONDON AND NEW YORK

Designed cover image: © Shutterstock Images / Tithi Luadthong

First published 2024
by Routledge
4 Park Square, Milton Park, Abingdon, Oxon OX14 4RN

and by Routledge
605 Third Avenue, New York, NY 10158

*Routledge is an imprint of the Taylor & Francis Group, an informa
business*

*British Library Cataloguing-in-Publication Data*
A catalogue record for this book is available from the British Library

*Library of Congress Cataloging-in-Publication Data*
Names: Steinmetz, Kevin F., author.
Title: Against cybercrime : toward a realist criminology of
computer crime / Kevin F. Steinmetz.
Description: Abingdon, Oxon; New York, NY: Routledge, 2024. |
Series: New directions in critical criminology |
Includes bibliographical references and index. |
Identifiers: LCCN 2023012784 | ISBN 9781032235097 (hardback) |
ISBN 9781032235059 (paperback) | ISBN 9781003277996 (ebook)
Subjects: LCSH: Computer crimes. | Criminology.
Classification: LCC HV6773 .S7349 2024 |
DDC 364.16/8–dc23/eng/20230627
LC record available at https://lccn.loc.gov/2023012784

ISBN: 978-1-032-23509-7 (hbk)
ISBN: 978-1-032-23505-9 (pbk)
ISBN: 978-1-003-27799-6 (ebk)

DOI: 10.4324/9781003277996

Typeset in Sabon
by Newgen Publishing UK

*For Pamela, Elsie, and little Alice.*

# CONTENTS

# ACKNOWLEDGMENTS

This book has been a long time coming. The idea for it began as I was wrapping up my first book, *Hacked*, around 2016. Other obligations—grants, teaching, service work, family, etc.—kept me from actively working on it. Sometimes ideas are like mold, though. If we leave them unattended, they flourish and take over. That's exactly what the idea for a "realist criminology of the internet" did. The only remedy was to write the damn book and to take out my excitement and frustration during the process on friends and family alike. I got in the habit of firing off random ideas or interesting quotes I found to friends like Brian Schaefer, Eddy Green, and Carl Root. I'd coax my colleague, Travis Linnemann, out of his office with the promise of coffee and then ramble about what I was writing. For these folks, and anyone else who dealt with me during this period, you have my sincerest gratitude (and apologies).

An extra-special thanks go to Carl Root, Majid Yar, Travis Linnemann, Jordana Navarro, and Cassandra Cross who reviewed chapter drafts and provided useful feedback. I thank Travis Pratt and Jill Turanovic for giving me the opportunity to write a chapter for their *Revitalizing*

*Victimological Theory* (Routledge), which served as the genesis for this book. Adrienne McCarthy helped co-author that initial chapter and introduced me to the work of André Gorz—her contributions are appreciated. I also wish to thank Elliot Currie who graciously answered my questions about the history of realist criminology in America and consented to allow excerpts of his explanations to be included in this book (Chapter 2). Similarly, Vic Kappeler was kind enough to provide me with a transcript of a talk he gave many years ago, an excerpt of which appears in Chapter 7. Any weaknesses or mistakes in the text are entirely my own.

My friend and department head Don Kurtz also deserves appreciation for his support. Heavy is the head that wears the crown, especially when I am one of their subjects!

I also need to thank my editor, Tom Sutton, who encouraged me to write this book as well as Walter DeKeseredy, who runs the *New Directions in Critical Criminology* series, thus providing this book a home (with plenty of outstanding neighbors).

During the entire writing process, my poor wife, Pamela, had to endure my dinner-table rants on realist criminology and computer crimes more generally—which were likely both patronizing and needlessly verbose. Fortunately, she takes such things in stride and is endlessly supportive. This book, and indeed my career, would not have been possible without her.

My youngest daughter Alice was born during this time. She is ceaselessly mirthful and provided a welcome reprieve from writing. Similarly, my oldest daughter, Elsie, encouraged time away by insisting we watch her favorite movies together … many, many, many times over (she is four). I love them both.

# 1

# INTRODUCTION

In July 2021, media outlets reported that the Pegasus spyware had been found on the phones of scores journalists and activists across the world and may have been used against tens of thousands more (Amnesty International, 2021; Rueckert, 2021). The software, developed by the Israeli NSO Group, provided access to, among other things, a target's contacts, messages, calls, photos, emails, camera, microphone, and even encrypted messages on platforms like Signal, WhatsApp, and Telegram (Kirchgaessner, Lewis, Pegg, Cutler, Lakhani, & Safi, 2021). Though early iterations of the software required the phone user to click on a fraudulent link in an email or a SMS text message to be installed on their device, later versions used "zero-click" methods to covertly install the program by exploiting "zero-day" exploits or vulnerabilities which a developer is unaware of and therefore has not patched (Amnesty International, 2021). NSO Group licensed Pegasus to government entities under the auspices of criminal investigation and terrorist surveillance.

The existence of the software itself is unsurprising as it had been used for years by governments around the world

DOI: 10.4324/9781003277996-1

(Follis & Fish, 2020a; 2020b). What set this incident apart was the suggested scope of abuse of the spyware by governmental entities. While likely used for its intended investigative purposes in some instances, countries like India, Mexico, Morocco, the United Arab Emirates, and others may have used it to monitor the activities of journalists, activists, and political opponents (Rueckert, 2021; Slater & Masih, 2021). Potentially tens of thousands of such abuses may have occurred (Amnesty International, 2021; Perrigo, 2021). Some allegations are egregious, if true. For instance, reports suggest that the software may have been used to surveil Jamal Khashoggi, the Saudi journalist who was brutally murdered in 2018, and his associates (Kirchgaessner et al., 2021).

The Pegasus spyware problem highlights one of the most pressing issues confronting the regulation of online behavior: many of the tools and strategies developed to combat online crime and related threats give significant power to states and corporations which can—and have—been abused. Individual privacy and autonomy shrink. Control concentrates into the hands of the few. We live in an era where police regularly use surveillance technologies and big data analytic techniques to track suspects, gather evidence, and predict criminal activity (Brayne, 2017). Intelligence agencies have created world-spanning surveillance programs that track inconceivable amounts data on regular citizens (Snowden, 2019). Entire industries have formed around the creation, collection, distribution, and analysis of personal information—data that can be appropriated for law enforcement or intelligence purposes (Zuboff, 2015). In total, nearly every move made by anyone using a computer connected to the internet or carrying a smartphone is tracked in some capacity. While such powers may be justified for the purposes of security or marketing, there is significant potential for exploitation and abuse.

Of course, not all methods of online crime control are surveillance-based. There exist, for instance, a variety of technological target-hardening measures designed to protect systems from intrusion or other forms of malfeasance (e.g. antivirus and firewalls) (McGuire, 2016). Online platforms and services use content moderation methods to reduce the circulation of offensive, obscene, or illegal material on their systems (Roberts, 2019). More and more police agencies feature computer crime units or task forces (Jewkes & Andrews, 2005; McGuire, 2016). All these strategies are rooted in the idea that crime and victimization are a problem of improperly deterred individuals seizing available criminal opportunities. They thus seek to circumscribe these opportunities, detect and deter criminal behavior, and encourage self-policing among internet users and platforms.

Unfortunately, these strategies generally do not address the conditions which gave rise to such criminality in the first place (Hall, 2012). Little consideration is needed for why these opportunities proliferate, what factors shape the drives of perpetrators, why certain populations are more or less likely to be offenders or victims, how to ameliorate the suffering of victims, the relations of power and powerlessness that may shape criminal involvement and victimization, or how crime control methods might be abused or lead to unintended collateral consequences. They are therefore incomplete strategies for online crime control.

These approaches share their classical roots with "terrestrial" crime control strategies like situational crime prevention and hot spots policing, which similarly rely on institutional coercion (or the threat thereof), the acquisition of crime control technologies (e.g. surveillance cameras), and the removal of "incivilities" from neighborhoods (e.g. Braga, Papachristos, & Hureau, 2014; Clarke, 1980; Wilson &

Kelling, 1982). For these approaches, identifying and addressing the underlying causes of crime are unnecessary if criminal events themselves can be disrupted. Unfortunately, the effectiveness of these strategies appears rather limited. Despite massive investments in policing and prisons since the 1970s, crime rates appear mostly independent of criminal legal operations. Further, the collateral consequences of these strategies have been staggering, perpetuating systemic injustices and doing little to—or even increasing—the suffering of the downtrodden (e.g. Clear, 2007; Gottschalk, 2013; Meares, 2015; Muller & Wildeman, 2013; Platt et al., 1977; Rojek, Rosenfeld, & Decker, 2012; Steinmetz, Schaefer, & Henderson, 2016; Websdale, 2001). In other words, we cannot say with any degree of certainty that these strategies have made us safer but we can readily conclude that they have increased the power of the criminal legal system, the growth of private security and prison industries, and the suffering experienced by many who are pulled into crime control's vacuous maw.

Just as Hall and Winlow (2015, p. 23) argue that "the insidious harms inflicted on society by intensive securitization and incarceration in many ways outweigh the harms caused by street crime," so too should it be concerning that the massive expansion of online surveillance in the name of crime control and national security concentrate power online within state and commercial institutions, potentially causing more harm than online crimes themselves.[1] The imaginative among us can envision a trajectory toward a the dystopian future envisioned in cyberpunk fiction. Scholars and activists alike have denounced the threat such programs and capabilities pose for political resistance, free speech, online equity and access, privacy, life, and limb. All the while, crime continues to proliferate online.

At the same time, there is also a need to take crime seriously. Real harms are created by the predatory behavior of others (Clevenger, Navarro, Marcum, & Higgins, 2018; Mawby & Walklate, 1994). In the digital realm, research has clearly established that significant physical, emotional, psychological, financial, and other harms are experienced by victims of computer crimes like child exploitation, stalking and harassment, and fraud, to name only a few (e.g. Button & Cross, 2017; Clevenger et al., 2018; Cross, Dragiewicz, & Richards, 2018; Cross, Richards, & Smith, 2016; Domhardt, Münzer, Fegert, & Goldbeck, 2015; Dreßring, Bailer, Anders, Wagner, & Gallas, 2014; Gewirtz-Meydan, Walsh, Wolack, & Finkelhor, 2018; Whitty & Buchanan, 2016). Consider, for instance, the case of Anna, a victim of romance fraud recently featured in *The Guardian* (Cernik, 2022). Looking for companionship years after a difficult marriage and divorce, she met "Andrew" online. This person, unbeknownst to Anna, was a fabrication. But the fraudster (or fraudsters) nurtured Anna's feelings toward Andrew. Though the perpetrator evaded requests to meet in person, her feelings blossomed. Eventually, Andrew claimed to be in crisis and asked Anna for financial help. She agreed, like any good and devoted partner would. The requests began to "snowball" (ibid). Andrew befell crisis after crisis, pleading with Anna for aid each time. Eventually, he claimed to have "been taken hostage by loan sharks and was being tortured" (ibid). Months later, he asserted he was still being held hostage. At this point, the fabrication began to fall apart after she appealed to a Facebook group for information about Andrew. She was contacted and informed that the picture she posted was that of an actor. Though the abuser tempered her doubts, Anna's Facebook friend continued to insist Andrew was a fraud. She finally ended the relationship after almost two and a half years of abuse and reported the crime to the authorities. By the end of the ordeal, she had lost £350,000. She was also emotionally devastated: "It felt like losing a husband that I loved with every inch of my heart and soul."

How can we avoid or resist the concentration of power in online spaces into the hands of government or corporate officials? How can we avoid the subsequent intended and unintended consequences of such control regimes? And how can we do so while also preventing, mitigating, or ameliorating the real harms experienced by victims of computer-related crimes? To address these questions, this book advances a criminological perspective that, to date, has been underappreciated in the examination of computer crimes—*realist criminology*. Involved is a kind of "radical" or "critical victimology" that aims to reduce victimization through social policies designed to address crime *and* their structural antecedents (DeKeseredy & Schwartz, 1991; Jones, MacLean, & Young, 1986, pp. 2–3; Lea & Young, 1984; Phipps, 1986; Walklate, 2015). It accepts that there are real, tangible harms experienced by victims that cannot be dismissed as artifacts of public panic, political discourse, and media reporting. At the same time, realist criminology rejects the position that crime is purely a product of opportunistic choices by improperly deterred individuals that can be squelched through tough-on-crime policies and surveillance. While choice may certainly be a factor, realist criminologists acknowledge that social structure and power shape the material conditions from which crime and victimization emerge. Thus, to address crime and victimization effectively and ethically, criminologists must look to identify and address underlying causes and find ways to reduce suffering.

Realist criminology began with the emergence of Left Realism or "New Left Realism" in Britain during the 1980s (Lowman & MacLean, 1992). During this period, radical criminologists like John Lea and Jock Young (1984) recognized that one of the most significant problems confronting British working classes were intra-class forms of crime and victimization, particularly violence. These criminologists focused on creating crime control policies that work "in and against" the system to ameliorate the harms caused by crime while also addressing those caused by social structure and circumstance (Matthews, 2016, p. 3). Similar movements emerged in the United States, Canada, and Australia (e.g. Brown & Hogg, 1992; Currie, 1998; 2010; DeKeseredy & Schwartz, 1991; Lowman & MacLean, 1992).

Moving beyond the Left Realism of the 1980s and 1990s, a smattering of criminologists forged new theoretical directions for realist criminology. The late Roger Matthews, for example, advanced a "critical realist criminology" situated in the philosophy of critical realism (Archer, 1995; Bhaskar, 1978). He also established firm methodological foundations for the perspective and explicitly traced the relationship between structure and agency at the heart of the realist enterprise. Most recent is ultra-realism, an amalgamation of critical realism, psychoanalysis, and political economic theory informed by Marx, Žižek, Freud, Lacan, and Bhaskar (Hall, 2012; Hall & Winlow, 2015). This perspective doubles down on the Marxist underpinnings of realist criminology, developing and advancing general explanations of criminal behavior stemming from the machinations of capitalism. In addition, ultra-realism diverges from other realist criminological perspectives by arguing for both short-term *and* long-term solutions to address the myriad social harms created under capitalism.

To date, most realist criminological research addresses street crime—violence most of all. This emphasis is understandable. Violence can be devastating to the physical and psychological well-being of victims and the social fabric of communities (e.g. Currie, 2020). Yet this focus on violence comes at the expense of other kinds of social harms. This book details a path forward for a realist criminology that addresses the harms created by computer-related crimes.

In short, a realist criminology of the computer crimes should be dedicated to three central objectives. First, it should center the variegated harms to individual victims (and the environment) created or amplified by computer-based or computer-facilitated crimes. Second, it should generate theoretically and empirically sound explanations of the crimes and harms in question while developing harm reduction strategies. Third, these solutions should be mindful of the role of power and structure in the organization of the social relations of the internet to avoid promoting policies and programs which unduly contribute to the erosion of online civil liberties, unnecessarily concentrate power into the hands of governments and corporations (at least without proper social democratic regulations and oversight), and otherwise perpetuate social harm.

To accomplish these objectives, it is not sufficient to simply *apply* realist criminology to the problem of computer crime. Instead, it is necessary to update and modify realist criminology to grapple with the challenges and idiosyncrasies presented by the internet. First is the problem of scope—what are the harms which should comprise the focus of a realist criminology of computer crime? The answer is necessarily broad. Given realist criminology's emphasis on addressing both structural and interpersonal harms, there exist a wide assortment of social harms considered "fair game" for consideration. These include damages stereotypically associated with computer crimes like online fraud, child exploitation, computer intrusions, malware, harassment, and hate speech. Additionally, it also considers those created by the actions of the powerful, which may or may not be criminalized under law including threats to privacy, malign neglect of systems and users, and damages caused by tech development and manufacturing (e.g. plundering of natural resources and exploitation of child labor).

Though often not explicit, realist criminology is a criminology of "place" as its analyses and policies tend to focus on locally situated communities, likely because of its general focus on street crime and violence (DeKeseredy & Schwartz, 1991, p. 256; Matthews, 2014, p. 4). For the study of online crimes, this presents an acute challenge as places are abstractions in the digital realm and are not fixed in physical locations. Yet, the concepts of space and place are not useless in analyses of the internet and online crime—they need only be reconceptualized. Related is the problem of community. This work treats communities as composed of *networks* of relationships, including those between offenders, victims, state actors, and members of the public (the "square of crime" or "social relations of crime control" described by left realists) (Jones, MacLean, & Young, 1986; Lea, 2002; 2016). In working toward a realist criminology of the internet, it is worth ruminating on the social networks engendered by contemporary telecommunications technologies, the methods through which such networks can be mapped, and how realist notions of social organization and structure may need to be loosened to deal with the unique problems presented by the internet.

This approach also considers the centrality of class within realist criminology. Critical perspectives that draw on Marxist thought—including realist criminology—tend to be critiqued as economic reductionists, distilling myriad social harms to problems of class relations (Bridges &

Gilroy, 1982; Gilroy & Sim, 1985; Renzetti, 2016; Wood, 2019; Wood, Anderson, & Richards, 2020). Despite the importance of class in understanding the essential causes of crime and victimization, not all social problems are reduceable to the undulations of the political economy. The tendency of realist criminologists to attribute crime and victimization to capitalism may diminish the importance of other variables of social stratification like gender, race, and sexuality. To be fair, realist criminologists have earnestly attempted to bridge the gaps between left realism, feminist criminology, and other perspectives to address this shortcoming (e.g. Hall & Winlow, 2015; Schwartz & DeKeseredy, 2010). Still, a paucity remains (Renzetti, 2013; 2016). This study thus continues the prior work of realist criminologists by building toward a perspective that considers how other structures may operate independently and concomitantly with the political economy to generate the underlying conditions of crime and victimization.

This analysis also considers the tension between the pursuit of piecemeal reform and the necessity of structural change. Traditionally, left and critical realist criminologists have embraced short-term reforms as such strategies have more immediate potential for the alleviation of harm. Such a focus has left them open to criticisms of being liberal rather than radical in the approach to harm reduction in that they ultimately fail to address the structural antecedents of crime (Michalowski, 1992). Ultra-realists, on the other hand, ask us to consider what "what *must* be done" to create long-term harm reduction, leaning more toward the revolutionary proclivities of other critical criminologists (Hall & Winlow, 2018, p. 51). Having established that the objective of a realist criminology of the internet is to reduce the harms of online crimes while not unduly contributing to the concentration of power in the hands of the powerful, it follows that the position advanced in this book sits between these poles—embracing piecemeal reform when possible while keeping an eye on long-term change.

To address these challenges, it is also necessary to revisit and reconsider the philosophical underpinnings of realist criminology. Rather than rely upon the critical realism favored by Matthews and the ultra-realists, this analysis instead considers the philosophical tradition of pragmatism. Pragmatism emerged in the late 1800s and early 1900s among American philosophers like Charles Peirce, William James, and John Dewey (Misak, 2013; Menand, 1997; 2001). Though there exist significant differences among pragmatist philosophers, there are marked consistencies, namely that they are united by the "pragmatic maxim" that "our theories and concepts must be linked to experience, expectations, or consequences" (Misak, 2013, p. 29). Involved is a skepticism toward transcendental truths that exist beyond the realm of human experience (Baert, 2003, p. 93). Pragmatism also holds that knowledge is impossible to fully disentangle from the social and historical contexts of its production. That is not to say it is a purely subjectivist endeavor. It does not deny the existence of an external reality, only that our ability to fully ascertain it is limited (Peirce, 1966). The only way to advance knowledge is to subject it to the gauntlet of experience and assess the consequences. We should favor, from this perspective, those beliefs, theories, and concepts whose outcomes contribute to "human flourishing" (Putnam, 1997) and if there exists no consequence either way, then "it is empty or useless for inquiry and deliberation" (Misak, 2013, p. 30).

As a philosophy of social science, pragmatism shares many commonalities with critical realism though, as will be discussed, important distinctions exist (Baert, 2005; Matthews, 2014; Hall, 2012; Hall & Winlow, 2015; Ritz,

2020). I admit that my preference for pragmatism may be a result of my nationality—pragmatism is predominantly, though not exclusively, an American school of philosophy. It also stems from my training in American criminology, which has been deeply influenced by pragmatism through its impacts on the Chicago School, symbolic interactionism, learning theories, subcultural theories, and more contemporary critical perspectives like cultural criminology (Baert, 2003; Joas, 1993; Ferrell, Hayward, & Young, 2015; McDermott, 2002; Ulmer, 2017; Wheeldon, 2015). But there are, as will be explored later in this book, legitimate reasons to consider pragmatism a useful social scientific foundation for realist criminology.

It is also necessary to consider the relationship between pragmatism and critical theory as a foundation for realist criminology. Usually, these two approaches are considered antithetical as pragmatism has often been associated with political liberalism. There also exist significant disagreements between pragmatist philosophers, who generally balk at the idea of absolute truth claims, and Marxists, who often attempt to describe the machinations of capitalism in law-like terms (e.g. Baert, 2005; Diggins, 1970, p. 905; Frega, 2014; Joas, 1993, pp. 84–85; Putnam, 1997). Yet there is reason to believe that the two are not irreconcilable. W.E.B. DuBois, C. Wright Mills, Cornell West, and Jürgen Habermas, for instance, have—to varying degrees—married the two traditions in their works (Aronowitz, 2012; Baert, 2005; Dunn, 2018; Frega, 2014, p. 59; Mills, 1959; West, 1989). Similarly, this union shows promise for a realist criminology of the internet. In the spirit of Wheeldon's (2015) "pragmatic criminology," we could refer to this approach as "critical pragmatism" (Kadlec, 2006, p. 520). Yet, that indicates too strong a divergence with prior theorizing by realist criminologists. I view this more of a modification and dialogue with existing strains of realist criminology than a reinvention.

## A Note on Nomenclature

Clarification is needed for some of the terminology used (or not used) throughout this book. I will generally refrain from using the term "cybercrime"—despite the term appearing in the title of this book! I have made my aversion to the term known elsewhere (Steinmetz, 2018; Steinmetz & Nobles, 2018; Yar & Steinmetz, 2019). In short, "cyber" is unnecessarily political, sensationalist, and unclear. Defining, for instance, exactly what constitutes "cybercrime" has been no small matter of debate within criminology (e.g. Furnell, 2002; 2017; McGuire, 2020; Wall, 2007; Yar & Steinmetz, 2019). In the early days of the web, "cyber" was affixed to almost anything performed through computer networks—"cybersex," "cybershopping," and other terms were all the rage. Today, the prefix has generally fallen out of favor except when applied to something illicit or malicious activities (e.g. "cybercrime," "cyberterrorism," or "cyberwarfare"). It is my contention that the term offers little analytic clarity while being mired in the politics of fear. The title of this book, *Against Cybercrime,* thus has two meanings—it captures the effort made here at providing a scaffolding for earnestly combating computer crime issues *and* notes my disdain for the politics of "cyber."

Other terms exist including "ecrime" and "technocrime," which are less ideologically charged but still do not, for me, capture the *je ne se quoi* of the relationship between computing technologies and crime (McGuire, 2020). I recently drew from the work of Shoshanna Zuboff (1988) to advance the concept of "informated crime" (Steinmetz, 2022). From this perspective, crime is viewed as a kind of work shaped and mediated by computer technologies. As machines, computers not only automate labor processes but they "informate" them as well—they transform physical processes into data. In this way, information technology "both accomplishes tasks and translates them into information" (Zuboff, 1988, p. 9). For this reason, the machine requires a different battery of abstract reasoning skills, which Zuboff (1988) terms "intellective skills." The informated perspective on computer-related crimes contradicts the idea of computer crimes as separate and unique form of criminality. Instead, crime is placed on a continuum based on the degree to which computers are necessary for the act in question, available to the actor, and the actor actively chooses to engage with such technologies—dimensions which dictate the level of intellective skills required in criminal activity. I recognize, however, that despite the conceptual precision the term offers, "informated crimes" is not very catchy. As such, I will generally use "computer crimes" throughout this book. The term is commonly used in the field to denote crimes involving the internet or related technologies but does not have the same political charge as "cybercrime."

## Chapter Summaries

*Against Cybercrime* is committed to two goals. It outlines my own reimagining of the realist criminology enterprise *and* how that perspective may be brought to bear in the study of computer crimes. It is not intended as the final word on the matter. I hope that others will build on its ideas and engage in thoughtful critique. The book is thus structured in broad terms, making specific arguments at times and, at others, gesturing at possibilities. Chapter 2 begins this work by charting the history of realist criminology, starting with the development of New Left Realism in the United Kingdom in the 1980s and its adoption among a small but influential band of Western criminologists. The chapter then considers the significant theoretical advancements forged by the critical realist approach of Roger Matthews and the ultra-realism of folks like Steve Hall and Simon

Winlow. This chapter also explores the various criticisms that have been leveled at realist criminology over time.

As mentioned, recent developments in realist criminology—specifically critical realist criminology and ultra-realism—have incorporated the philosophy of critical realism. Given the newfound pervasiveness of this ontological and epistemological approach in the area, it seems appropriate to explain why I've chosen to avoid it. These matters are the focus of Chapter 3. Chapter 4 then turns to American pragmatism and its viability as a foundation for realist criminology.

With these philosophical matters aside, Chapter 5 updates realist criminology to grapple with computer crimes and related harms. As foreshadowed above, the realist criminology advanced herein takes a broad view of the kinds of social harms related to computer network technologies considered fair game for analysis and redress. It also considers the problem of "space" presented by the internet and the challenges involved in mapping the social relations of crime control online. The chapter then ruminates on the question of class. Though realist criminology has been traditionally focused primarily on political economic concerns, there is a need to open our analytic horizons to other structural possibilities. Finally, this chapter tackles the classic debate between short- and long-term solutions—should a realist criminology of computer crimes prioritize short-term reforms or aim toward necessary revolutionary change?

No exploration of realist criminology would be complete without an exploration of research methodology. Drawing works like C. W. Mills' *The Sociological Imagination* and Young's (2011) *The Criminological Imagination*, Chapters 6 critiques the current state of computer crime research, particularly the burgeoning domain of computational criminology—an approach to the study of crime which makes use of computationally intensive research strategies like big data analyses, machine learning, and the like. Chapter 7 then considers how the sociological or criminological imagination can be applied to the study of computer crimes (Mills, 1959; Young, 2011). Involved is an orientation which actively grapples with the values endemic to the study of social problems, considers structural and historical contexts, and explores both objective circumstances and subjective experiences. The chapter then makes a case for the primacy of qualitative methods in the study of computer crimes—though, as I am ever reluctant to throw the baby out with the bathwater, it acknowledges the importance of quantification.

Chapter 8 attempts to show how realist criminologists can adopt a "big picture" perspective toward approach crime issues while determining points of intervention and potential solutions. Two case studies are used to demonstrate this approach. The first, illicit computer hacking, is used to show how realist criminologists might approach computer crime-reduction. The second, fraud, demonstrates how we might address the needs of victims. Together, these two case studies should give some idea to how criminologists and social scientists in general can envision social policies and institutional changes to address computer crimes without unduly relying on authoritarian technologies.

In addition to summarizing primary points made throughout, the conclusion of this book charts future directions in the development of a realist criminology of the internet. It also makes a case for integrating realist criminology with other areas of critical criminology, specifically cultural criminology. Realist criminology has a history of being rather antagonistic to other kinds of critical criminology. The democratic sensibilities of pragmatism dictate that realist criminologist look to possible points of convergence with other strains of criminological thought.

## Note

1   Countries and international bodies have adopted statutory measures which attempt to curb potential abuses of mass personal data collection by both governments and corporations like the EU's General Data Protection Regulation. Unfortunately, such measures appear to have done little to curb the expansion and intrusiveness of surveillance.

## References

Amnesty International. (2021, July 18). Forensic methodology report: How to catch NSO Group's Pegasus. Retrieved July 19, 2021, at www.amnesty.org/en/latest/research/2021/07/forensic-methodology-report-how-to-catch-nso-groups-pegasus/#_ftnref1

Archer, M. (1995). *Realist social theory: The morphogenic approach.* Cambridge: Cambridge University Press.

Aronowitz, S. (2012). *Taking it big: C. Wright Mills and the making of political intellectuals.* New York: Columbia University Press.

Baert, P. (2003). Pragmatism, realism and hermeneutics. *Foundations of Science, 8,* 89–106.

Baert, P. (2005). *Philosophy of the social sciences: Towards pragmatism.* Malden, MA: Polity Press.

Bhaskar, R. (1978). *A realist theory of science.* Atlantic Highlands, NJ: Humanities Press Inc.

Braga, A. A., Papachristos, A. V., & Hureau, D. M. (2014). The effects of hot spots policing on crime: An updated systematic review and meta-analysis. *Justice Quarterly, 31*(4), 633–663.

Brayne, S. (2017). Big data surveillance: The case of policing. *American Sociological Review, 82*(5), 977–1008.

Bridges, L. & Gilroy, P. (1982, June). Striking back: The police use of race in crime statistics is a political act. *Marxism Today.* Retrieved November 21, 2019 at http://banmarchive.org.uk/collections/mt/pdf/82_06_34.pdf

Brown, D. & Hogg, R. (1992). Essentialism, radical criminology and left realism. *Australian and New Zealand Journal of Criminology, 25,* 195–230.

Button, M., & Cross, C. (2017). *Cyberfrauds, scams and their victims*. New York: Routledge.

Cernik, L. (2022, January 10). 'It felt like losing a husband': The fraudsters breaking hearts—and emptying bank accounts. *The Guardian*. Retrieved January 6, 2023 at www.theguard ian.com/lifeandstyle/2022/jan/10/it-felt-like-losing-a-husb and-the-fraudsters-breaking-hearts-and-emptying-bank-accounts

Clarke, R. V. G. (1980). "Situational" crime prevention: Theory and practice. *British Journal of Criminology, 20*(2), 136–147.

Clear, T. R. (2007). *Imprisoning communities: How mass incarceration makes disadvantaged neighborhoods worse*. New York: Oxford University Press.

Clevenger, S., Navarro, J. N., Marcum, C. D., & Higgins, G. E. (2018). *Understanding victimology: An active-learning approach*. New York: Routledge.

Cross, C., Dragiewicz, M., & Richards, K. (2018). Understanding romance fraud: Insights from domestic violence research. *British Journal of Criminology, 58*, 1303–1322.

Cross, C., Richards, K., & Smith, R. G. (2016). The reporting experiences and support needs of victims of online fraud. *Trends & Issues in Crime and Criminal Justice, 518*, 1–14.

Currie, E. (1998). *Crime and punishment in America*. New York: Metropolitan Books.

Currie, E. (2010). Plain left realism: An appreciation, and some thoughts for the future. *Crime, Law and Social Change, 54*, 111–124.

Currie, E. (2020). *Peculiar indifference: The neglected toll of violence on Black America*. New York: Metropolitan Books.

DeKeseredy, W. S., & Schwartz, M. D. (1991). British and U.S. Left Realism: A critical comparison. *International Journal of Offender Therapy and Comparative Criminology, 35*(3), 248–262.

Diggins, J. P. (1970). Ideology and pragmatism: Philosophy or passion? *The American Political Science Review, 64*(3), 899–906.

Domhardt, M., Münzer, A., Fegert, J. M., & Goldbeck, L. (2015). Resilience in survivors of child sexual abuse: A systematic review of the literature. *Trauma, Violence, & Abuse, 16*(4), 476–493.

Dreßring, H., Bailer, J., Anders, A., Wagner, H., & Gallas, C. (2014). Cyberstalking in a large sample of social network users: Prevalence, characteristics, and impact upon victims. *Cyberpsychology, Behavior, and Social Networking, 17*(2), 61–67.

Dunn, R. G. (2018). *Toward a pragmatist sociology: John Dewey and the legacy of C. Wright Mills*. Philadelphia, PA: Temple University Press.

Ferrell, J., Hayward, K., & Young, J. (2015). *Cultural criminology: An invitation* (2nd ed.). Thousand Oaks, CA: Sage.

Follis, L., & Fish, A. (2020a). *Hacker states*. Cambridge, MA: MIT Press.

Follis, L., & Fish, A. (2020b). State hacking at the edge of code, capitalism and culture. *Information, Communication & Society*. https://doi.org/10.1080/1369118X.2020.1776368

Frega, R. (2014). Between pragmatism and critical theory: Social philosophy today. *Human Studies, 37*, 57–82.

Furnell, S. (2002). *Cybercrime: Vandalizing the information society*. London, England: Addison-Wesley.

Furnell, S. (2017). The evolving landscape of technology-dependent crime. In M. R. McGuire & T. J. Holt (eds.) *The Routledge handbook of technology, crime and justice* (pp. 65–77). New York: Routledge.

Gewirtz-Meydan, A., Walsh, W., Wolak, J., & Finkelhor, D. (2018). The complex experience of child pornography survivors. *Child Abuse & Neglect, 80*, 238–248.

Gilroy, P., & Sim, J. (1985). Law, order and the state of the left. *Capital & Class, 9*, 15–55.

Gottschalk, M. (2013). The carceral state and the politics of punishment. In J. Simon & R. Sparks (eds.) *The Sage handbook of punishment and society* (pp. 205–241). Thousand Oaks, CA: Sage.

Hall, S. (2012). *Theorizing crime and deviance: A new perspective*. Thousand Oaks, CA: Sage.

Hall, S., & Winlow, S. (2015). *Revitalizing criminological theory: Towards a new ultra-realism*. New York: Routledge.

Hall, S., & Winlow, S. (2018). Ultra-realism. In W. S. DeKeseredy & M. Dragiewicz (eds.) *Routledge handbook of critical criminology* (pp. 43–56). New York: Routledge.

Jewkes, Y., & Andrews, C. (2005). Policing the filth: The problems of investigating online child pornography in England and Wales. *Policing and Society, 15*(1), 42–62.

Joas, H. (1993). *Pragmatism and social theory.* Chicago, IL: University of Chicago Press.

Jones, T., MacLean, J., & Young, J. (1986). *The Islington crime survey.* Aldershot, England: Gower.

Kadlec, A. (2006). Reconstructing Dewey: The philosophy of critical pragmatism. *Po+lity, 38*(4), 519–542.

Kirchgaessner, S., Lewis, P., Pegg, D., Cutler, S., Lakhani, N., & Safi, M. (2021, July 18). Revealed: Leak uncovers global abuse of cyber-surveillance weapon. *The Guardian.* Retrieved July 19, 2021 at www.theguardian.com/world/2021/jul/18/revea led-leak-uncovers-global-abuse-of-cyber-surveillance-wea pon-nso-group-pegasus

Lea, J. (2002). *Crime and modernity.* London: Sage.

Lea, J. (2016). Left realism: A radical criminology for the current crisis. *International Journal for Crime, Justice and Social Democracy, 5*(3), 53–65.

Lea, J., & Young, J. (1984). *What is to be done about law and order?* New York: Penguin.

Lowman, J., & MacLean, B. D. (1992). Introduction: Left realism, crime control, and policing in the 1990s. In J. Lowman & B. D. MacLean (eds.) *Realist criminology: Crime control and policing in the 1990s* (pp. 3–29). Toronto, Ontario: University of Toronto Press.

Matthews, R. (2014). *Realist criminology.* New York: Palgrave Macmillan.

Matthews, R. (2016). Realist criminology, the new aetiological crisis and the crime drop. *International Journal for Crime, Justice and Social Democracy, 5*(3), 2–11.

Mawby, R. I., & Walklate, S. (1994). *Critical victimology.* Thousand Oaks, CA: Sage.

McDermott, M. J. (2002). On moral enterprises, pragmatism, and feminist criminology. *Crime & Delinquency, 48*(2), 283–299.

McGuire, M. (2016). Cybercrime 4.0: Now what is to be done? In R. Matthews (ed.) *What is to be done about crime and punishment: Towards a 'public criminology'* (pp. 251–279). London: Macmillan.

McGuire, M. R. (2020). It ain't what it is, it's the way that they do it? Why we still don't understand cybercrime. In R. Leukfeldt & T. J. Holt (eds.) *The human factor of cybercrime* (pp. 3–28). New York: Routledge.

Meares, T. (2015). Broken windows, neighborhoods, and the legitimacy of law enforcement or why I fell in and out of love with Zimbardo. *Journal of Research in Crime and Delinquency, 52*(4), 609–625.

Menand, L. (ed.) (1997). *Pragmatism: A reader.* New York: Vintage Books.

Menand, L. (2001). *The metaphysical club: A story of ideas in America.* New York: Farrar, Straus, and Giroux.

Michalowski, R. (1992). Crime and justice in socialist Cuba: What can left realists learn? In J. Lowman & B. D. MacLean (eds.) *Realist criminology: Crime control and policing in the 1990s* (pp. 115–138). Toronto, Ontario: University of Toronto Press.

Mills, C. W. (1959). *The sociological imagination.* New York: Oxford University Press.

Misak, C. (2013). *The American pragmatists.* New York: Oxford University Press.

Muller, C. & Wildeman, C. (2013). Punishment and inequality. In J. Simon & R. Sparks (eds.) *The Sage handbook of punishment and society* (pp. 169–185). Thousand Oaks, CA: Sage.

Peirce, C. S. (1966). Reality. In A. W. Burks (ed.) *Collected papers of Charles Sanders Peirce* (vol. 7, pp. 207–211). Cambridge, MA: The Belknap Press of Harvard University Press.

Perrigo, B. (2021, July 19). Governments used spyware to surveil journalists and activists. Here's why revelations about Pegasus are shaking up the world. *Time.* Retrieved July 19, 2021 at https://time.com/6081433/pegasus-spyware-monito red-journalists-activists/

Phipps, A. (1986). Radical criminology and criminal victimization. In R. Matthews & J. Young (eds.) *Confronting crime* (pp. 97–117). London: Sage.

Platt, T., Frappier, J., Ray, G., Schaeuffler, R., Trujillo, L., Cooper, L., Currie, E., & Harring, S. (1977). *The iron fist and the velvet glove: An analysis of the U.S. police* (3rd ed.). San Francisco, CA: Crime and Social Justice Associates.

Putnam, H. (1997). Fact and value. In L. Menand (ed.) *Pragmatism: A reader* (pp. 338–362). New York: Vintage Books.

Renzetti, C. (2013). *Feminist criminology*. New York: Routledge.

Renzetti, C. (2016). Critical realism and feminist criminology: Shall the twain ever meet? *International Journal for Crime, Justice and Social Democracy, 5*(3), 41–52.

Ritz, B. (2020). Comparing abduction and retroduction in Peircean pragmatism and critical realism. *Journal of Critical Realism, 19*(5), 456–495.

Roberts, S. T. (2019). *Behind the screen: Content moderation in the shadows of social media*. New Haven, CT: Yale University Press.

Rojek, J., Rosenfeld, R., & Decker, S. (2012). Policing race: The racial stratification of searches in police traffic stops. *Criminology, 50*(4), 993–1024.

Rueckert, P. (2021, July 18). Pegasus: The new global weapon for silencing journalists. *Forbidden Stories*. Retrieved July 19, 2021 at https://forbiddenstories.org/pegasus-the-new-global-weapon-for-silencing-journalists/

Schwartz, M. D. & DeKeseredy, W. S. (2010). The current health of left realist theory. *Crime, Law & Social Change, 54*, 107–110.

Slater, J., & Masih, N. (2021, July 19). The spyware is sold to governments to fight terrorism. In India, it was used to hack journalists and others. *The Washington Post*. Retrieved July 19, 2021 at www.washingtonpost.com/world/2021/07/19/india-nso-pegasus/

Snowden, E. (2019). *Permanent record*. New York: Metropolitan Books.

Steinmetz, K. F. (2018). Technocrime at the margins: Introduction to the special issue on critical or marginal perspectives and issues in the study of technocrime. *Journal of Qualitative Criminal Justice and Criminology, 6*(2), 131–135.

Steinmetz, K. F. (2022). Crime in the age of the smart machine: A Zuboffian approach to computers and crime. *International Journal of Crime, Justice and Social Democracy, 11*(1), 225–238.

Steinmetz, K. F., & Nobles, M. R. (2018). Introduction. In K. F. Steinmetz & M. R. Nobles (eds.) *Technocrime and criminological theory* (pp. 1–10). New York: Routledge.

Steinmetz, K. F., Schaefer, B. P., & Henderson, H. (2016). Wicked overseers: American policing and colonialism. *Sociology of Race and Ethnicity, 3*(1), 68–81.

Ulmer, J. T. (2017). The extensive legacy of symbolic interactionism in criminology. In R. A. Triplett (ed.) *The Wiley handbook of the history and philosophy of criminology* (pp. 103–122). Indianapolis, IN: Wiley.

Wall, D. S. (2007). *Cybercrime: The Transformation of crime in the information age.* Malden, MA: Polity Press.

Walklate, S. (2015). Jock Young, Left Realism and critical victimology. *Critical Criminology, 23,* 179–190.

Websdale, N. (2001). *Policing the poor: From slave plantation to public housing.* Boston, MA: Northeastern University Press.

West, C. (1989). *The American evasion of philosophy.* Madison, WI: The University of Wisconsin Press.

Wheeldon, J. (2015). Ontology, epistemology, and irony: Richard Rorty and re-imagining pragmatic criminology. *Theoretical Criminology, 19*(3), 396–415.

Whitty, M. T., & Buchanan, T. (2016). The online dating romance scam: The psychological impact on victims–Both financial and non-financial. *Criminology & Criminal Justice 16*(2), 176–94.

Wilson, J. Q., & Kelling, G. L. (1982, March). The police and neighborhood safety: Broken windows. *The Atlantic Monthly, 249,* 29–38.

Wood, M. A. (2019). What is realist about ultra-realist criminology? A critical appraisal of the perspective. *Journal of Theoretical & Philosophical Criminology, 11,* 95–114.

Wood, M. A., Anderson, B., & Richards, I. (2020). Breaking down the pseudo-pacification process: Eight critiques of ultra-realist crime causation theory. *British Journal of Criminology, 60,* 642–661.

Yar, M., & Steinmetz, K. F. (2019). *Cybercrime & Society* (3rd ed.). Thousand Oaks, CA: Sage.

Young, J. (2011). *The criminological imagination.* Malden, MA: Polity Press.

Zuboff, S. (1988). *In the age of the smart machine: The future of work and power.* New York: Basic Books.

Zuboff, S. (2015). Big other: Surveillance capitalism and the prospects of an information civilization. *Journal of Information Technology, 30,* 75–89.

# PART I
# Foundations

# 2

# REALIST CRIMINOLOGY

## An Overview

British Left Realism emerged as a reaction to the intellectual climate of its time. A useful starting point for understanding the genesis of the perspective is the National Deviancy Conference (NDC), sometimes referred to as the National Deviancy Symposium. Starting in 1968 as a defection from the University of Cambridge's National Conference of Teaching and Research on Criminology, the NDC was an act of rebellion against what was viewed as a staunchly conservative and control-oriented criminology, which considered criminals either pathological or under-deterred (Young, 1988, p. 164; see also: Downes, 1988). The new generation of British criminologists—including folks like Jock Young, Stan Cohen, Ian Taylor, Paul Rock, and Mary McIntosh—instead viewed crime as both a meaningful activity for its perpetrators and a product of cultural and political conflicts (Linnemann & Martinez, 2017, p. 226). The NDC had a significant impact on the trajectory of British as well as American criminology, which was undergoing its own radical turn during this period. Members of the NDC produced touchstone works in criminology including Cohen's (1972) *Folk Devils*

DOI: 10.4324/9781003277996-3

*and Moral Panics,* Hall, Critcher, Jefferson, Clarke, and Roberts's (1978) *Policing the Crisis,* and Ian Taylor, Paul Walton, and Jock Young's (1973) *The New Criminology.*

While the NDC presented a significant challenge to the prevailing criminology of its day, it was also marred by its own intense disagreements. As Downes (1988, pp. 48–49) explains, "the creative, productive aspect of the NDC was accompanied by much factious and turbulent in-fighting... It was a dizzying scene, more a paradigmatic kaleidoscope than a clear-cut progression of superior paradigms delivering a knock-out blow to the inferior." One notable schism concerned the appreciative stance toward crime and deviance taken by many members of the NDC. The same year as the first meeting of the NDC, Alvin Gouldner (1968) published "The Sociologist as Partisan: Sociology and the Welfare State," a critique of Howard Becker's (1967) classic "Whose Side Are We On?" Under fire was the tendency of many liberal criminologists of the time to romanticize crime and criminals, shedding any pretense of objectivity to present the views of the "unflawed underdog" (Young, 1988, p. 174). For Gouldner (1968, p. 106), a sociologist who unabashedly claimed to adopt the perspective of the downtrodden risked becoming a "zookeeper of deviance"—a researcher who,

> expresses the Romanticism of the zoo curator who preeningly displays his rare specimens. And like the zookeeper, he wishes to protect his collection; he does not want spectators to throw rocks at the animals behind the bars. But neither is he eager to tear down the bars and let the animals go.

From this view, the researcher does not question the values or behaviors of the so-called deviant but instead regards their behavior as authentic self-expression in the face of oppressive circumstances. Such a position was untenable for Gouldner for many reasons, not least of which was its tendency to frame social problems as matters between the subordinates and superiors rather than to consider how structures and institutions shape the contexts of social conflicts for all parties involved (Gouldner, 1968, p. 111). In addition, Becker's position struggles to problematize the behaviors of the downtrodden. For Gouldner, it should be entirely possible for criminologists to appreciate the plight of the marginalized while recognizing the social harms caused by their actions—constrained as they might be.

Just as Gouldner (1968) demonstrated the moral and philosophical limitations of Becker's view, his critique also served as an indictment of many works produced by members of the NDC. As the NDC sought to distance itself from the positivistic and administrative approaches to crime adopted by the dominant criminological institutions of the time, like the Home Office Research Unit and the Institute of Criminology at Cambridge University, many in the NDC committed themselves to an incomplete sociology of deviance that romanticized but refused to criticize the actions and values of those they studied. Elliot Currie (1974, pp. 135, 141) remarked that works like *The New Criminology* contained little consideration of "the social *consequences*" of the various theories explored within—that "where traditional criminology tended to see pathology everywhere, Taylor et al. see it *nowhere*; both positions seem to me to be essentially static, impoverished, and divorced from close attention to the behavior of real people in the real world." He further lamented that this hands-off approach to crime and criminality meant that "there is almost no discussion of the way in which any of these theories has been translated into social policy; in short, virtually no analysis of the impact of criminology theories on real people living in the real world" (ibid).

One of the authors of *The New Criminology,* Jock Young, seemed to take such criticisms to heart. In "Working Class Criminology" (1975, pp. 63–64) he contended that the intellectual rebellion of the NDC and its American counterpart, the Society for the Study of Social Problems (SSSP), had fallen into a "trap" by advancing an "alternative position" that was "crass inversion" of the "positivist" or "correctionalist" criminology of the time. For him, positivist criminology was deterministic, atomizing, detached, and policy-oriented (Young, 1975, pp. 64–66). Deviance, from this view, is the result of improper socialization into a consensual social order or by latent criminality embedded in "fixed, psychological, physiological and/or genetic propensities" (ibid, p. 66). This perspective maintains an "antagonism to the idea that social circumstances cause crime, and a lack of interest in the causes of crime" (Hough, 2014, p. 215). Thus, in their pursuit of crime control, this conservative criminology—dubbed "right realism" or "administrative criminology" by left realists—advanced policies that directly contributed to the over-policing of poor communities, adding to the structural burden such populations bear (e.g. Hough, 2014; Matthews, 2014; Meares, 2015; Young, 2007).

The new radical criminology, however, was the inverse—a relativistic and non-deterministic criminology that views deviance as simultaneously a product of self-selection into subcultures and the imposition of rules by more powerful groups (Young, 1975, p. 66). This "new deviancy theory" was said to be uninterested in "utilitarian crime," instead prioritizing "expressive deviancy" or "crimes without victims" like drug use and sex work (ibid, p. 68). Young argued that this deviancy theory was "voyeuristic" or "non-interventionist," echoing Gouldner's (1968) "zookeepers of deviance" accusations—that such criminologists would preserve deviants within a glass cage of abstraction divorced from "social and political power relations" and "define away any notion of personal integrity, autonomy and authentic existence" (Lea, 2014, p. 433). These criminologists, according to Young, did little to recognize or reduce the harms produced by offending. He further lamented the tendency of this work to romanticize crime—to frame deviance in all its forms as an act of rebellion against the social order: "if an activity was anti-State in any conceivable sense, this was sufficient for it to be celebrated or approved" (Young, 1975, p. 70). He similarly echoed Currie's (1974) criticisms, explaining that this version of radical criminology abstained from policy discussions or short-term harm reduction strategies, instead viewing crime and deviance as "irrelevant to the struggle for socialism," likely to disappear once capitalism were overcome, or at least be treated more humanely after the revolution (Young, 1975, p. 70). He also intimated that leftist criminologists may have avoided the subject of violent crime and victimization out of a fear of "pathologizing the poor, 'whipping up' support for severe punishment, and supporting racist arguments," or victim blaming (DeKeseredy, 2003, p. 31; Young, 1975, p. 89). Such criminologists would later be derided by left realists as "left idealists."

The solution for Young (1975) was to create a criminology which bridges the gaps between the correctionalist criminology and the criminology of the NDC while maintaining its radical center. This new version of radical criminology would be explicitly Marxist in orientation, elevating the role of power and class in their analyses. This program would also need to carefully utilize official crime statistics, which cannot be dismissed outright as social constructions—they may, albeit imperfectly, convey the scope and scale of real problems confronting working-class communities. It would need to reject an absolutist view of freedom as people may not always be making rational decisions and these decisions may be structured by material and ideological circumstances beyond their control. Also necessary is a more earnest engagement with the problem of intervention. A hands-off approach does nothing to address the issues faced by the disproportionately working-class victims of crime. Finally, this new criminological endeavor was to be fundamentally socialist, working toward "a culture which takes up the progressive components in pluralism, whilst rejecting those activities which are directly the product of the brutalizations of existing society" (Young, 1975, p. 90). This program set the stage for what would become the "New Left Realism."

As the intellectual headwinds began to turn for British radical criminology, the 1980s also saw significant political changes in British society and elsewhere. This was a time of post-Fordist deindustrialization with a strong conservative social and economic shift under Thatcherism (Brown & Hogg, 1992; Walklate, 2015; Young, 2007). Involved was, among other things, a neoliberal attack on the British welfare state, economic deregulation, and a strident embrace of capitalism. There also existed a prevailing sense of precariousness and anxiety among the general population, including a growing discontent toward the Labour Party and their handling of crime. As Jones, Maclean, and Young (1986, p. 6) explain,

> It had become increasingly obvious that there was an extra-ordinary hiatus in Labour Party policy over crime. Despite the fact that socialist administrations control virtually every inner-city high crime area in Britain (as is true, incidentally, of most Europe), the Labour Party had come to regard law and order as the natural and exclusive realm of Conservatives.

This meant that the left was largely incapable of responding to growing public anxiety about crime and victimization. As British radical criminologists began to take violence and property crimes more seriously, however, they became more involved in higher-level policy discussions, accepting, for instance, invitations to work with the Home Office's Research and Planning Unit. These criminologists also got involved in the development and administration of domestic victimization surveys, which the UK Home Office had been implementing after such surveys had been pioneered in the United States with its National Crime Survey (Jones, Maclean, & Young, 1986; Rock, 1988).

The 1982 wave of the British Crime Survey, the earliest state-run victimization survey in the country, led the UK Home Office and others to conclude that public fear of crime was "irrational" and "out of proportion with their actual risk from crime" (Walklate, 2015, p. 181). The burgeoning realist criminologists, however, noted that such a conclusion from this data was misleading (Matthews, 2014, p. 13). Local victimization surveys like those conducted in Islington and Merseyside revealed that crime "when situated in its local context and in relation to what people knew went on in their neighbourhood, was a problem for people" that could not be dismissed as "irrational" (Walklate, 2015, p. 181). Comparing public fears of crime with national crime trends unfairly dismissed the real crime risks confronting certain populations in particular locations as victimization is not evenly distributed socially and geographically (Jones, Maclean, & Young, 1986; Like-Hailsip & Miofsky, 2011; Walklate, 2015).

Most discussions of the history of Left Realism focus upon the development of the perspective in Britain. That said, contemporaries in the United States, Canada, and Australia were arriving at similar conclusions (Mooney,

2022). For instance, Canadian criminologist Brian MacLean was a visiting professor at the Center for Criminology at Middlesex Polytechnic during the heyday of British Left Realism (ibid). Here he worked alongside Young, Lea, Matthews, Kinsey, and Kate Painter and contributing to foundational works in the area (ibid). Other Canadians similarly advanced realist criminological works including Walter DeKeseredy and Shahid Alvi (ibid). In Australia, criminologists like Kerry Carrington, Dave Brown, and Russell Hogg took up the mantle (ibid).

In America, Elliot Currie emerged as one of the most profound voices of Left Realism. His landmark book *Confronting Crime* (1985, p. 14) dismantles the harsh, unjust, and ineffective handling of crime by the American right, the "noninterventionist" stance adopted by many on the liberal left, and the "scattershot" approach taken by other liberals. He then details a comprehensive crime reduction strategy grounded in creating economic, community, and familial stability and security while addressing inequality. Given his profound influence on the development of realist criminology and that he had expressed similar ideas to the British Left Realists prior to the publication of Young's (1975) "Working Class Criminology," I wanted to learn more about the development of realist criminology in the American context. I reached out to Currie through email where he explained that

> The emergence of the perspective that ultimately got to be known as Left Realism happened pretty much simultaneously in the US and the UK (and Canada) and was driven by the same set of concerns—notably the idea that by not taking crime seriously, what passed for the left had ceded the issue to the right. So, it was time to take back the issue and lay the blame for rising crime, especially serious violence that affected poor and

working-class people, on the policies of the resurgent right. I don't think either side of the pond had much influence in the beginning on the other—this was a home-grown perspective rooted, especially, in political developments in society generally and within the academic left in particular in the various countries.

According to Currie, criminologists in various countries were independently arriving at similar conclusions during the late 1970s and early 1980s—that the left needed to start "taking crime seriously." These parallel developments, however, would eventually converge through academic dialog:

> But then a bunch of us got to know each other. This may indeed have taken off originally with my review of Taylor, Walton, and Young's book back in the day, and took off when Ian Taylor and I started talking on the phone after I published my *Confronting Crime* in the mid-80s. There were a couple of international events that helped further these personal and intellectual relationships, including a conference at Islington in London in, I think, 1990, where I met Jock Young and some other folks who leaned in this direction, and one in Vancouver, BC, initiated by Canadian left realists in 1991. There were a bunch of Brits there, including Roger Matthews, who I got to know very well. The Canadians included Walter DeKeseredy, John Lowman, and Brian Maclean. DeKeseredy became one of the most prolific left realists on the international scale. Lowman and Maclean edited a book out of that conference that's illustrative—*Realist Criminology*, which came out in 1992.

Thus, realist criminology emerged across the UK, the United States, Canada, and Australia in academic and political climates that made the inadequacies of crime policies on both the right and left apparent. Collectively, these scholars and their ideas coalesced into what Currie (2010, p. 113) terms left realism "without capitals" or "plain" left realism (e.g.). Realist-minded leftist criminologists sought to take working class crime and victimization more seriously and to get involved in policy interventions. It was a result of a changing intellectual landscape and increasing political pressures for the left to confront crime.

## What Is Left Realism?

As left realism's influence expanded, it retained certain general principles which Currie (2010) details in "Plain Left Realism: An Appreciation, and Some Thoughts for the Future." First, he argues that, as opposed to the views of left idealists or what he terms "liberal minimalists," "crime isn't *just* a matter of social construction—not just a phantom issue stirred up by governments, right wing politicians, or the mass media, playing on the exaggerated fears of a deluded (or racist) public" (Currie, 2010, p. 114). They also resist the notion that crime rates are purely a byproduct of overzealous policing efforts (Currie, 2010; DeKeseredy & Schwartz, 1991, p. 249). Instead, left realists recognize that while fears about crime may be inflamed by moral panics or other distortions, they cannot be dismissed outright as irrational. Crime occurs, likely at rates loosely corresponding to official measures, and it hurts folks.

Second, left realists argue that victimization is not evenly distributed across space and demography. Crime—particularly serious crimes—affect "some people, in some kinds of places, far more than others" (Currie, 2010, p. 114). Violent crimes, for example, tend to be disproportionately leveled against the socially, economically, and politically marginalized. From this position the failure of leftist criminologists to address crime and victimization is tantamount to complicity in structures that organize such social inequalities and their collateral consequences.

Third, left realism insists that reforms can make meaningful change as opposed to some radical scholars who assert that any reform short of a full revolution will only be absorbed into its machinations and new forms of the same oppression will manifest (Currie, 2010). While not unsympathetic to this position, left realists recognize that real harms occur because of crime here and now. As Schwartz and DeKeseredy (2010, p. 109) explain, "purposeful inattention to policing... also means dooming to misery those women and men who are right now being raped, robbed, beaten and burglarized." Left realists have been criticized for this commitment to policy—that they stand accused of complicity in the social harms wrought by repressive criminal justice policies because they work with agents and agencies of the system (such criticisms will be discussed in greater detail below). Yet, as Currie (2010, p. 117) argues, left realists are also critical of "repressive criminal justice strategies in controlling crime" (see also: Lea & Young, 1984, p. 194). Such repression is one of the key reasons that left realists argue for leftist criminologists to be directly involved in crime control. Without such involvement, leftists are surrendering crime control to the right, which has repeatedly demonstrated an unwillingness to consider the role of social structure, power, inequality, and oppression in the creation and organization of crime, criminality, and victimization (Currie, 2016, p. 25; DeKeseredy & Schwartz, 2018, p. 31).

Left realism is also "'social democratic' in its core analysis and implications" (Currie, 2010, p. 115). Lea (2010, p. 144) refers to this proclivity as left realism's "democratic imperative." A social democratic orientation views capitalism as inherently harmful but argues that its harms can be ameliorated by bringing multiple parties together to generate informed, effective, and holistic analyses and policies to address social problems, including crime. One method of developing such analyses and policies is to utilize the "square of crime" (Jones, MacLean, & Young, 1986) or what Lea (2002, p. 144) later described as "the social relations of crime control" (Lea, 2016, p. 56). These concepts refer to "the interaction between law enforcement, the wider community and public, the victim and the offender" (Lea, 2010, p. 144). Any effective policy must consider the relationships between these parties while also allowing for each party to have a voice in the process, particularly victims, offenders, and the public, who are often omitted from inclusion in the conversation typically dominated by criminal justice agencies and politicians. For left realists, the relations between these parties may vary depending on the type of crime under examination as well as the specific communities under consideration (Lea, 2016). Thus, left realists are tasked with understanding the social relations of crime in each context before working to reorient those relations in a more democratic fashion. The process also necessitates a sensitivity to the role of social structure and power in the contexts under scrutiny including those based on "class, gender, ethnicity, politics, law and the state and… the economy" (Lea, 2016, p. 59).

From this platform, Currie (2010, p. 118) summarizes the general thrust of left realist criminology:

> Taking crime seriously, recognizing that it dispropor- tionately afflicts the most vulnerable, understanding its roots in the economic disadvantages, social deficits and cultural distortions characteristic of (but not limited to) predatory capitalism; insisting that those conditions are modifiable by concerted social action,

and acknowledging the usefulness of some smaller-scale interventions that stand the test of evidence—while rejecting as counterproductive and unjust the massive expansion of repression as a response to crime: those are, I'd say, the fundamental principles of "plain" left realism.

In this manner, left realism is not so much a theory of crime as it is an approach to research and addressing crime and victimization problems. As Lea and Young (1993, p. vii) explain, "left realism originated as a political platform—an injunction to the political left to 'take crime seriously'—rather than as an academic theory." Yet, it would be a mistake to conclude that left realists eschew theory and theorizing altogether. Theory informs their epistemological and moral choices—the choice to focus on the role of social structure in shaping crime and victimization, to embrace a diverse assortment of data sources, oppose repressive criminal justice strategies, etc. Yet, they also engage in explanatory theory as they seek to holistically make sense of and address the crime problems at hand.

For instance, in what is now a keystone work in left realism, Lea and Young's (1984, p. 218) *What Is to Be Done About Law and Order?* argues that street crime is a result of *discontent* produced by *relative deprivation*, an "excess of expectations over opportunities" where individuals perceive themselves as less well off than others. It is thus not poverty that causes crime but the perception that one is unfairly deprived of that which is afforded to others. Discontent is a mental or emotional state where a person feels activated to address the perceived unfairness. Yet, the populations most blighted by crime and victimization are also politically and economically *marginalized*—unable to resolve their discontent by participation in adequate economic opportunities or through local political institutions. In an argument harkening back to Merton's (1938) "Social Structure and Anomie," the discontented are said to cope or adapt to this situation—one such adaptation being crime (Lea & Young, 1984, p. 74). As they explain, "the equation is simple: relative deprivation equals discontent; discontent plus lack of political solution equals crime" (ibid, p. 88).

They further elaborate on the role of *subculture*. Adopting a position close to that of Albert Cohen (1955) in *Delinquent Boys*, Lea and Young (1984) argue that subcultures may arise as mechanisms to help the discontented find solutions to the various problems plaguing their station. In the process, subculture participants may develop and share values and rationalizations which facilitate deviance and predation. These shared cognitive and linguistic tools may evolve over time as the material and social circumstances in which subcultures and their participants are embedded shift.

Lea and Young (1984) also describe the causal role of factors like fear of crime, moral panics, community disorganization, and related elements in both crime causation and reactions to crime. The point, however, is that left realists were committed not only to finding solutions but also to developing theoretical tools to grapple with crime and victimization—to situate the phenomenon in their proper contexts and to trace appropriate relationships between social structure, culture, policy, and individual action.

## Criticisms of Left Realism

Given its polemic framing, it is unsurprising that left realism has garnered significant criticism. To start, left realists have been accused of treating left idealism as a strawman, exaggerating, or even misrepresenting the arguments and sensibilities of so-called left idealists (Cottee, 2002; Linnemann & Martinez, 2017, p. 230). Cottee (2002), for instance, accuses Young and other left realists of perpetuating a false dichotomy between left idealism and left realism, which may overlook the diversity of thought among critical criminologists. Essentially, he concludes that the works associated with left idealism do not (1) consistently downplay or minimize the harms caused by crime, (2) uniformly consider crime to be a "proto-revolutionary act," or (3) diametrically opposed to practical interventions. While Cottee's (2002) criticism has merit, it does not negate the fact that the problems attributed to left idealism do exist, even if the simplistic binary fails to capture critical criminology's variety. (In their rebuttal, Cohen and Young (2004) argue that Cottee himself conjures an unfair characterization of Young's work. Additionally, the authors were apoplectic over Cottee's refusal to consider the merits of the left realist framing of the matter.)

Others have accused left realism of giving too much credence to police-generated crime statistics, particularly those pointing to disproportionate offending among certain racial groups, and overly accepting legal definitions of crime (Bridges & Gilroy, 1982; Gilroy & Sim, 1985; Hall & Winlow, 2015, pp. 63–64). Left realists most certainly recognize the limitations of police-driven crime statistics but argue that such measures are not wholly invalid indicators of crime problems (Lea & Young, 1984). For instance, changes in crime rates observed within the U.S. Uniform Crime Report often correspond with similar changes in crime rates noted in the National Crime Victimization Survey, even if the latter is a better indicator of the "dark figure" of crime, those crimes not recorded by or reported to the police. Further, the categories of crime measured by these data sources, particularly for violent forms of crime, are generally not controversial—most people will agree that assault and murder are problems. Yet, the point remains that use of official statistics privileges state definitions of crime and divert attention toward certain kinds of crime and victimization and away from other kinds of harm.

Scholars have also argued that left realism tends to overly prioritize class in its analyses and treat the working class as a relatively homogenous group, failing to consider its diversity—particularly in terms of race and gender (Bridges & Gilroy, 1982; Gilroy & Sim, 1985; Renzetti, 2016). The contention is that not every group within the working class is equally likely to be involved in crime or be victimized by it. Nor are they equal in how they will be impacted by criminal justice policy and policing strategies. For instance, within social classes, Blacks are generally more likely to be violent victimized or be involved in crime than their White counterparts in the United States, particularly Black *men*—the reasons for which likely result from the historical political and economic circumstances confronting such populations that cannot be reduced to class position (see: Currie, 2020).[1] Regarding gender, men and women are not equally likely to be victimized by various kinds of crime—for instance, men are more likely to be violently assaulted but women are more likely to experience sexual violence (Morash, 2006). Not to mention the victimization experiences of LGTBQ+ populations and other historically marginalized groups.

As will be discussed further in Chapters 4 and 5, balancing the causative, mediating, and moderating dimensions of different social structures and identity markers is an extraordinarily complex matter, one where reasonable people can easily disagree. My understanding is that realist criminologist generally privileges the role of class and capitalism because of the important role these factors play in structuring licit and illicit opportunities, the availability of social support mechanisms, nutrition, education, childcare, and the priorities of law enforcement and legislative bodies. Further, the effects of social class and capitalism are differentially distributed and felt by other historically marginalized groups, thus indicating that social class intermingles with other kinds of social stratification. As Matthews (2009, p. 347) explains, "class continues to be one of the most important explanatory concepts for understanding the nature of crime and punishment." It would be disingenuous, however, to pretend that left realists were blind to these variations. Many major works in the area, such as *What Is To Be Done?*, speak to these differences while giving priority to the role of class. Yet, it warrants noting that the importance of the political economy does not mean that mean that other types of social stratification are secondary, unimportant, or do not have effects independent of social class. Striking a balance is difficult and thus decisions must be made when crafting theoretical or practical frameworks, for better or worse. (That said, I do feel that this criticism is a bit unfair toward left realists who often had considered the role of factors like race and gender, even if they centered class.)

Perhaps due to the criticisms leveled at the perspective—or the flightiness of a trend-chasing criminology—left realism fell out of favor since its heyday in the 1980s and 1990s. It did not die out entirely, however. The mantle is currently borne by a minority of critical criminologists. Further, adherents have sought to expand the perspective, updating it to account for new social trends and intellectual developments. One is the realist criminology most prominently associated with the work of the late Roger Matthews. The other is the "ultra-realism" of Steve Hall,

Simon Winlow, and their merry band. It is toward these perspectives we now turn.

## Matthew's Realist Criminology

In the decades since Left Realism crawled out from the muck of the Thatcher–Reagan era, expansions and revisions have emerged. Folks like Jock Young eventually abandoned the project (he would go on to become a powerhouse in cultural criminology). Others, however, remained committed to the project of realist criminology. One such individual was Roger Matthews. As might be expected of a realist criminologist, his work is characterized by a deep appreciation of theory, an adamant demand for empirical evidence and methodological rigor, and a desire to connect these elements to policy and practice, to "engage in theoretically informed interventions employing an appropriate methodology" (Matthews, 2009, p. 343). In the late 2000s, he turned toward the philosophical tradition of critical realism—a perspective he had first encountered as a graduate student at the University of Sussex (South & Brisman, 2020, p. 303)—to provide a foundation upon which theory, method, and practice could be more fruitfully combined (Archer, 1995; Bhaskar, 1978; Sayer, 2000).

Critical realism is considered in greater depth in Chapter 3. For now, it is sufficient to state that critical realism, as described by Matthews (2014, p. 55), "embodies the view that there is a reality independent of our knowledge and that this reality is stratified, containing emergent properties whose effects should not be conflated with our experience of them [citations omitted]." Wilkinson, Quraishi, Irgan, and Prudie (2021) explain that "stratified" and "emergent" mean that "phenomena at one level of reality are scientifically to be explained in terms of structures or mechanisms located a deeper level that generate or produce these phenomena" (Wilkinson et al., 2021, p. 6). In other words, researchers must determine the fundamental or basic elements that constitute, shape, or cause a phenomenon while also acknowledging that the whole can be more than the sum of its parts. Further causality is viewed in multifaceted and complex terms, particularly as phenomena occur in the context of "open systems" which thus require explanations that acknowledge a diverse array of causes. Rather than focus purely on correlations, an accusation he makes toward empiricists, critical realists—according to Matthews (2014)—seek the deeper processes and mechanisms through which changes are produced. The result is an ontology (view of reality) and epistemology (view of knowledge and knowledge production) that eschews the relativism of certain strains of critical criminology *and* the shallow or altogether atheoretical proclivities of positivist criminology.

Matthew's most thorough treatment of this critical realist criminology was likely in his 2014 book, *Realist Criminology*. Here, he claims that critical realists advance left realism by placing it "upon a firmer epistemological and methodological foundation" (Matthews, 2014, p. 28). He details the requirements for conducting a critical realist criminological research agenda, including prioritizing a process often briefly discussed in research methods classes but frequently given a short shrift in research practice, *conceptualization*. As he explains, "where loose and sloppy abstractions are used, they are unable to bear the explanatory weight placed upon them" (Matthews, 2014, p. 31).[2] Recognizing the issues endemic to legal definitions of crime, for example, Matthews (2014, pp. 46–48) instead defines crime as the production of harm stemming from the violation of human rights and dignity. This definition decouples crime and social harm from the confines of the state while also providing a new basis for grounding a consistent definition of harm. Additionally, critical realist criminology holds that theory without evidence is as useless as evidence without theory. "Naïve realists" or administrative criminologists are viewed as prioritizing evidence while applying only the most vestigial of theory whereas some left idealists might be engaged in "theoreticism" or theoretical abstraction that divorces itself from reality. Like the left realists before him, Matthews (2014) prioritizes social class and political economy in analysis to provide the scaffolding through which theory and evidence can be wed.

Methodologically, this critical realist criminology adopts a pluralistic approach, embracing a sweeping array of quantitative and qualitive approaches. As he explained in "Beyond 'So What?' Criminology," this version of realist criminology "is compatible with a relatively wide range of research methods, depending upon the object under study and what one wants to find out about it" (Matthews, 2009, p. 353). In this sense, he rejects "cookbook criminology" or a criminology that utilizes "one favoured method in all situations" or believes "that one method is superior to all others" (Matthews, 2009, p. 354).

Matthews (2014, p. 14) also explicitly tackles the structure versus agency debate. Consistent with critical realist philosophy, he argues that structure and agency are "analytically separable" and not to be "conflated" with one another. For the purposes of temporal ordering, "structure necessarily pre-dates action, which leads to its reproduction and transformation and that structure also post-dates action sequences that have given rise to it" (Matthews, 2014, p. 39). Building from this position, realist analyses should therefore examine the situational relationships between structure and agency as well as identify factors that mediate these relationships. Relatedly, critical realists also conceptualize power beyond the two-dimensional repressive function of the state and law. Drawing from Foucault, Matthews (2014, p. 45) argues that power incorporates "a multiplicity of forces involving ceaseless struggles and confrontations," which can be both repressive and productive. In this manner, critical realist criminologists seek to advance a more fully formed epistemic position to advance criminological and victimological research that will form the basis of crime prevention policies.

## Ultra-Realism

The most significant advancement in realist criminology is the relatively recent *ultra-realism* (e.g. Hall, 2012; Hall and Winlow, 2015). The perspective was established in 2015, though its architects, namely Steve Hall and Simon Winlow, had laid its groundwork for years (Raymen & Kuldova, 2020, pp. 243, 246). It is difficult to summarize succinctly as the perspective is nuanced and draws from unorthodox (at least within the realm of criminology) philosophy and social theory. Nevertheless, I will try to give it due diligence herein.

Ultra-realism constitutes an amalgamation of critical realist, psycho-social, and political economic theory informed by Marx, Žižek, Freud, Lacan, and Bhaskar. It takes the left realist criticisms of left idealism further, arguing that contemporary liberal criminologists have turned a blind eye to the reality of crime and victimization as a matter of political prudence—that they purposefully ignore key facts about crime and victimization to avoid hard discussions or because such facts contradict their own political agenda. Building from Žižek, Hall (2012) accuses the left of engaging in "fetishistic disavowal" where "we can continue not wanting to know what we already know and therefore continue to live and act as if we don't know" (Hall, 2012, p. 93). He accuses criminologists of engaging in "political and intellectual cowardice" by failing to take seriously basic facts about crime. For instance, that criminals are not always the victims of circumstance, that moral agency has a role to play in crime, and that not all crimes can be viewed as forms of proto-revolutionary behavior (ibid).

For ultra-realists, the failure to properly address crime and victimization is not just a failure of the left, but a failure of liberalism more generally (Winlow & Hall, 2019). Liberals, from this perspective, are accused of ignoring—or, at best, given a passing consideration to—the role of the root causes of crime and instead wallowing in fragmentary identity politics (a term used as a pejorative in this context). Further, ultra-realists accuse such criminologists of ultimately upholding the status quo by failing to challenge the underlying causal mechanisms at play.

Like Matthews, ultra-realists incorporate the philosophy of critical realism into their perspective. Unlike prior realist criminologists, however, ultra-realists subscribe to *transcendental materialism*, a position influenced by Žižek and formally articulated by Johnston (2008), which holds that,

> All humans are, paradoxically, hard-wired for plasticity, which carries a natural tendency to dysfunctionality; in other words, we are *naturally unnatural*. This allows us to create various cultures and practical ways of doing things in order to adapt to widely divergent environments, some benign and some difficult and demanding.
>
> *(Hall & Winlow, 2015, p. 111)*

Here, crime is understood as something which humans are energized toward by social structural circumstances, ideology, experience, emotions, and physiology (Hall,

2012, p. 253). The tendency for humans to be pliable in their circumstances make them intrinsically vulnerable to energizing forces—notably capitalism—that encourage certain kinds of self-serving and predatory behaviors, though not deterministically so.

"Criminal actions" from this view "are those of an individual who is both ideologically and neurologically motivated to *undertake* to go considerably further than the law-abiding citizen" (Hall, 2012, p. 193). "Undertakers" are "functionally ruthless" and motivated to step over others to "get things done" (Hall, 2012, p. 199). Criminal undertakers are those who direct their energies in unsanctioned ways. Both legal and illegal undertakers share ruthlessness and aggression to compete in the marketplace. Undertakers are thus imbued with what ultra-realists describe as "special liberty" or a "sense of entitlement felt by an individual who will risk harm to others in order to further his own instrumental or expressive interests," which is fostered by the logic of capital accumulation (Hall & Winlow, 2015, p. 91). Related to special liberty is the concept of *pseudo-pacification*. Contrary to the *civilizing process* advanced by theorists like Norbert Elias (2000), Hall (2012) argues that violence has declined over time not because humans have become more civil, but that the individualist and self-serving behaviors energized by capitalism have found alternative avenues to be exercised, such as through cutthroat participation in competitive markets (hence *pseudo*-pacification).

Ultra-realism is zemiological, like Matthews's critical realist criminology, focusing on crime as the creation of harm rather than rule-violation. From this perspective, regardless of how crime is defined, it should be grounded in how such actions "inflict harm on individuals, their environments and their fragile social systems" with harm being defined as "action that leaves whatever it impacts in a worse condition" (Hall & Winlow, 2018, pp. 47–48). Since the drive to harm is informed by characteristics like "special liberty," ultra-realists argue that the engine of contemporary harm and social inequality is the capitalist mode of production and neoliberalism (Hall, 2012; Hall & Winlow, 2018; Winlow & Hall, 2019). In this sense, ultra-realism definitively places capitalism and class at the center of crime and crime control. Any failure to address these root causes reduces criminology, according to ultra-realists, to "symptomology rather than aetiology" (Winlow & Hall, 2016, p. 88).

Importantly, ultra-realists differ from other realist criminologists in their orientation toward policy. Both embrace the need for effective policy solutions to address the harms caused by crime. Left realist and critical realist criminologies, however, are criticized for being too near-sighted in their approach, focusing primarily on short-term policy achievements and neglecting long-term solutions, becoming mired in "administrative pragmatism" (Hall & Winlow, 2015, p. 63). Ultra-realists argue that the "pragmatic investigation of what *can* be done must be replaced by the realistic investigation of what *must* be done to effect long-term transformation of the system in such a way as to reduce its propensity for multiple harms" (Hall & Winlow, 2018, p. 51; Winlow & Hall, 2019). Additionally, ultra-realists argue that policy should be secondary to critique because the "imperative to be 'policy relevant' enforces firm limits on what can be thought and said" (Winlow, 2019, p. 47).

Ultra-realism has not been without its detractors (e.g. Lea, 2016; Walklate, 2016; Hayward, 2016; Wood, 2019; Wood, Anderson, & Richards, 2020). Critics have lambasted the theory's minimization of important factors like gender in the structuring of crime and victimization, failure to consider "the array of values, beliefs and vocabularies of motive for crime that are not solely an expression of capitalism," and reduction of other possible causes of crime to epiphenomenon of the political economy (Wood, Anderson, & Richards, 2020, p. 644; see also Hayward, 2016; Wood, 2019). Further, the theory has been critiqued for its contradictory use of psychoanalytic theory, arguing that the pseudo-pacification process "naturalizes violent drives," which contradicts their transcendental materialist claim that humans are "hardwired for plasticity" (Wood, Anderson, & Richards, 2020, p. 643). Their use of transcendental materialism has also been critiqued for (1) failing to account for neuroscience that contradicts their thesis that humans are purely wired for plasticity, (2) being "incongruous with the psychoanalytic notion of a 'dynamic unconscious' of drives that the perspective builds upon," and (3) rehashing "a 'tabula rasa' subject whose desires and drives, as well as their beliefs and ethics, are determined by society" (Wood, 2019, p. 101). Clement and Mennell (2020) argue that the ultra-realists' critiques of Elias's civilizing process are based on fundamental misunderstandings of his work, that Elias was not so blind to the decivilizing processes nor on the role of the state and other institutions to shape and redirect the drives and energies of actors. The authors also take the ultra-realists to task for their pessimism regarding the ability of the public to engage in meaningful resistance to capitalism. They further lament ultra-realism's seeming short shrift of subcultural theory, a perspective with a long history of criminology in highlighting how individuals navigate competing, conflicting, divergent, or convergent value systems—that "criminology has long recognized that there are elements of incorporation *and* opposition within motivations and justifications for crime" (Clement & Mennell, 2020, p. 13). Finally, Lea pointed out that ultra-realism provides a bleak and totalizing portrayal of the power of capitalism with relatively little hope of amelioration and no direction toward social change. As he asks, "who is the subject, the bearer of change" in ultra-realism? (Lea, 2017, p. 1274).

Ultra-realists, ever willing to engage in spirited debate, have replied to these criticisms, particularly those offered by Wood and colleagues (Wood, 2019; Wood, Anderson, & Richards, 2020). The long and short of the rebuttal is that, according to the ultra-realists, the critique hinges on fundamental misreadings or mischaracterizations of the ultra-realist perspective—that they do not, for instance, adopt a uni-directional "hydraulic" perspective toward motivation nor do they believe they are advancing a purely biological conception of human nature but, rather, a holistic and flexible one (Raymen & Kuldova, 2020). Further, they contend that some criticisms, including the relegation of gender to an "epiphenomenon" of class, are not only a misreading but directly countered by the empirical work conducted by ultra-realists. Instead, they stated that "ultra-realists have simply refused to elevate these cultural forces to a pedestal of some free-floating autonomous causative force unaffected by politics, economic change and the spectre of history" (Rayman & Kuldova, 2020, p. 254). Criticisms aside, it is hard to dispute the fact that the ultra-realists have brought a much-needed energy to critical criminological discourse.

## Conclusion

Despite their differences, the various strains of realist criminology described in this chapter share certain commonalities. They eschew atheoretical or shallow analyses, instead favoring approaches which robustly consider both macro- and micro-level factors, including a prioritization of the role of the political economy and other social structures in shaping the circumstances, drives, motives, opportunities, and consequences of both crime and victimization. They similarly reject oppressive, tough-on-crime approaches which tend to only perpetuate various social harms rather than provide any net harm reduction benefits. At the same time, they call for crime to be "taken seriously"—that many crime problems cannot be dismissed as merely social constructions or moral panics. Criminologists, in this sense, are tasked with developing robust theoretical approaches which consider the multifaceted dimensions of crime while working toward reducing social harm. They also tend to be methodological pluralists, though this does not count the ultra-realists, who favor ethnographic methods.

To be perfectly honest, I have no significant devotion to any of these realist camps. They all have made significant contributions to building a criminology that is both radical and interventionist. My primary interest is in charting a pathway forward for a realist criminology of computer crimes. Involved is a consideration of the core elements of realist criminology and how they can be tweaked for the context of the internet and related technologies. The only point of conflict I will wade into with the prior generations is the application of critical realism as I favor the philosophical tradition of American pragmatism. But this is a subject for the next chapter.

## Notes

1 Violent crime rates can vary significantly among Black populations as well, such as between native born and foreign born (see Gabbidon & Greene, 2019; Lee & Martinez, 2009; Light, He, & Robey, 2019).
2 In this capacity, though critical realists criticize social constructionists for minimizing the harms caused by crime, they also recognize that social constructionism can be useful for problematizing such taken-for-granted concepts (Matthews, 2014, p. 37).

## References

Archer, M. (1995). *Realist social theory: The morphogenic approach*. Cambridge: Cambridge University Press.

Becker, H. S. (1967). Whose side are we on? *Social Problems, 14*(3), 239–247.

Bhaskar, R. (1978). *A realist theory of science*. Atlantic Highlands, NJ: Humanities Press Inc.

Bridges, L. & Gilroy, P. (1982, June). Striking back: The police use of race in crime statistics is a political act. *Marxism Today*. Retrieved November 21, 2019 at http://banmarchive. org.uk/collections/mt/pdf/82_06_34.pdf

Brown, D. & Hogg, R. (1992). Essentialism, radical criminology and left realism. *Australian and New Zealand Journal of Criminology, 25*, 195–230.

Clement, M., & Mennell, S. (2020) Elias, ultra-realism and double-binds: Violence in the streets and the state. *European Journal of Criminology*. DOI: 10.1177/1477370820977889.

Cohen, A. K. (1955). *Delinquent boys: The culture of the gang*. New York: Free Press.

Cohen, S. (1972). *Folk devils and moral panics: The creation of the Mods and Rockers*. London: McGibbon and Kee.

Cohen, S., & Young, J. (2004). Comments on Simon Cottee's "Folk devils and moral panics: 'Left idealism' reconsidered". *Theoretical Criminology, 8*(1), 93–97.

Cottee, S. (2002). Folk devils and moral panics: 'Left idealism' reconsidered. *Theoretical Criminology, 6*(4), 387–410.

Currie, E. (1974). Beyond criminology: *The new criminology: For a social theory of deviance* by Ian Taylor, Paul Walton and Jock Young. *Issues in Criminology, 9*(1), 133–142. Accessed Jun 8, 2022 at: www.jstor.com/stable/42909699

Currie, E. (1985). *Confronting crime: An American challenge*. New York: Pantheon Books.

Currie, E. (2010). Plain left realism: An appreciation, and some thoughts for the future. *Crime, Law and Social Change, 54*, 111–124.

Currie, E. (2016). The violence divide: Taking "ordinary" crime seriously in a volatile world. In R. Matthews (ed.) *What is to be done about crime and punishment? Towards a "public criminology"* (pp. 9–30). London, England: Palgrave Macmillan.

Currie, E. (2020). *Peculiar indifference: The neglected toll of violence on Black America.* New York: Metropolitan Books.

DeKeseredy, W. (2003). Left realism on inner-city violence. In M. D. Schwartz & S. E. Hatty (eds.) *Controversies in critical criminology* (pp. 29–41). Cincinnati, OH: Anderson Publishing Co.

DeKeseredy, W. & Schwartz, M. D. (2018). Left realism: A new look. In W. S. DeKeseredy & M. Dragiewicz (eds.) *Routledge handbook of critical criminology* (pp. 30–42). New York: Routledge.

DeKeseredy, W. S. & Schwartz, M. D. (1991). British and U.S. left realism: A critical comparison. *International Journal of Offender Therapy and Comparative Criminology, 35*(3), 248–262.

Downes, D. (1988). The sociology of crime and social control in Britain, 1960–1987. *British Journal of Criminology, 28*(2), 45–57.

Elias, N. (2000). *The civilizing process (revised edition).* Hoboken, NJ: Wiley-Blackwell.

Gabbidon, S., & Greene, H. T. (2019). *Race & crime* (5th ed.). Thousand Oaks, CA: Sage.

Gilroy, P., & Sim, J. (1985). Law, order and the state of the left. *Capital & Class, 9,* 15–55.

Gouldner, A.W. (1968). The sociologist as partisan: Sociology and the welfare state. *The American Sociologist, 3*(2), 103–116.

Hall, S. (2012). *Theorizing crime and deviance: A new perspective.* Thousand Oaks, CA: Sage.

Hall, S., Critcher, C., Jefferson, T., Clarke, J., & Roberts, B. (1978). *Policing the crisis: Mugging, the state, and law and order.* London: Macmillan Press.

Hall, S., & Winlow, S. (2015). *Revitalizing criminological theory: Towards a new ultra-realism.* New York: Routledge.

Hall, S. & Winlow, S. (2018). Ultra-realism. In W. S. DeKeseredy & M. Dragiewicz (eds.) *Routledge handbook of critical criminology* (pp. 43–56). New York: Routledge.

Hayward, K. J. (2016). Cultural criminology: Script rewrites. *Theoretical Criminology, 20*(3), 297–321.

Hough, M. (2014). Confessions of a recovering "administrative criminologist": Jock Young, quantitative research, and policy research. *Crime Media Culture, 10*, 215–226.

Johnston, A. (2008). *Žižek's ontology: A transcendental materialist theory of subjectivity.* Evanston, IL: Northwestern University Press.

Jones, T., MacLean, J., & Young, J. (1986). *The Islington crime survey.* Aldershot, England: Gower.

Lea, J. (2002). *Crime and modernity.* London, England: Sage.

Lea, J. (2010). Left realism, community, and state-building. *Crime, Law & Social Change, 54*, 141–158.

Lea, J. (2014). New deviancy, Marxism and the politics of left realism: Reflections on Jock Young's early writings. *Theoretical Criminology, 18*(4), 423–440.

Lea, J. (2016). Left realism: A radical criminology for the current crisis. *International Journal for Crime, Justice and Social Democracy, 5*(3), 53–65.

Lea, J. (2017). Book review: *Revitalizing criminological theory: Towards a new ultra-realism.* By Steve Hall and Simon Winlow. *British Journal of Criminology, 57*(5), 1272–1275.

Lea, J., & Young, J. (1984). *What is to be done about law and order?* New York: Penguin.

Lea, J., & Young, J. (1993). Introduction: Ten years on. In J. Lea & J. Young (authors) *What is to be done about law and order?* (pp. vii–xxxix). New York: Pluto Press.

Lee, M. T., & Martinez, R. (2009). Immigration reduces crime: An emerging scholarly consensus. In W. F. McDonald (ed.) *Immigration, crime and justice (Sociology of crime, law and deviance, vol. 13)* (pp. 3–16). Bingley: Emerald Group Publishing Limited.

Light, M. T., He, J., & Robey, J. P. (2019). Comparing crime rates between undocumented immigrants, legal immigrants, and native-born US citizens in Texas. *PNAS.* https://doi.org/10.1073/pnas.2014704117

Like-Haislip, T. Z. & Miofsky, K. T. (2011). Race, ethnicity, gender, and violent victimization. *Race and Justice, 1*(3), 254–276.

Linnemann, T., & Martinez, K. (2017). Let fury have the hour: The radical turn in British criminology. In R. Triplett (ed.) *The Wiley handbook of the history of philosophy of criminology* (pp. 222–236). New York: Wiley.

Matthews, R. (2009). Beyond 'so what?' criminology. *Theoretical Criminology, 13*(3), 341–362.

Matthews, R. (2014). *Realist criminology.* New York: Palgrave Macmillan.

Meares, T. (2015). Broken windows, neighborhoods, and the legitimacy of law enforcement or why I fell in and out of love with Zimbardo. *Journal of Research in Crime and Delinquency, 52*(4), 609–625.

Merton, R. K. (1938). Social structure and anomie. *American Sociological Review, 3*(5), 672–682.

Mooney, J. (2022). Left Realism: "Taking crime seriously." In H. N. Pontell (ed.) *Oxford encyclopedia of criminology and criminal justice.* https://doi.org/10.1093/acrefore/978019 0264079.013.671

Morash, M. (2006). *Understanding gender, crime, and justice.* Thousand Oaks, CA: Sage.

Raymen, T., & Kuldova, T.O. (2020). Clarifying ultra-realism: A response to Wood et al. *Continental Thought & Theory: A Journal of Intellectual Freedom, 3*(2): 242–263.

Renzetti, C. (2016). Critical realism and feminist criminology: Shall the twain ever meet? *International Journal for Crime, Justice and Social Democracy, 5*(3), 41–52.

Rock, P. (1988). The present state of criminology in Britain. *British Journal of Criminology, 28*(2), 58–69.

Sayer, A. (2000). *Realism and social science.* Thousand Oaks, CA: Sage.

South, N., & Brisman, A. (2020). Remembering Roger Matthews (1948–2020) and editors' introduction to "new times" and "environmental crimes." *Critical Criminology, 28,* 303–307.

Taylor, I., Walton, P., & Young, J. (1973). *The new criminology: For a social theory of deviance.* New York: Routledge & Kegan Paul.

Walklate, S. (2015). Jock Young, Left Realism and critical victimology. *Critical Criminology, 23,* 179–190.

Walklate, S. (2016). Steve Hall and Simon Winlow (2015) *Revitalizing criminological theory: Towards a new ultra-realism* [book review]. *International Journal for Crime, Justice and Social Democracy, 5*(3), 111–113.

Wilkinson, M., Quraishi, M., Irgan, L, & Purdie, M.S. (2021). Building on the shoulders of Bhaskar and Matthews: A critical realist criminology. *Journal of Critical Realism*, DOI: 10.1080/14767430.2021.1992736.

Winlow, S. (2019). What lies beneath? Some notes on ultra-realism, and the intellectual foundations of the 'deviant leisure' perspective. In T. Raymen & O. Smith (eds.) *Deviant leisure: Criminological perspectives on leisure and harm* (pp. 45–65). London: Palgrave Macmillan.

Winlow, S., & Hall, S. (2016). Realist criminology and its discontents. *International Journal for Crime, Justice and Social Democracy, 5*(3), 80–94.

Winlow, S., & Hall, S. (2019). Shock and awe: On progressive minimalism and retreatism, and the new ultra-realism. *Critical Criminology, 27,* 21–36.

Wood, M. A. (2019). What is realist about ultra-realist criminology? A critical appraisal of the perspective. *Journal of Theoretical & Philosophical Criminology, 11,* 95–114.

Wood, M. A., Anderson, B., & Richards, I. (2020). Breaking down the pseudo-pacification process: Eight critiques of ultra-realist crime causation theory. *British Journal of Criminology, 60,* 642–661.

Young, J. (1975). Working-class criminology. In I. Taylor, P. Walton, & J. Young (eds.) *Critical criminology* (pp. 63–91). New York: Routledge.

Young, J. (1988). Radical criminology in Britain: The emergence of a competing paradigm. *British Journal of Criminology, 28*(2), 159–183.

Young, J. (2007). *The exclusive society: Social exclusive, crime and difference in late modernity.* Thousand Oaks, CA: Sage.

# 3

# ESCHEWING CRITICAL REALISM

Early left realists did not spend much time addressing the philosophical questions like "what is the nature of reality?" or "how can we *know* anything?" These criminologists were principally concerned with trying to bridge the gap between radical sensibilities and practical concerns. It wasn't until the new millennium that realist criminologists grappled with these matters in earnest. As mentioned in Chapter 2, realist criminologists like Roger Matthews and the ultra-realists have embraced critical realism as their philosophical foundation. Yet, I am not sure that this position is adequate, at least for my own project. For this reason, this chapter briefly details the basics of critical realism and presents my reservations.[1] In short, I am skeptical about its arguments regarding the *irreducible* causal powers of social structure and its separation of social structure from agency. In Chapter 4, I will detail what I consider to be a more useful social scientific philosophy for realist criminology—American pragmatism.

DOI: 10.4324/9781003277996-4

## Critical Realism

Critical realism is an approach to social science ontology (the nature of social reality). It is a growing field with many contributors, but it is perhaps most prominently associated with the work of Roy Bhaskar. It is "realist" in that it argues there exists a reality independent of subjective experience. Though our ability to fully ascertain that reality may be constrained, it does not diminish this fact. As Bhaskar (2002, p. 8) states, "clearly there would be things, and there would be events, actual phenomena, even if humanity was not here to observe it." This view contradicts subjectivist ontologies which can tend to conflate individual experience of reality with reality itself.

For Bhaskar (2002, p. 8), this reality is subdivided into three domains for the purposes of social scientific inquiry: *the actual, the empirical,* and *the real.* Hall and Winlow (2015, p. 99) explain that the empirical refers to the "experiences of knowing subjects." We know the world through our experiences of it. The actual "represents real events or absences that often sit outside of our everyday experiences but can nevertheless shape subjective experience at the empirical level" (Kotzé & Lloyd, 2022, p. 12). Events may happen which we may not directly experience or have knowledge of that may still impact our lives. Or there may exist absences that create similar effects—failures to act, removal of resources, and the like. The real refers to "underlying generative mechanism that cause the events that are open to experience" (Kotzé & Lloyd, 2022, p. 12). It constitutes the realm "beyond sense perception," which has "a causative effect on the events and experiences at the actual and empirical level" (Kotzé & Lloyd, 2022, p. 12). This is an "intransitive realm," which cannot be directly observed or experienced but is still said to have fundamental causative impacts. Critical realists argue that positivist and empiricist social sciences only extend into the empirical and actual whereas the objective of social sciences should be to craft explanations which move beyond these domains to the deep structures and mechanisms situated in the real.

As a result of this ontology, critical realists tend to prioritize the role of social structure and similar elements as central causative mechanisms, though they do recognize the importance of factors like culture and materiality. The perspective thus tackles the structure–agency debate head-on. For critical realists, structure and agency operate in mutually reinforcing ways. Structure shapes and constrains action and action, in turn, recreates, reinforces, or changes social structure. Structure, however, precedes agency in the temporal ordering of causation. As Bhaskar (2002, p. 20) explains, "we never create social structure, we never create the social circumstances into which we are born. We never create it from scratch, it always pre-exists us." Further, while humans can change social structure, such changes are likely to be slight and incremental. There is thus a kind of inertia to social structure. In this sense, structure has a life both dependent upon and independent from human action. Critical realists also hold that both structure and agency are "irreducible" to one another (Archer, 1995, p. 14). Structures cannot be understood simply as amalgamated individual action where structure is "passive" (Archer, 1995, p. 4). At the same time, individuals are not servile automatons whose actions are wholly determined by the machinations of structure.

In this manner, critical realism understands reality as "stratified" and "emergent" (Archer, 1995). Emergence refers to the idea that social structures are not conjured out of thin air fully formed. Instead, they emerge over time through a developmental process. For instance, capitalism did not suddenly appear one day. It gradually arose as economic relations among individuals changed.

Further, this emergence is a continual process as social structures incrementally change due to human action and historical circumstance. Stratification means that entities, including social structures, may be composed of constituent parts, but the whole cannot be reduced to the elements of its composition. Water is a popular natural science corollary among critical realists. A water molecule can be understood as a combination of two hydrogen atoms and one oxygen—it cannot exist without both elements. Yet, the characteristics and behavior of water cannot be understood by examining hydrogen and oxygen in isolation as water behaves in a manner distinct from its base atoms and molecules (e.g. stable liquid state within a given temperature range, capillarity, etc.). This is what is meant by the irreducibility of strata, that one level cannot be explained by only examining strata above or below it. Similarly, structure and agency are said to comprise different strata, which cannot be reduced to one another because each possesses characteristics and causative powers which are their own (Archer, 1995, pp. 3–14).

The tension between structure and agency also means that critical realism views causation probabilistically rather than deterministically. Structures and other generative mechanisms may encourage, constrain, or otherwise influence action, but do not determine it absolutely (Bhaskar, 1978, p. 14; 2002; Hall & Winlow, 2015; Kotzé & Lloyd, 2022). In other words, causation under critical realism is not a simplistic formula where a change in X causes a direct corresponding change in Y. Rather, change in X increases the *probability* that there will be a change in Y.

Critical realists thus argue that (1) reality is real, (2) our ability to understand this reality is limited, (3) the best kinds of knowledge attempt to connect observations with underlying structural mechanisms in the intransitive realm of the real, (4) structure and agency are distinct, albeit interrelated, causal forces which cannot be reduced to one another, and (5) causation refers to probabilistic tendencies. There are other elements of critical realism, but these elements likely suffice for present purposes (with apologies to any slighted critical realists).

## Reservations

Critical realism is a fascinating and insightful philosophy. Yet, I am hesitant to embrace the perspective outright. Specifically, the argument that the causative power of social structures is *irreducible* to the actions of its constituent agents seems problematic or, at the very least, introduces some confusion. As Kaidesoja (2007, p. 3) points out, Bhaskar never fully justifies why we must "refer to social structures which possess causal powers that are ontologically distinct from agents and their interactions" and that he needs to clarify "why descriptions and explanations of social phenomena necessarily require reference to such causally efficacious social structures which are separated from the interactions of individuals." The justification for irreducibility appears incomplete.

The language of critical realists, including its descriptions of irreducibility, confers an ontologically privileged status to social structure that may be unwarranted. It is populated with what Kivinen and Piiroinen (2004, p. 232) call "heavy ontological furniture." For critical realists, social structure is *real* and *separate* from human action (Kaidesoja, 2005, p. 32). In the preface of *A Realist Theory of Science,* Bhaskar (1978, p. 9) explicitly states that "the basic principle of realist philosophy of science, viz. that perception gives us access to things and experimental activity access to structures that *exist independently of us* [emphasis added]." In *The Possibility of Nautralism,* he responds to the question "what properties to societies and people possess that might make them possible objects of knowledge for us?" by stating:

> It is important to note that I must establish that any such properties, and *a fortiori* their bearers, *are real*. That is to say, I must show not only that in explanations in the domain of the human sciences social (and psychological) predicates are irreducible (which is consistent with a transcendental idealist interpretation of their status), but that a realistic interpretation of social scientific (and psychological) theory is in principle acceptable; that is, that some possible objects designated by social scientific (and psychological) theory *are real*. [emphasis added]
>
> *(ibid, p. 14)*

Further still, he states explicitly that "I argue that social forms are a necessary condition for any intentional act, that their *pre-existence* establishes their *autonomy* as possible objects of scientific inquiry and that their *causal power* establishes their *reality* [emphasis in original]" (ibid, p. 25). Later he states that "people and society are not, I shall argue, related 'dialectically'. They do not constitute two moments of the same process. Rather they refer to radically different kinds of things" (ibid, p. 33). These are only some examples that indicate that Bhaskar seems to impart a very literal reality to social structures rather than a purely conceptual one.[2]

This is not to say that critical realists hold that social structure is entirely independent of individual action. Bhakar (2002, p. 20), for instance, explicitly denies reifying social structure in this manner:

> What I argued was, against voluntarism, that we never create social structure, we never create the social

circumstances into which we are born. We never create it from scratch, it always pre-exists us. Therefore we must acknowledge the presence of the past, we must acknowledge the presence of the structures which we inherit. We can reproduce and change them as radically as we want or as conditions allow us, but they pre-exist us and that legacy of the past must be acknowledged. *At the same time, against those who commit the opposite error to voluntarism, that of reification, these social structures would not be ongoing unless we reproduced them or transformed them in our conscious intentional activity.* So we have a view of the social structure pre-existing humanity, but existing only in virtue of our ongoing human activity. This was the basis of the transformational model of social activity.

*(emphasis added)*

Here there is a clear statement that human action and social structure are intractably intertwined. Yet, by arguing that social structure has causative powers *irreducible* to the collective action of individuals, there is at least some element of independence at play. They are ontologically separate and distinct and have causative powers all their own (Bhaskar, 1998, p. 37).

It is not my interpretation alone that Bhaskar ascribes a literal independent existence to social structure. Kemp (2022, p. 313), for instance, cites Bhaskar (1978) to explain that:

the idea that scientists are trying to investigate deep structures that exist *independently* of them allows realists to distinguish themselves from positivists who focus on surface events and (quasi)-idealists who see the natural world as constructed in/by scientific theories.

*(emphasis added)*

Pleasants (1999, pp. 110–111) explores Bhaskar's distinction between "knowledge (the 'transitive' realm) and that which knowledge is *about* (the 'intransitive' realm of ontology)," noting that the intransitive is "strictly non-relativistic—it consists of objects, powers, mechanisms, structures and relations which operate and endure 'transfactually', regardless of their state of empirical manifestation." It thus does not appear controversial to recognize that Bhaskar speaks of the literal reality and independence of social structures and related mechanisms operating within an intransitive realm. In this way, "Bhaskar claims that social structure both has a *sui generis* real, separable existence from people, and does not exist independently of people" (Pleasants, 1999, p. 112).

I am personally unconvinced that the causative powers of social structures are irreducible to the actions of their constituent agents. And yet, for critical realists, good social analyses *must* account for these hidden, invisible, and irreducible social structural powers. I agree with Bruno Latour (2005, p. 53) that explanations which rely on literal "invisible and unaccountable social forces" constitute "conspiracy theory, not social theory." If these arguments were framed epistemologically, I would be much more sympathetic. Bhaskar's arguments could be seen as a framework through which reality can be *understood*—that structure would be a concept used to make sense of social patterns and stabilities. Because critical realism's descriptions of social structure are an attempt to describe the nature of reality itself (Elder-Vass, 2022, p. 273), accepting its arguments means accepting their transcendental basis.

Pleasants (1999, p. 111) similarly contends that Bhaskar's arguments might not be so problematic if they were framed epistemologically rather than ontologically:

If emergence is to be seen as an (intransitive) ontological property of certain phenomena, and not as a (transitive) epistemological limit on our ability to explain or understand the relationship between levels, then we are back to Humean scepticism (against which—to put it mildly—Bhaskar is passionately opposed). If emergent phenomena really are "ontologically" irreducible, then all we can do is note what are in effect only "constant-conjunction" relations between higher and lower orders.

Using the brain–mind analytic dualism, he adds that:

Thus we know that brains are composed of physical stuff, and that mind and its powers are "*sui generis* real", but we must not try to say *how* it emerges from its physical basis because any such (reductionist) move *ipso facto* subverts the unique, "emergent" reality of mental powers.

*(ibid)*

This same problem applies to Bhaskar's view on the causal relationship between structure and agency as well (Pleasants, 1999, p. 112). In other words, the irreducibility argument means that we cannot accomplish much more than state that social structures and other causative mechanisms occur alongside their effects, but cannot explain how these causal powers emerge *because then they would be reducible*. Thus, it would make more sense, for Pleasants (1999, p. 112), for critical realism to consider "emergence" and "irreducibility" to be "transitive concepts" rather than "intransitive phenomena."

To this effect, it is perhaps best to view social structures conceptually rather than as real entities suspended aloft above humanity. What we call "social structures" are concepts which help us make sense of the complex patterns and conflicts evident among relationships and interactions found among individuals (Harré & Bhaskar, 2001, pp. 22–28).[3] These concepts may endure if they are useful for making sense of social behavior, its patterns, stability, *et cetera*, but we must always bear in mind that these concepts may be incomplete, imperfect, inaccurate, or otherwise ill-fitted to our analysis, especially if used carelessly and haphazardly. And their utility may change over time, requiring an update to our conceptions of these social structures or to invent new conceptions to better explain the current situation. Critical realists do not necessarily disagree with these points as they similarly adopt a fallibilist view of epistemology—that our ability to comprehend reality may be limited. But as an ontology, critical realism elevates social structure to the status of real, causative entities with powers all their own. Instead, what we describe as the causative power of social structures is the collective causal impact of individual action. We *can* reduce social structure in this manner.

Imagine that we, as social scientists, were omnipotent and all-powerful and, by virtue of our newly found god-like status, could instantaneously study all the social interactions, relationships, conflicts, and other activities of people, tracing them meticulously and documenting them in voluminous tomes. If we were to do that, we would have all the causative explanations necessary to understand our present without appealing to unseen invisible forces irreducible to the actions of individuals, which we have thoroughly documented (Latour, 2005). We could, for example, see how capitalists manage to elevate themselves to positions where they could coerce others into compliance, how social stratification and inequities formed, how political institutions were established and maintained, and so on. Assuming an equally timeless and omnipotent reader, they could digest our descriptions and themselves arrive at a comprehensive understanding of the present. We might be able to identify general patterns or even social laws. We might not be able to generate deterministic predictions of the future (we are not advocating for Laplace's demon here), but certainly we could make probabilistic ones.[4] But I see no reason in this scenario why we would identify social structural causal powers *irreducible* to the relations described in our infinite document.

Yet, we are not all-powerful and omnipotent. If we hope to do "big picture" studies of society, we have to rely on heuristics like "social structure" to do some heavy lifting for us. And, to be clear, we *should* use these concepts. They can be incredibly useful for social analysis and for political action. But we should never lose sight of the fact that they are, at the end of the day, tools to make sense of an otherwise overwhelming world (Harré & Bhaskar, pp. 22–28; Kivinen & Piiroinen, 2004, p. 235). In other words, social structure is a useful epistemological device but an ontologically awkward one. Likely this view is, as will be discussed in the following chapter, a reflection of my pragmatic leanings. As Elder-Vass (2022, p. 274) explains, "scepticism about ontological claims is common amongst sociological pragmatists, and connects to a belief that they can manage perfectly well without them." And to this point, I suppose guilty as charged. This view toward social structure will be revisited in Chapters 4 and 5 (we will properly beat a dead horse).

Relatedly, I am uncomfortable with the metaphysics of critical realism. It requires a belief in intransitive and unobservable realm of "the real"—a kind of parallel dimension where social structures loom and their tendrils can slip through the veil to influence our actions in the realm of the actual or empirical. Such structures emerge from collective human activity and then exist within a parallel dimension. Here again, I cannot help but agree with Latour (2020, p. 287): " 'emergence' has always been for me an apparently scientific way to say 'here a miracle occurs!' " Indeed, believing in the emergent production of social structural entities seems to require a spiritual belief that human collective action can birth ontologically independent, invisible objects in an aethereal realm. That is a leap of faith I cannot make.

In *The Myth of Sisyphus*, Albert Camus (1942) argues that there is no ultimate meaning to existence—the universe is chaotic and life is a cosmic accident—and that the search for meaning is not only futile, but ultimately *absurd*. Rather than give meaning to life, religion and other systems of belief only offer the *illusion of meaning* to existence. Retreat from the absurdity of life, for him, constitutes "philosophical suicide," grasping at figments of meaning while disavowing the cold, bleak reality of the absurd (Camus, 1942, pp. 28–50). Similarly, retreating from the complexity and nuance of human collective existence into the intransitive realm of the real and the irreducible power of social structure is itself a kind of *sociological suicide*. The insistence of the causative presence of social structure within the transitive realm requires the researcher to view structural causative powers as a matter of faith—as if we are to believe in gods and devils—and imbue them with an unwarranted metaphysical significance.

The likely critical realist response against this argument is that a failure to treat social structure transcendentally engenders a tendency toward individualistic analyses (Elder-Vass, 2022, p. 262; Kemp, 2022).[5] Such concerns are not without merit. For instance, Latour (2005) argues that social scientists should adopt a flattened ontology where the analyst eschews social structure altogether and, instead, prioritizes tracing associations among actors within a network, keeping their nose to the ground like a good little "ant" (see also: Kemp, 2022; Latour's version of actor network theory will be revisited in Chapter 5). Yet, I do not think we need to accept the ontological view of structure advanced by critical realists to make use of social structure as an analytic tool. As previously stated, concepts related to social structures—capitalism, organizations, institutions, *et cetera*—can be useful. They have been employed across a range of theoretical and philosophical perspectives that do not subscribe to the same ontological suppositions of critical realism.

Further, I worry that the insistence on reaching toward these deep generative causal mechanisms within "the real" limits our analytical horizons. In his critique of functionalism, Lévi-Strauss (1963, p. 13) once remarked that "to say that something functions in a society is a truism, to say that everything is functional is an absurdity." He was lamenting the tendency of functionalists to view *everything* as functional—the result being that researchers would bend their analyses to conform to the assumption of functionality. Similarly, to say social explanations must reach toward depth structures within the intransitive realm of the real seems similarly problematic. Surely is there some room for non-intransitive explanations in criminology? Further, because objects within the realm of the real are, by their very nature, unobservable and can only be known through their effects, my concern is that anyone who wants to find these structural causes within the realm of the real will be able to find them, whether they exist or not. Explanations for observations could be bent to conform with the assumption of generative structural mechanisms, with any shortcomings attributed to probability or capricious agency. Such explanations may never fail to be correct because how could we know otherwise (Pleasants, 1999, pp. 114–115)?

The next chapter considers an alternative philosophy of social science—pragmatism. Matters of structure and agency will be revisited along with views toward knowledge and knowledge production. Additionally, though pragmatism has been much maligned—and not without good reason—as liberal and relativistic, Chapter 4 will consider the critical potential of pragmatism for realist criminology.

## Notes

1  I will not review all the criticisms made against critical realism. For those interested, there are more eloquent and thoughtful critiques available (e.g. Pleasants, 1999; Kivinen & Piiroinen, 2004).

2  Bhaskar (1998, pp. 21–22) does note that critical realism "can sustain the *transfactuality* of social structures, while insisting on their *conceptuality* (or concept-dependence)." He elaborates elsewhere that "critical realism accepts the hermeneutical thesis of the conceptuality of social life. But it argues that social life, though concept-dependent, is not exhausted by its conceptuality. It has a material as well as a conceptual dimension" (Bhaskar, 2020, p. 116). Here, he argues that there is a material element of social life independent of its conceptuality—essentially a restatement of its realist orientation that there does exist a reality independent of our individual beliefs and experiences. But to say that there is a material element of reality (an example he gives is the carnage of war) is not the same as affirming the existence of irreducible social structures.

3  The reference to Harré and Bhaskar (2001) refers specifically to Harré's arguments presented in this piece, which are separate from Bhaskar's.

4  Thanks to Graham Leach Krouse for introducing me to the Laplace's demon thought experiment.

5  While reading a prior draft of this chapter, Majid Yar offered what I thought was a novel and spot-on observation:

> It seems to me that realist criminologists are forever conflating the *epistemological* and *ontological* with the *political* and *moral*. They fear that an ontology that favors the subject as the constitutive element of "the social" automatically

endorses moral and political *individualism*. Likewise, they seem to think that granting ontological privilege to that which transcends the individual automatically favors a political and moral valuation of the collective and communal. This, for me, is simply unwarranted and unhelpful.

## References

Archer, M. (1995). *Realist social theory: The morphogenic approach.* Cambridge: Cambridge University Press.

Bhaskar, R. (1978). *A realist theory of science.* Atlantic Highlands, NJ: Humanities Press Inc.

Bhaskar, R. (1998). Philosophy and scientific realism. In M. Archer, R. Bhaskar, A. Collier, T. Lawson, & A. Norrie (eds.) *Critical realism: Essential readings* (pp. 16–47). New York: Routledge.

Bhaskar, R. (2002). *From science to emancipation: Alienation and the actuality of enlightenment.* New York: Routledge.

Bhaskar, R. (2020). Critical realism and the ontology of persons. *Journal of Critical Realism, 19*(2), 113–120.

Camus, A. (1942). *The myth of Sisyphus.* New York: Vintage Books.

Elder-Vass, D. (2022). Pragmatism, critical realism and the study of value. *Journal of Critical Realism, 21*(3), 261–287.

Hall, S., & Winlow, S. (2015). *Revitalizing criminological theory: Towards a new ultra-realism.* New York: Routledge.

Harré, R. & Bhaskar, R. (2001). How to change reality: Story v. structure–A debate between Rom Harré and Roy Bhaskar. In J. López & G. Potter (eds.) *After postmodernism: An introduction to critical realism* (pp. 22–39). New York: The Athlone Press.

Kaidesoja, T. (2005). The trouble with transcendental arguments: Towards a naturalization of Roy Bhaskar's early realist ontology. *Journal of Critical Realism, 4*(1), 28–61.

Kaidesoja, T. (2007). The concept of social structure in Roy Bhaskar's critical realism. *Sociologia, 44*(2), 79–94. English translation retrieved July 10, 2022 from www.researchgate. net/profile/Tuukka-Kaidesoja/publication/307475809_The_ Concept_of_Social_Structure_in_Roy_Bhaskar's_Critical_ Realism/links/57c68d7308aefc4af34a9eb0/The-Concept-of-Social-Structure-in-Roy-Bhaskars-Critical-Realism.pdf

Kemp, S. (2022). Organizational de-structuring? Latour's potential contribution to the critical realist–pragmatist dispute. *Journal of Critical Realism, 21*(3), 309–330.

Kivinen, O., & Piiroinen, T. (2004). The relevance of ontological commitments in social sciences: Realist and pragmatist viewpoints. *Journal for the Theory of Social Behaviour, 34*(3), 231–248.

Kotzé, J., & Lloyd, A. (2022). *Making sense of ultra-realism: Contemporary criminological theory through the lens of popular culture.* Bingley, United Kingdom: Emerald Publishing Limited.

Latour, B. (2005). *Reassembling the social: An introduction to actor-network theory.* New York: Oxford University Press.

Latour, B. (2020). Afterword: Politics—A glimpse at bodybuilding. In B. Latour, S. Schaffer, and P. Gagliardi (eds.) *A book of the body politic: Connecting biology, politics and social theory* (pp. 285–302). Venice: Fondazione Giorgio Cini.

Lévi-Strauss, C. (1963). *Structural anthropology.* New York: Basic Books.

Pleasants, N. (1999). *Wittgenstein and the idea of a critical social theory: A critique of Giddens, Habermas and Bhaskar.* New York: Routledge.

# 4

# EMBRACING PRAGMATISM

Given the "heavy ontological furniture" involved with critical realism, realist criminology may be better served by a different philosophical foundation—something more flexible and unburdened by unnecessary metaphysics and structural commitments.[1] At the same time, there is much to admire about critical realism including its fallibilistic view toward knowledge, assumption of the existence of an external reality beyond sense-perception, appreciation of empirical evidence in the scientific enterprise, and willingness to consider values to be a legitimate domain of analysis. In this chapter, it is argued that American Pragmatism may be a better base for realist criminology as it shares many of critical realism's strengths while avoiding its metaphysical trappings (Elder-Vass, 2022, pp. 261–262; Elder-Vass & Zotzman, 2022).[2]

Pragmatism emerged in the late 1860s and early 1870s as part of the "Metaphysical Club" in Cambridge, Massachusetts (Misak, 2013; West, 1989). Its members included Charles S. Peirce, William James, Oliver Wendell Holmes, Chauncey Wright, and other figures in

DOI: 10.4324/9781003277996-5

the American intellectual scene of the time. Pragmatism became a preeminent school of American philosophy with pronounced intellectual impacts that shaped the trajectories of sociology, psychology, criminology, and many other disciplines. Its themes have appeared across a diverse array of philosophical works outside of the pragmatist tradition including those by Ludwig Wittgenstein, W. V. O. Quine, Donald Davidson, Wilfred Sellars, and Jacques Derrida (Bernstein, 2010, pp. 1–31; Misak, 2013). Despite its waning popularity throughout the mid-20th century, the perspective has undergone a resurgence in recent decades, with prominent philosophers and social theorists reinvigorating pragmatist ideas including Hilary Putnam, Richard Rorty, Richard Bernstein, Cheryl Misak, Jürgen Habermas, Hans Joas, and Cornel West, to name only a few.

My objective is to utilize pragmatism as basic philosophical foundation for advancing the social scientific and practical endeavor of realist criminology.[3] This chapter details a pragmatist approach toward knowledge and knowledge production, the critical potential of pragmatist thought, and its approach to the structure–agency problem. The account provided herein is by no means definitive or comprehensive. The philosophy has a long and storied history. I hope, however, that this review convinces the reader to at least consider the benefits of such an approach. Even if the connections are not always explicit, my objective is that the realist criminology described throughout this book be consistent with the pragmatist foundations described herein. More work is necessary to fully develop a criminological "critical pragmatism" (Kadlec, 2006). Any mistakes or inconsistencies in this regard are, of course, mine and mine alone. For those interested in more complete accounts of pragmatism, I recommend Cheryl Misak's (2013) *The American Pragmatists,* Cornel West's

(1989) *The American Evasion of Philosophy,* Richard Bernstein's (2010) *The Pragmatic Turn,* and Dave Elder-Vass's (2022) "Pragmatism, Critical Realism, and the Study of Value" in the *Journal of Critical Realism.*

## Belief, Doubt, and Inquiry

Like critical realists, pragmatists, at least those following in the footsteps of Peirce, believe that there does exist an external reality but that our ability to know this reality is limited (Peirce, 1997, p. 58; Ritz, 2022).[4] In other words, knowledge is fallible.[5] Grappling with this problem, pragmatists carefully consider how knowledge is developed and rendered useful despite the gap between reality and experience. Peirce (1955a, p. 29) describes the basic unit of knowledge as "belief" or a position held by an individual or group, which serves as a readymade basis to guide action. It is the formation of a disposition (or "habit") which primes a person to act a particular way under certain circumstances.[6] The reader should note the connection drawn between belief and action—the two are intrinsically intertwined. Pragmatism is known for its emphasis on outcomes. If beliefs matter, then they should result in consequences of some kind. If two beliefs differ on their face but generate no discernable differences in outcome, then they are not *really* different, at least according to Peirce.

For pragmatists, we do not enter situations devoid of belief—we carry with us *a priori* beliefs, which provide readymade (though not determinative) foundations for action. It is perfectly logical and appropriate, according to Peirce (1955a, p. 26), for individuals to act as if their beliefs are true until such beliefs experience the "irritation of doubt." Doubt arises when a belief no longer works to achieve an objective or is otherwise countered by evidence or reason (Peirce, 1955a, p. 26). Such doubts are handled through "inquiry" or the process of evaluating, adjusting, jettisoning, or otherwise reconsidering beliefs and arriving upon a new belief that assuages our doubts. This new belief becomes the basis for action until new doubt is introduced and so on. A belief can be said to be good, roughly speaking, if it is useful as a platform for action and gives no reasonable basis for doubt. Bad beliefs, on the other hand, are those which fail to yield desired outcomes, provide no additional benefits over other beliefs, are contradicted by evidence and reason, or avoid the "irritation of doubt" through appeals to faith, dogma, or taboo.

As knowledge is framed as a process, pragmatists are deeply concerned with the development of legitimate and appropriate methods for the settlement of doubt. According to Misak (2013, pp. 17–18), pragmatism is not so much concerned with the origin of beliefs per se but, rather "what tests a belief must pass once we have it." "It is a view," she explains, "about what it is for a belief to count as nonspurious, genuine, or legitimate." Though the exact methods differ based on the subject matter at hand and the questions being asked, pragmatists generally favor a scientific approach, broadly conceived as a systematic mode of analysis requiring logic and evidence, grounded in experience (avoiding, as we will talk about later, appeals to transcendental phenomena outside the realm of experience). Ideally, the process of inquiry would continue until beliefs are arrived upon that so closely approximate reality that they can be considered "truth" or a "position unassailable by doubt" (Peirce, 1955b, p. 257). Such truths are beliefs that "will not disappoint; that will guide action on a safe course; that will continue to fit with experience, evidence and argument" (Misak, 2013, p. 35). Pragmatists therefore tend to be "anti-foundationalist" or opposed to the notion that "knowledge rests upon fixed foundations, and that we possess a special faculty of insight or intuition by which we can know these foundations" (Bernstein, 1997, p. 385; see also: Bernstein, 2010; West, 1989, p. 36). Instead, knowledge is produced through a dynamic process where our beliefs are put to test against experience, evidence, and reason to develop better beliefs.

Yet, it is not enough that a single inquirer arrives upon a doubt-resistant truth. Experiences vary and thus many inquirers may not be presented with the same reasons for doubt as others, leading to a plurality of "truths" and, thus, a descent into relativism, a tendency resisted by many pragmatists, especially those working in the tradition of Peirce.[7] To avoid such relativism, Peirce argued that it is necessary to examine beliefs within the context of a "community of inquirers." For many pragmatists, robust beliefs are those vetted by many through open and earnest dialog and analysis. The greater the consensus achieved and the less assailable by doubt a belief is, the greater truth value it contains.

Pragmatists, however, recognize that it is tremendously difficult to definitively settle belief, so much so that it may be difficult to know when absolute truths have been arrived upon (Misak, 2013, p. 34; Rorty, 2010, p. 3). Misak (2013, p. 229), however, explains that:

> Peirce does not think that rational inquirers must necessarily converge. He holds, rather, that for any given question we are inquiring into, *we must hope or assume that there would be an answer on which we would converge.*
>
> *(emphasis added)*

Thus, establishing that the pursuit of truth is a Sisyphean task, but one must maintain the hope of progress regardless (James, 1997c, p. 81). Pragmatism therefore holds a shred of epistemological utopianism that it is possible to arrive upon a collective idea of truth upon which there is no reasonable basis for doubt.

Pragmatists are hostile to dogmatic and absolutist beliefs, those that are not allowed to be questioned even in the face of legitimate doubt. Pragmatists are thus verificationists. All knowledge should be open to refutation through evidence and reason and there should exist connections between ideas and practice (James, 1997b, p. 114; Misak, 2013, p. 31; Peirce, 1955c, p. 54). Summarizing Peirce's "pragmatic maxim," Misak (2013, p. 29) states "our theories and concepts must be linked to experience, expectations, or consequences." In this spirit, pragmatists are generally opposed to any claims or arguments which preclude the possibility of investigation (Peirce, 1955c, p. 54). For this reason, pragmatists also tend to be methodological pluralists. Ethnography is certainly a valued methodology for pragmatists given their focus upon experience (Frega, 2014), but they are willing to consider all evidence relevant and appropriate for handling the question or problem at hand (Misak, 2013, p. 96). What they are uncomfortable with, however, as will be detailed further in Chapters 6 and 7, is with methodological fetishism or the primacy of method above theory or reason.

Yet, despite such reservations, pragmatists are equally careful to avoid unnecessary skepticism. Baseless and persistent interrogation of beliefs for its own sake is viewed as a path to intellectual paralysis. Questioning all beliefs all the time leaves us with no platform for action. As Bernstein (1997, p. 387) explains,

> we realize that although we must begin any inquiry with prejudgments and can never call everything into question at once, nevertheless there is no belief or

thesis—no matter how fundamental—that is not open to further interpretation and criticism.

Thus, the pragmatist simultaneously resists unnecessary skepticism while maintaining a perpetual openness to doubt.

Since pragmatists resist dogma, it also stands to reason that they tend toward naturalism in that they eschew "supernatural" or metaphysical explanations (Misak, 2013, p. x). For most pragmatists, there is little sense in appealing to some transcendental or extra-material plane as a source of causation because it "impedes inquiry, it fosters devotion and obedience, two attitudes that can only hobble science" (Misak, 2013, p. 18).[8] That said, pragmatists are also unwilling to throw the baby out with the bathwater. All matters are open to inquiry. For the pragmatist, there may be ideas and conflicts worth salvaging from the realm of metaphysics. The goal is to find "a way of discriminating between good meta-physics and bad" (Misak, 2013, pp. 19–20). Indeed, various pragmatists have grappled with metaphysical questions (e.g. James, Dewey, West). At every turn, however, pragmatists attempt to ground such analyses in the realm of experience and reason.

Additionally, the naturalism favored by pragmatists should not be confused with physicalism—the idea that all analysis must be rooted in the physical world. Pragmatism is distinguished from empiricism and positivism in that it considers matters like values and ethics fertile ground for inquiry (e.g. Dewey, 1998b). For example, Putnam (1997, p. 357) explains that "talk of 'justice,' like talk of 'reference,' can be *non*-scientific without being *un*scientific." In other words, while discussions of such matters may not be reducible to the language of physicality, there exists no reason why a scientific mindset cannot be brought to bear on politics, morality, culture, and similar matters. Pragmatists are also willing to examine mental processes and related phenomena which they consider to be very real even though the manifestations of the mind (e.g. dreams) may not themselves be valid reflections of reality.[9]

Further, pragmatists—like critical realists—recognize that values are intractably intertwined with the scientific process, problematizing the fact–value dichotomy (Putnam, 2002). Value judgments, for instance, are made when deciding upon knowledge relevance, applicability, and the kinds of rationality employed in any given analysis. Rather than feign objectivity, pragmatic social scientists are encouraged to examine the values endemic to their analysis and be open and honest about those values. This is not to say that knowledge cannot be sought rigorously and systematically in working toward some truth, only that we cannot assume our notions of objectivity and rationality may be permanently settled for every situation under all circumstances.

Finally, though pragmatists are interested in causality, they are anti-deterministic. They embrace the roles of "contingency" and "chance" as "ineradicable and pervasive features of the universe" (Bernstein, 1997, p. 388; see also: West, 1989, p. 52). Like critical realists, they recognize that "we can never hope to 'master' unforeseen and unexpected contingencies. We live in an 'open universe' which is always at once threatening and a source of tragedy and opportunity" (Bernstein, 1997, p. 389). When pragmatists speak of causation, they can only speak in probabilistic terms.

## The Critical Potential of Pragmatism

As previously mentioned, pragmatism is not an amoral or ethically agnostic perspective. It does involve certain value commitments. Unfortunately, the ethics and politics of pragmatism have been subjected to much debate and confusion. Pragmatism is often affiliated with what many consider liberal values—like individual autonomy, freedom of speech, and a deep commitment to democracy, perhaps most evident in the writings of John Dewey (Bernstein, 2010, p. 8; Dewey, 1971, p. 251; West, 1989). This commitment stems from pragmatism's democratic approach to knowledge production which values diverse perspectives (Bernstein, 1997, pp. 387–388; Misak, 2013, p. 23). As Bernstein (1997, p. 388) explains,

> It is only by submitting our hypothesis to public critical discussion that we become aware of what is valid in our claims and what fails to withstand critical scrutiny. *It is only by the serious encounter with what is other, different, and alien that we can hope to determine what is idiosyncratic, limited, and partial.*
>
> *(emphasis added)*

Of course, such a position is likely familiar to any student of the physical or social sciences. Pragmatists simply highlight this aspect as important for knowledge generation and connect it to a deeper democratic politics that permeates the tradition.

Critical and radical theorists have often dismissed pragmatism because of its associations with liberal values or have maligned the verificationist position of pragmatism as a veiled positivism (for an overview, see Joas, 1993, pp. 79–91). Gramsci, for instance, viewed pragmatism as "a crude apology for the *status quo*" and "steeped in a tradition of vulgar utilitarianism" (Kadlec, 2006, pp. 525–526). Horkheimer dismissed pragmatism as "nothing more than the philosophical residue of positivism" because of its qualified embrace of empiricism (Kadlec, 2006, p. 527). Others have argued that pragmatism tends to view knowledge production in a utopian manner—such that democratic processes will allow beliefs to progressively converge upon reality through processes of communal inquiry. This perspective, however, struggles to address how beliefs, trajectories of inquiry, and taboos may be shaped by power and conflict rather than earnest inquiry (Rytina & Loomis, 1970). In recent years, however, many scholars have complicated this understanding of pragmatism, gesturing toward the potential for a "critical pragmatism," which marries the pragmatists' epistemology and ethics with critical theory's focus on power, oppression, and resistance (Frega, 2014; Joas, 1993; Kadlec, 2006; Midtgarden, 2012; Ray, 2004).

Dewey is perhaps the pragmatist most committed to democratic principles in both his approach to inquiry and politics. As Ray (2004, p. 308) explains, "there is a political programme inherent in classical pragmatism, associated with John Dewey in particular, claiming that the conditions for establishing objective knowledge are the same as those sustaining democratic polity" (Ray, 2004, p. 308). It would be a mistake, however, to assume that democracy is used in this context to simply describe a method of governance. For Dewey, democracy is more broadly conceived as a modality of social organization. Frega (2014, p. 71) explains that a Deweyian conception of democracy,

> names every form of human association that complies with specific organizational principles, and in particular with (a) the principle of the freedom to experiment and of choice for individuals in undergoing social activities, and (b) the principle of the assignment of responsibilities to individuals in the undertaking of social tasks and in the shaping of social goals.
>
> *(citation omitted)*

In this sense, democracy is a broad term used to describe a way of organizing collectives, which highlights the importance of individual freedom *and* social responsibility.

Dewey's view of democracy goes hand-in-hand with his perspective on social conflict. Conflict, for him, is a problem of competing interests and fights for recognition. Domination occurs when one group's interests are legitimized as the interests of the whole society (Dewey, 1973; Frega, 2014, p. 73). Oppression, conversely, results when interests go unrecognized. Dewey was interested in exploring how social conflicts could restrict growth or the capacity of individuals and groups to engage in self-realization and full-democratic participatory potential. For him, oppression is harmful because it restricts the ability of folks to participate in, contribute to, and realize the benefits of collective engagement.

None of this is to say that Dewey provides a straightforward pathway toward a "critical pragmatism." But this discussion highlights its potential. His work shows a conceptualization of harm based in suppression of potential for self-realization and democratic contribution, a conception of power rooted in the legitimation of interests, and struggle rooted in fights for recognition. In addition, Dewey was all too aware of how the tyranny of the powerful, including capitalists, could undermine democracy, freedom, and individual autonomy. For instance, his descriptions of the state-of-affairs during his time would sound eerily familiar for the students of Marx:

> That the competitive system, which was thought of by early liberals as the means by which the latent abilities of individuals were to be evoked and directed into socially useful channels, is now in fact a state of

scarcely disguised battle hardly needs to be dwelt upon. That the control of the means of production by the few in legal possession operates as a standing agency of coercion of the many, may need emphasis in statement, but is surely evident to one who is willing to observe and honestly report the existing scene. It is foolish to regard the political state as the only agency now endowed with coercive power. Its exercise of this power is pale in contrast with that exercised by concentrated and organized property interests.

(Dewey, 1998c, p. 326)

He also argues against crass individualism endemic to some variations of liberalism. While he views social change best achieved through the judicious application of "intelligence," this is not a celebration of individual genius but, rather, Dewey recognizes that intelligence is a social characteristic—that knowledge is generated by a community (ibid, p. 327). Relatedly, he thought that individuals have a social responsibility toward one another. That said, it would be a mistake to assert that Dewey's thought was indistinguishable from Marx. Dewey could be quite hostile to Marxism, perhaps a prejudice endowed by his status as a preeminent American philosopher and his seeming unwillingness to jeopardize his own professional status (Rytina & Loomis, 1970).

Other scholars have done more to show the critical potential of pragmatism (e.g. Frega, 2014; Joas, 1993; Habermas, 1998; Kadlec, 2006; Midtgarden, 2012; Ray, 2004; West, 1989). For instance, Cornel West (1989) demonstrates the compatibility of pragmatist and radical thought in *The American Evasion of Philosophy*. Here, he articulates a "prophetic pragmatism," a synthesis merging pragmatism's embrace of community, democracy, diversity, and inclusion, radical theories' concerns with power, oppression, and inequality, and his own Christian faith. At the same time, he acknowledges that, though many pragmatists were ardently committed to justice and inclusion, many maintained "blindnesses and silences" toward certain kinds of exclusion from this democratic project, such as those made along race or gender lines (West, 1989, pp. 146–147, 180). Despite such shortcomings, West demonstrates that there is nothing endemic to the pragmatist tradition that forecloses opposition to ensconced power, oppression, exploitation, and abuse nor any inherent tendency which obstructs the quest for sweeping changes for the advancement of society. He explains that "the prophetic religious person, much like C. Wright Mills' activist intellectual, puts a premium on educating and being educated by struggling peoples, organizing and being organized by resisting groups" (West, 1989, p, 234).

Speaking of which, C. Wright Mills is another prominent example of how pragmatism and radical theory can be conjoined. Though sometimes controversial, Mills was a profound influence on the development of American critical sociology through works like *The Power Elite, The Sociological Imagination,* and *Power, Politics and People.* While it would be a stretch to claim Mills himself was a pragmatist, he was certainly steeped in the works of pragmatists—his dissertation was titled *A Sociological Account of Pragmatism: An Essay on the Sociology of Knowledge.* Though he was a radical thinker indebted to theorists like Marx and Veblen, his work possesses strong pragmatic commitments (Aronowitz, 2012; Dunn, 2018; Treviño, 2012). Dunn (2018, p. 3) highlights the influence of Dewey in particular, explaining that he and Mills shared "an abiding concern for the public role the social sciences should play as a normative science focused on societal problems, the well-being of the individual, and the moral, ethical, and political concerns of society and its members." These concerns not only shaped Mills's (1959, p. 8) dedication to examining the role of political and economic power in society, but also his view toward social science methodology—most thoroughly detailed in *The Sociological Imagination*—which looks to draw connections between "the personal troubles of milieu" and "the public issues of social structure" (this methodological orientation will be explored in greater depth in Chapter 7).

To this end, perhaps the strongest point of convergence between pragmatism and critical theory is that both share a commitment to generating *useful* knowledge including knowledge applicable to improving the human condition (Dunn, 2018; Rytina & Loomis, 1970). For the Marxist-oriented perspectives, this is usually framed as "praxis." In the *Theses on Feuerbach,* Marx (1970, p. 122) explains that "all social life is essentially practical. All mysteries which lead theory to mysticism find their rational solution in human practice and in the comprehension of this practice." He later stated that "the philosophers have only interpreted the world, in various ways; the point is to change it" (ibid, p. 123). Similarly, pragmatists are convinced that knowledge should be useful. Dewey (1998d, p. 46) remarked that philosophy "is unusually conservative—not, necessarily, in proffering solutions, but in clinging to problems." Elsewhere, he explains that philosophy should be "an intellectualized wish, an aspiration subjected to rational discriminations and tests, a social hope reduced to a working program of action, a prophecy of the future, but one disciplined by serious thought and knowledge" (Dewey, 1998b, p. 72). It is not enough for pragmatists that knowledge be useful in a crude utilitarian sense. Knowledge is best committed toward the uplifting of the human condition. Dewey (1998b, p. 73) argued that we should work in the pursuit of "wisdom" or "a conviction about moral values, a sense for the better kind of life to be led." Similarly, West's (1989, p. 229) vision of pragmatism "promotes the possibility of human progress and the human impossibility of paradise."

Though there exist points of convergence, significant divergences exist between pragmatists and critical scholars (too many, in fact, to cover in this chapter!). Perhaps the most notable distinction is that pragmatists are unwilling to privilege class as a central organizing concept for intellectual inquiry. Dewey, for instance, was an unabashed liberal skeptical of "class conflict," worried it would lead to simply replacing the tyranny of one class with that of another (Dewey, 1998c; 1998a; Midtgarden, 2012, p. 509). Similarly, West (1989, p. 235) claims that his prophetic pragmatism is not "confined to any preordained historical agent, such as the working class, black people, or women." Instead, "it invites all people of goodwill both here and abroad to fight for an Emersonian culture of creative democracy in which the plight of the wretched of the earth is alleviated" (ibid).[10] Conversely, radicals tend to privilege class within their analysis including many realist criminologists (Hall, 2012; Hall & Winlow, 2015; Matthews, 2014; Lea & Young, 1984; Young, 1975). Certainly, class is a key mechanism of organization and stratification in society, but it is also important not to reduce everything to "epiphenomenon" of the political economy (Wood et al., 2020). It is necessary to strike a balance—to examine how systems, institutions, and other mechanisms of social differentiation manifest, result in conflict and domination, and operate both independently *and* dependently of other mechanisms (Raymen & Kuldova, 2020, p. 254). Further, adopting a rigidly class-centered analytic approach risks requiring the researcher to impose an explanation and then cherry-pick or bend the evidence to conform to the explanation. Basically, everything is capitalism and capitalism is everything. As Frega (2014, p. 72, note 23) explains, however,

> Dewey wants to provide a general concept of social conflict that is not a general explanation to be imposed on any social situation from outside. Concepts are tools for exploring social reality, and the concept of conflict is no exception to this rule.

In other words, explanations should fit the evidence and not the other way around. We thus should resist the impulse to insert our explanations *a priori*.

Pragmatists and critical theorists may also differ in their views toward democracy. Dewey (1998a, 1998c), for instance, viewed the erosion of liberal rights as a failure to fight hard enough for the maintenance of democratic methods of social organization whereas Marxists and other radicals tend to view such erosions as a result of the dialectical contradictions endemic to liberalism—that liberal democracy will continually find ways to undermine itself, a tension between freedom and oppression (Losurdo, 2011; Harvey, 2014, pp. 199–215). Relatedly, pragmatists generally adopt a reformist view toward social change. This does not mean, however, that such reforms should be implemented in a haphazard or unstructured manner. Dewey (1998c, p. 325) once remarked that changes to the liberal regime cannot be overcome through "piecemeal policies undertaken *ad hoc*," he added that radical changes are best enacted through a gradual process guided by a clear "social goal based upon an inclusive plan." Though pragmatists are reformist, they call for careful planning and clear objectives in the realization of their goals. Conversely, radicals tend to argue that reforms—though they may bring mild or temporary relief to the oppressed— only allow a broken system to lurch forward, manifesting its mechanisms of control in new ways (Quinney, 1977, pp. 78–90; Tant, 2004).[11] That said, the tension between "revolution" and "reform" is by no means a settled debate among radicals (e.g. Gorz, 1967). The issue of reform will be taken up further in Chapter 5.

## On Structure and Agency

If it is possible to use pragmatism in analyses of power and oppression, then it is also necessary to consider how the perspective handles the structure–agency problem. Agency is a relatively simple matter. Like Marxists and, indeed, most contemporary social theorists, pragmatists generally contend that actors have agency but do not exercise their freedom under circumstances of their choosing. Joas (1993, p. 4) argues that pragmatists view humans as engaged in "creative action" and exercise "situated freedom." According to him, "actors confront problems whether they want to or not; the solution to these problems, however, is not clearly prescribed beforehand by reality, but calls for creativity and brings something objectively new into the world" (ibid).[12] These problems emerge under objective circumstances, filtered through subjective perception, and are acted upon within the context of the situation.[13] Simple enough.[14]

Discerning a pragmatist position on social structure is a more complicated matter, though not insurmountably so. While pragmatists tend to be wary of structural explanations of social phenomena (Elder-Vass, 2022, p. 262), some embrace their explanatory power. It is one thing to be careful about making transcendental arguments about structure and quite another to dismiss the idea of structure altogether. As previously explained in Chapter 3, the concept has significant utility for directing our attention to the "big picture," to get us out of the muck and mire of the immediate. Structural analysis can help us avoid becoming what C. Wright Mills (1943) referred to as "social pathologists." Astructural analyses, according to Mills (1943, p. 172), do not permit "points of entry for broader types of action, especially political action." If we are to make real, substantive change, then we must consider our problems within the entire fabric of society and not simply a swatch or thread.

Early pragmatists did not say much, if anything, about social structure, at least not in such terms. Glimmers of such thinking are evident in some of their writings, however. Consider the pragmatist notion of "habit." Peirce conceived of habit as a predisposition toward action. Like the transcendental materialism embraced by ultra-realists, James (1997a, p. 61) contended that the habits of creatures, including humans, are marked by varying degrees of "plasticity" in the sense that they are in "possession of a structure weak enough to yield to an influence, but strong enough not to yield all at once." In other words, organic life has an inherent capacity to change, though that capacity may vary and there are limits to the degree to which change may occur. These habits were said to be molded by circumstance and embedded into the circuitry of the brain. He then traces a connection between individual habit, social stability, and the durability of social roles:

Habit is thus the enormous fly-wheel of society, its most precious conservative agent. It alone is what keeps us all within the bounds of ordinance, and saves the children of fortune from the envious uprisings of the poor. It alone prevents the hardest and most repulsive walks of life from being deserted by those brought up to tread therein. It keeps the fisherman and the deck-hand at sea through the winter; it holds the miner in his darkness, and nails the countryman to his log-cabin and his lonely farm through all the months of snow; it protects us from invasion by the natives of the desert and the frozen zone. It dooms us all to fight out the battle of life upon the lines of our nurture or our early choice, and to make the best of a pursuit that disagrees, because there is no other for which we are fitted, and it is too late to begin again. It keeps different social strata from mixing.

*(James, 1997a, p. 63)*

He is describing what sociologists generally refer to as "socialization," that the behavioral dispositions and inclinations of individuals may be shaped by living among others. Plasticity is used to explain why such behavioral tendencies may be resistant (but not immune) to change. He is, however, not making a deterministic argument. Though some of the particulars may be dated, he is keen to explain that individuals can take charge of their lives to nurture positive or advantageous habits.

We can see the residues of structure in the work of Dewey as well. In *Lectures in China, 1919–1920*, Dewey (1973) examines the social conditions related to "growth" or those necessary "for the development of individual capacities that enable social and political participation" (Midtgarden, 2012, p. 507). Here, Dewey articulated how large-scale domination could inhibit the participatory potential of individuals in the democratic project. Social conflict is said to emerge as a result of a "pattern of suppression and legitimization of group interests" (Midtgarden, 2012, p. 508). In this manner, group domination is attributed to "asymmetric recognition" where the interests of the dominating party are privileged (Midtgarden, 2012, p. 509). Though not discussed in structural terms, this analysis has a structural character that mirrors the conflict theories which explain social organization and hierarchy as characterized by conflicts of interests between competing social groups (Snipes, Bernard, & Gerould, 2019).

More recently, some pragmatists explicitly use structural language for making sense of contemporary social problems.[15] Cornel West's (1989, p. 228) "prophetic pragmatism," for instance, frames structure as a result of the "inescapable and inexpungible character" of tradition. Tradition is the collective accumulation of habit transmitted through a process of "socialization and appropriation, of acculturation and construction" (ibid). Such an approach is not far removed from the arguments made by Bhaskar as he describes the "emergence" of social structure appearing through historically developed collective human action, though West does not appear to ontologically privilege structure as an independent entity. While tradition can be "smothering," it can also be "liberating" especially when combined with creative freedom. For instance, West and Buschendorf (2014) describe the need to counter the effects of capitalism among Black communities by reinvigorating the "black prophetic tradition" affiliated with the likes of Frederick Douglas, Martin Luther King, Jr., W. E. B. Du Bois, Ella Baker, and others. This tradition is, according to them, one defined by struggle, passion, community, and recognition—it is dedicated to combating injustice and making the world better for all. In other words, tradition may not be totalizing and may provide cultural and cognitive tools for resisting oppression if one chooses to use them in such a manner. For West (1989, p. 228), human agency is instrumental for combating the "evils" wrought by traditions steeped in oppression and domination. His prophetic pragmatism "confronts candidly individual and collective experiences of evil in individuals and institutions—with little expectation of ridding the world of *all* evil" (ibid). At the same time, it views such evils to be the results of "choices and actions" taken by humans, meaning that such evils are "neither inevitable nor necessary" (ibid). For him, "human struggle" is the vehicle through which social change occurs—the exercise of agency against the weight of tradition and the harms inflicted by both individuals and institutions.

Taken together, there is a collective sense that, for pragmatists, structure can be understood as beliefs or habits accrued into traditions over time which inform and shape the circumstances of activity, generating consequences in a complex web of interpretation, action, and interaction. It is both a process (the historical transmission of tradition or the widespread fixation of belief) and a property of human collectives (the stability or inertia of social patterns, rules, and hierarchies). Agency, then, is the (constrained) ability of folks to transcend tradition to reshape the trajectories of their lives and the lives of others.[16] Agency is the modality through which such traditions are challenged, disrupted, or otherwise changed.

Another approach to social structure can be found in symbolic interactionism, which was deeply shaped by pragmatic thought (Lewis, 1976; Shalin, 1986; Ulmer, 2017; Wheeldon, 2015). Shalin (1986) argues that both pragmatism and symbolic interactionism view social structure as a conceptual vehicle for understanding collective behavior and shared meaning. While critical realism ontologically separates structure from agency as independent (though intertwined) phenomena, pragmatists and symbolic interactionists view "society" and "the individual" as inseparable and mutually constitutive, such that they are "neither opposed to each other nor separated from each other" (Dewey, 1972, p. 55; as quoted in Shalin, 1986, p. 14) and that they are "simply collective and distributive aspects of the same thing" (Cooley, 1962, p. 314; as quoted in Shalin, 1986, p. 14). From this view, talk of "society" or "structure" is a way to understand the way the individual is influenced, enabled, or constrained by the actions of others and how individuals themselves contribute to or detract from the collective. Contradicting the critical realists' arguments of Bhaskar, Shalin (1986, p. 14) explains that

> The originality of this approach consists in the fact that it eschews both sociological realism with its reified view of society as a superhuman entity existing before and apart from individuals, and sociological nominalism with its flawed notion of society as a convention set up at will by individuals endowed by nature with minds.

Here we see another view of structure as process, a continual product of the collective actions of individuals. According to Dewey (1958, p. 72, as quoted in Shalin, 1986, p. 15), "the isolation of structure from changes whose stable ordering it is, renders it mysterious." In other words, structure *can* be reduced to the actions of individuals.

Pragmatism thus adopts a view toward structure that "treats concepts as mere *representations* of reality [emphasis in original]" (Dunn, 2018, p. 21). From this view, "the proper function of sociological concepts is heuristic and analytical, and they are not to be confused with actual phenomena" (ibid). This position stands in stark contrast to critical realism which confuses representation with reality through its transcendental metaphysics.[17]

The point here is not to endorse one single approach to social structure. Rather, it is to demonstrate that while pragmatism may not center social structure—it is primarily a method of knowledge production—it is *not incompatible* with structural analysis. The objective is also not to advance pragmatism as a mature theory of power and inequality. It isn't. But it *is,* for me, a mature theory of knowledge and knowledge production upon which fruitful analyses of structure, power, and oppression can be constructed. A pragmatist approach also permits analysis of structure and power that avoids unnecessary transcendental assumptions—structure is a conceptual apparatus for making sense of stabilities, patterns, and effects evident amidst human collectivities and the associations between individuals within them.[18]

## Conclusion

Finding perfect and universal answers to philosophical problems, particularly ones of epistemology and ontology, is likely an impossible task. The best we can hope for is to discern between "better and worse ways of thinking" (Putnam, 1990, p. 19).[19] Perhaps pragmatism is a better way or simply one that I prefer. It does certainly have its shortcomings. Though I have attempted to detail its view toward social structure, its approach is not nearly as clearly delineated or uniform as those found in other philosophies like critical realism. In addition, pragmatists are rightly criticized for their optimism toward democracy and community, overlooking how such methods of organizing can be corrupted. For them, such problems are often a result of not being democratic enough. Yet there is the potential that democratic methods of organizing are prone to self-defeating internal contradictions (Losurdo, 2011; Harvey, 2014, pp. 199–215). Additionally, perhaps this approach is too quick to dismiss transcendental ontological arguments. It could be that the utility of a transcendental approach to structure offsets the weighty metaphysics—only time will tell. Overall, pragmatism has been subjected to heavy criticism over the years, much of which stems from inconsistencies and disagreements among pragmatists themselves. Regardless, pragmatism, from my view, provides a more grounded, approachable, flexible, useful, and applicable foundation than the alternatives.

Pragmatism is a philosophy that embraces uncertainty, democracy, inclusivity, and diversity while mistrusting anything antithetical to these values (in this way, pragmatism seems to advance its own version of Popper's tolerance paradox). To simplify matters, below is a summary of the pragmatist insights explored in this chapter, a set of guiding principles for a "critical pragmatism":

1 There exists a reality independent of our subjective experiences (realism), but our ability to know this reality is limited (fallibilism).
2 Distrust of dualisms, dogmas, absolutes, and transcendental truths.
3 Knowledge can be made better (more durable against doubt) over time through inquiry.
4 Knowledge must be connected to outcomes. If beliefs do not result in actions or consequences, then what is the point?
5 Knowledge is to be developed democratically among diverse communities of inquirers.
6 Humans are endowed with creative freedom, though this freedom is not without constraints.
7 Structure can be understood as both a process (the historical transmission of tradition or the widespread fixation of belief) and a property of human collectives (the stability or inertia of social patterns, rules, and hierarchies).
8 It is necessary to maintain a radical vision of democracy; to fight barriers and obstructions to human flourishing.

9 Vigilance is needed against power and domination in all its forms.

10 Reform is favored over revolutionary change, though reforms should be made according to thoughtful and articulated plans toward established objectives.

The principles described here are not foreign to criminology. Indeed, as mentioned previously, pragmatism has had a pronounced impact on the development of sociological criminology especially, though not exclusively, the American traditions (Ulmer, 2017; Wheeldon, 2015).

Indeed, it is both the historical relevance and flexibility of pragmatism that makes it appealing as a base for realist criminology. In fact, I contend that the original Left Realism was itself heavily influenced by pragmatism, even if those influences have largely gone unacknowledged. For instance, Left Realism drew from subcultural theories which themselves were rooted in both the Chicago School of sociology and symbolic interactionism (Lea & Young, 1984; Ulmer, 2017). Though it was critical of labeling theory, Left Realists incorporated insights from labeling perspectives as well—another criminological tradition rooted in symbolic interactionism (ibid). The attentive reader has also likely noticed that pragmatism's embrace of democracy echoes the "democratic imperative" of left realism which advocates bringing together multiple community members involved in the "square of crime" or "social relations of crime" to understand the problem at hand, develop an explanation, and chart a pathway toward resolution (Jones, MacLean, & Young, 1986; Lea, 2002; 2016). In fact, though imperfect, the original Left Realism is a case study in how pragmatist social theory can be synthesized with Marxist thought.

Unfortunately, the potential of pragmatism was perhaps underutilized. There are additional advantages that pragmatism can offer realist criminology. First, because pragmatism is not "confined to any preordained historical agent," as demonstrated by West (1989, p. 235), it may help realist criminology overcome one of its biggest criticisms—that it overemphasizes class at the expense of other forms of social stratification and domination like those operating along the axes of race, gender, and sexual orientation, to name a few (Bridges & Gilroy, 1982; Gilroy & Sim, 1985; Renzetti, 2016; Wood, 2019; Wood, Anderson, & Richards, 2020). Of course, as previously noted, realist criminologists have made significant efforts to incorporate such concerns (e.g. Hall & Winlow, 2015; Schwartz & DeKeseredy, 2010). Yet, the centering of class in their analysis has sometimes left their analyses of other matters of oppression and inequality feeling vestigial, particularly among the works of early left realists. To put it another way, realist criminologists should consider opening themselves up to some level of intersectional analysis (Crenshaw, 1989).

While pragmatism encourages the decentering of class—a move likely to irritate committed Marxists—it opens our analytic horizons to a broader constellation of oppression, alienation, exploitation, and abuse. The Marxist counterargument to this position is that such analytic pluralism will result in liberal individualism and reactive identity politics, losing sight of the role of the political economy. While such concerns are not unfounded, such outcomes are not inevitable. It is possible to examine other axes of oppression while also considering how these axes intersect with other structural forms of domination (Raymen & Kuldova, 2020). In fact, Elliot Currie, a towering figure in realist criminology, demonstrates this possibility admirably in his 2020 book, *A Peculiar Indifference: The Neglected Toll of Violence on Black America*. In this book, he traces the historical development of structural circumstances that have contributed to disproportionate Black violence in America and links them to the present situation, recognizing the unique role of race-based discrimination and oppression while also considering the impacts of material, economic, and political conditions. This is not saying that Currie utilized pragmatism, only that pragmatism encourages such analyses and resists demands that explanations *must* be reduced to class-based explanations. This matter will be revisited in Chapter 5.

In this manner, using a pragmatic base for our realist criminology allows us to borrow ideas more successfully from other domains of inquiry. Pragmatists are, after all, generally unwilling to throw the baby out with the bathwater. Critical criminologists—myself included—have often been quick to dismiss the evidence and explanatory frameworks developed through mainstream criminological perspectives. The typical criticism is that mainstream criminology tends to be too liberal and positivistic, ignoring the role of structure and power in the production of both crime and criminality. While this may be true, pragmatism encourages us to consider such perspectives and incorporate those insights that are useful and stand up against the weight of evidence, experience, and reason. Critical criminologists have also sometimes been overly willing to dismiss other critical criminological perspectives. The potential for such theoretical synthesis via pragmatism will be further explored in Chapter 9.

## Notes

1 As a reminder, the phrase "heavy ontological furniture" is attributed to Kivinen and Piiroinen (2004).
2 It should be noted that not all pragmatists adopt a "realist" view toward reality. Richard Rorty, at the most extreme, has suggested that we should give up the notion of reality altogether in his *Pragmatism and Anti-Authoritarianism*

(2021). Here, he argues that the notion of "reality" supplanted "God" during the enlightenment, liberating inquiry to move onto new heights previously restricted under religious dogma. Yet, he argues now we are being similarly constrained by the very idea of reality. In my read, however, I do not think that Rorty ever actually says "there is no reality," only that the question "is there an external reality?" is not a particularly philosophically productive one. He makes a compelling argument, but for the purposes of social scientific analysis directed toward practical implications, I think it behooves us to at least assume an external reality and proceed accordingly.

3 It could be argued that Wheeldon (2007) has hinted at the possibility of using pragmatism as a foundation for realist criminology, but this was never really developed. Wheeldon's work, however, does provide a primordial glimmer. He does not, as far as I can tell, actually argue for using pragmatism as a social scientific foundation for left realism.

4 Peirce's view of realism does warrant a qualification. As Ritz (2022, p. 2) explains, this is a view of the realism of causation that is "independent of whether or what anyone thinks about it."

5 Dewey (1998b, p. 75) usefully captures this view in his definition of reality as "the world of existence accessible to verifiable inquiry."

6 Peirce (1955a, p. 29) himself explains that "the essence of belief is the establishment of a habit." Peirce was, admittedly, sometimes vague in his use of the term "habit" (Shapiro, 1973). It can generally, however, be understood as a disposition toward action, how one is likely to act under certain circumstances. Tracing the linkages between belief, habit, and action is perhaps not a straightforward endeavor, but what is important is that a belief can hardly be said to be an earnestly held belief (if we can use that word) if it is not, in some form, reflected in action.

7 Unfortunately, pragmatism became associated with just such a relativism largely because of the writings of Peirce's contemporary, William James. Many interpreted James as adopting a more individualistic approach to truth and belief

and sliding into relativism by arguing that something can be considered true if it is good, satisfying, or influential for an individual (Misak, 2013, p. 66). Misak (2013, p. 104), however, is careful to note that James sometimes broached the subject of truth and subjectivity more carefully and more consistent with Peirce, but this was not the iteration which would become the frequent target of critics. From this line of reasoning, God can be considered to exist because such a belief provides some good for some people. For Peirce, such "passional evidence—that one, cannot, for instance, emotionally or psychologically do without the belief— is pertinent to the question of whether or not religion is good for human beings, but not pertinent to the question of whether God exists" (Misak, 2013, pp. 66–67). The Jamesian perspective threatens to allow the subjective to obliterate the external. James (1997d, pp. 109–111) later attempted to qualify his claims but, by then, the damage was done. Pragmatism was dismissed by many critics as a wholly relativist enterprise. Others, however, have defended James from the critiques of relativism. For instance, Cornel West (1989, p. 67) argued that James "rejects all forms of epistemological foundationalism yet preserves a realist ontology," though admits that his theory of truth is "less rigorously worked out" than Peirce's. In short, pragmatism embraces fallibilism and eschews pure relativism.

8 Peirce (1955b, p. 259) himself is rather terse in this regard:

it will serve to show that almost every proposition of ontological metaphysics is either meaningless gibberish— one word being defined by other words, and they by still others, without any real conception ever being reached— or else is downright absurd; so that all such rubbish being swept away, what will remain of philosophy will be a series of problems capable of investigation by the observational methods of the true sciences—the truth about which can be reached without those interminable misunderstandings and disputes which have made the highest of the positive sciences a mere amusement for idle intellects, a sort of chess—idle pleasure its purpose, and reading out of a book its method.

9 Peirce (1955a, p. 36) was clear on this point, noting that things like mental processes can be very real even if they give rise to subjective experiences that are not:

> There are, however, phenomena within our own minds, dependent upon our thoughts which are at the same time real in the sense that we really think them. But though their characters depend on how we think, they do not depend on what we think those characters to be. Thus, a dream has a real existence as a mental phenomenon, if somebody has really dreamt it; that he dreamt so and so, does not depend on what anybody thinks was dreamt, but is completely independent of all opinion on the subject. On the other hand, consider, not the fact of dreaming, but the thing dreamt, it retains its peculiarities by virtue of no other fact than that it was dreamt to possess them. *Thus we may define the real as that whose characters are independent of what anybody may think them to be.*
>
> (emphasis added)

10 It should be noted here that West (1989) is merging radical and pragmatic thought within this quote, with evident traces of John Dewey, Ralph Waldo Emerson, and Frantz Fanon.

11 The interview with Howard Zinn cited here (Tant, 2004) has apparently disappeared from the internet since I first read it back in 2012. The original quote stated that

> A liberal thinks that the system is basically good, but that it has a few flaws. … Liberals think that you can work within the system and maybe get a better president. Radicals think that the whole system is so corrupt that it will swallow you up and spit you out. Radicals also think that you need to create powerful social movements outside the system that will put pressure on the system, what has been called a permanent culture of resistance.

I chose to keep the source here because it is such an iconic description of the perceived differences between liberals and radicals.

12 Generally, pragmatists treat agency as an assumption, like most theories, as the idea is difficult, if not impossible, to test. Thus it makes what Peirce calls a "regulative assumption," or

"a statement about a practice and what that practice requires in order to be comprehensible and in order to be sensibly carried out" (Misak, 2013, p. 51).

13 Some pragmatists appear disinterested or ambivalent toward the question of agency. One reason is that any answer to the question of agency may yield few meaningful consequences or outcomes. For instance, Richard Rorty, a sometimes-controversial pragmatist figure, provides a particularly flippant response to the agency question. He has argued that there is a possibility that "we shall someday be able, 'in principle', to predict every movement of a person's body" (Rorty, 1980, p. 354). He points out, however, that such exacting determinism would be "too difficult to carry out except as an occasional pedagogical exercise" (ibid). Pleasants (1999: 105) explains that this is a result of taking a "compatibilist" view of the natural world that refuses to distinguish humans as a special entity within the natural world whereas perspectives like critical realism tend to be "incompatibilist"—that humans are somehow special within the natural realm. It is important to note, however, that Rorty is not necessarily staking a definitive position on the agency debate here. Rather, he is playing the role of the ever-uncertain pragmatist by gesturing toward possibilities. My read of Rorty is that he likely considers the question of agency to be relatively unimportant.

14 Or maybe my description of the pragmatist view of agency is overly simplistic. Joas (1993, p. 130) more robustly elaborates on the "pragmatist theory of action" in the following passage:

> This theory does not conceive of action as the pursuit of ends that the contemplative subject establishes a priori and then resolves to accomplish; the world is not held to be mere material at the disposal of human intentionality. Quite to the contrary, pragmatism maintains that we find our ends in the world, and that prior to any setting of ends we are already, through our praxis, embedded in various situations. There is an interplay between the manifold impulses of the actor and the possibilities of a given situation, which can be interpreted in various ways. Between impulses and possibilities of action, the actor experimentally establishes connections, of which, in any

given instance, only one is realized; that one, however, is influenced in its particular manner of realization by the other possibilities that have been mentally played through. The course followed by an action then is not one that has been established once and for all time; rather, it must be produced over and over again by construction and is open to continual revision.

15 Interestingly, James (1997b, p. 120) points out the need to engage in shared terminologies—to not reinvent the wheel, so to speak. As he explains,

> All human thinking gets discursified; we exchange ideas; we lend and borrow verifications, get them from one another by means of social intercourse. All truths thus get verbally built out, stored up, and made available for everyone. Hence, we must *talk* consistently just as we must *think* consistently: for both in talk and thought we deal with kinds. Names are arbitrary, but once understood they must be kept to.
>
> (emphasis in original)

16 West (1989, p. 230) summarizes this approach:

> All that human beings basically have are traditions— those institutions and practices, values and sensibilities, stories and symbols, ideas and metaphors that shape human identities, attitudes, outlooks, and dispositions. These traditions are dynamic, malleable, and reviseable, yet all changes in a tradition are done in light of some old or newly emerging tradition. Innovation presupposes some tradition and inaugurates another tradition.

17 It could be argued that some pragmatist-influenced thinkers, like C. Wright Mills, adopt non-nominalist views toward social structure. For Mills (1959, p. 134), social structure is defined as "the combination of institutions classified according to the functions each performs." And he speaks so often of social structures that it would be easy to construe that he considers these to be actual objects that exist in some transcendental realm, like the critical realists. But if one pays attention to his words, he almost always seems to describe social structure as a matter of social organization and classification—indicating a heuristic or nominalist view

toward social structure. While it may be difficult to say one way or the other on Mills, my point is that there is room for reasonable people to disagree. In this sense, Mills may be an example of how one can do structural analyses *without* committing to transcendental metaphysics.

18 Consider, for example, Dewey's (1998c, p. 330) description of capitalism as "*a rough designation* of a complex of political and legal *arrangements* centering about a particular mode of economic *relations* [emphasis added." Here he notes that capitalism is a concept ("a rough designation") used to describe actions, interactions, and relations ("arrangements" and "relations") to carry out a specific kind of economic activity. There is not a transcendental wink to this description. It treats capitalism as concept—albeit a useful one—for describing a complex situation.

19 Here, Hilary Putnam (1990, p. 19) rephrases the following quote attributed to Stanley Cavell (1983, p. 9): "while there may be no satisfying answers to such questions in *certain forms*, there are so to speak, directions to answers, *ways to think*, that are worth the time of your life to discover."

## References

Aronowitz, S. (2012). *Taking it big: C. Wright Mills and the making of political intellectuals*. New York: Columbia University Press.

Bernstein, R. J. (1997). Pragmatism, pluralism, and the healing of wounds. In L. Menand (ed.) *Pragmatism: A reader* (pp. 382–401). New York: Vintage Books.

Bernstein, R. J. (2010). *The pragmatic turn*. Malden, MA: Polity.

Bridges, L. & Gilroy, P. (1982, June). Striking back: The police use of race in crime statistics is a political act. *Marxism Today*. Retrieved November 21, 2019 at http://banmarchive.org.uk/collections/mt/pdf/82_06_34.pdf

Cooley, C. H. (1962). *Social organization*. New York: Schocken Books.

Crenshaw, K. (1989). Demarginalizing the intersection of race and sex: A Black feminist critique of antidiscrimination doctrine, feminist theory and antiracist politics. *University of Chicago Legal Forum, 1989*(1), 139–167.

Currie, E. (2020). *Peculiar indifference: The neglected toll of violence on Black America.* New York: Metropolitan Books.

Dewey, J. (1958). *Experience and nature.* New York: Dover.

Dewey, J. (1971/2008). Moral approbation, value and standard. In J. a. Boydston (ed.) *John Dewey–The early works, 1882–1898* (vol. 4, pp. 247–291). Carbondale, IL: Southern Illinois University Press.

Dewey, J. (1972/1897). Ethical principles underlying education. In *John Dewey, The early works, 1882–1898* (vol. 5, pp. 54–83). Carbondale, IL: Southern Illinois University Press.

Dewey, J. (1973). *Lectures in China, 1919–1920.* Honolulu, HI: The University of Hawai'i Press.

Dewey, J. (1998a/1937). Democracy is radical. In In L. A. Hickman & T. M. Alexander (eds.) *The essential Dewey, Volume 1: Pragmatism, Education, Democracy* (pp. 337–339). Bloomington, IN: Indiana University Press.

Dewey, J. (1998b/1919). Philosophy and democracy. In L. A. Hickman & T. M. Alexander (eds.) *The essential Dewey, Volume 1: Pragmatism, education, democracy* (pp. 71–78). Bloomington, IN: Indiana University Press.

Dewey, J. (1998c/1935). Renascent liberalism. In L. A. Hickman & T. M. Alexander (eds.) *The essential Dewey, Volume 1: Pragmatism, education, democracy* (pp. 323–336). Bloomington, IN: Indiana University Press.

Dewey, J. (1998d/1917). The need for a recovery of philosophy. In L. A. Hickman & T. M. Alexander (eds.) *The essential Dewey, Volume 1: Pragmatism, education, democracy* (pp. 46–70). Bloomington, IN: Indiana University Press.

Dunn, R. G. (2018). *Toward a pragmatist sociology: John Dewey and the legacy of C. Wright Mills.* Philadelphia, PA: Temple University Press.

Elder-Vass, D. (2022). Pragmatism, critical realism and the study of value. *Journal of Critical Realism, 21*(3), 261–287.

Elder-Vass, D., & Zotzman, K. (2022). Overlapping traditions with divergent implications? Introduction to the special issue on pragmatism and critical realism. *Journal of Critical Realism, 21*(3), 257–260.

Frega, R. (2014). Between pragmatism and critical theory: Social philosophy today. *Human Studies, 37,* 57–82.

Gilroy, P., & Sim, J. (1985). Law, order and the state of the left. *Capital & Class, 9*, 15–55.

Gorz, A. (1967). *Strategy for labor: A radical proposal*. Boston, MA: Beacon Press.

Habermas, J. (1998). *On the pragmatics of communication*. Cambridge, MA: MIT Press.

Hall, S. (2012). *Theorizing crime and deviance: A new perspective*. Thousand Oaks, CA: Sage.

Hall, S., & Winlow, S. (2015). *Revitalizing criminological theory: Towards a new ultra-realism*. New York: Routledge.

Harvey, D. (2014). *Seventeen contradictions and the end of capitalism*. New York: Oxford University Press.

James, W. (1997a). Habit. In L. Menand (ed.) *Pragmatism: A reader* (pp. 60–68). New York: Vintage Books.

James, W. (1997b). Pragmatism's conception of truth. In L. Menand (ed.) *Pragmatism: A reader* (pp. 112–131). New York: Vintage Books.

James, W. (1997c). The will to believe. In L. Menand (ed.) *Pragmatism: A reader* (pp. 69–92). New York: Vintage Books.

James, W. (1997d). What pragmatism means. In L. Menand (ed.) *Pragmatism: A reader* (pp. 93–111). New York: Vintage Books.

Joas, H. (1993). *Pragmatism and social theory*. Chicago, IL: University of Chicago Press.

Jones, T., MacLean, J., & Young, J. (1986). *The Islington crime survey*. Aldershot, England: Gower.

Kadlec, A. (2006). Reconstructing Dewey: The philosophy of critical pragmatism. *Polity, 38*(4), 519–542.

Kivinen, O., & Piiroinen, T. (2004). The relevance of ontological commitments in social sciences: Realist and pragmatist viewpoints. *Journal for the Theory of Social Behaviour, 34*(3), 231–248.

Lea, J. (2002). *Crime and modernity*. London: Sage.

Lea, J. (2016). Left realism: A radical criminology for the current crisis. *International Journal for Crime, Justice and Social Democracy, 5*(3), 53–65.

Lea, J., & Young, J. (1984). *What is to be done about law and order?* New York: Penguin.

Lewis, J. D. (1976). The classic American pragmatists as forerunners to symbolic interactionism. *The Sociological Quarterly, 17*(3), 347–359.

Losurdo, D. (2011). *Liberalism: A counter-history*. New York: Verso.

Marx, K. (1970). Theses on Feuerbach. In C.J. Arthur (ed.) *The German ideology: Part one with selections from parts two and three and supplementary texts* (pp. 121–123). New York: International Publishers.

Matthews, R. (2014). *Realist criminology*. New York: Palgrave Macmillan.

Midtgarden, T. (2012). Critical pragmatism: Dewey's social philosophy revisited. *European Journal of Social Theory, 15*(4), 505–521.

Mills, C. W. (1943). The professional ideology of social pathologists. *The American Journal of Sociology, 49*(2), 165–180.

Mills, C. W. (1959). *The sociological imagination*. New York: Oxford University Press.

Misak, C. (2013). *The American pragmatists*. New York: Oxford University Press.

Peirce, C. S. (1955a). How to make our ideas clear. In J. Buchler (ed.) *Philosophical writings of Peirce* (pp. 23–41). New York: Dover Publications.

Peirce, C. S. (1955b). The essentials of pragmatism. In J. Buchler (ed.) *Philosophical writings of Peirce* (pp. 251–268). New York: Dover Publications.

Peirce, C. S. (1955c). How to make our ideas clear. In J. Buchler (ed.) *Philosophical writings of Peirce* (pp. 42–59). New York: Dover Publications.

Peirce, C. S. (1997). A definition of pragmatism. In L. Menand (ed.) *Pragmatism: A reader* (pp. 56–58). New York: Vintage Books.

Pleasants, N. (1999). *Wittgenstein and the idea of a critical social theory: A critique of Giddens, Habermas and Bhaskar*. New York: Routledge.

Putnam, H. (1990). *Realism with a human face*. Cambridge, MA: Harvard University Press.

Putnam, H. (1997). Fact and value. In L. Menand (ed.) *Pragmatism: A reader* (pp. 338–362). New York: Vintage Books.

Putnam, H. (2002). *The collapse of the fact/value dichotomy and other essays*. Cambridge, MA: Harvard University Press.

Quinney, R. (1977). *Class, state, and crime.* New York: David McKay Company, Inc.

Ray, L. (2004). Pragmatism and critical theory. *European Journal of Social Theory, 7*(3), 307–321.

Raymen, T., & Kuldova, T.O. (2020). Clarifying ultra-realism: A response to Wood et al. *Continental Thought & Theory: A Journal of Intellectual Freedom, 3*(2): 242–263.

Renzetti, C. (2016). Critical realism and feminist criminology: Shall the twain ever meet? *International Journal for Crime, Justice and Social Democracy, 5*(3), 41–52.

Ritz, B. (2022). Peircean realism: A primer. *Journal of the Theory of Social Behaviour.* DOI: 10.1111/jtsb.12340.

Rorty, R. (1980). *Philosophy and the mirror of nature.* Oxford: Blackwell.

Rorty, R. (2010). Intellectual autobiography. In R. E. Auxier & L. E. Hahn (eds.) *The philosophy of Richard Rorty* (pp. 3–24). Chicago, IL: Open Court.

Rorty, R. (2021). *Pragmatism as anti-authoritarianism.* Cambridge, MA: The Belknap Press of Harvard University Press.

Rytina, J. H. & Loomis, C. P. (1970). Marxist dialectic and pragmatism: Power as knowledge. *American Sociological Review, 35*(2), 308–318.

Schwartz, M. D., & DeKeseredy, W. S. (2010). The current health of left realist theory. *Crime, Law & Social Change, 54*, 107–110.

Shalin, D. N. (1986). Pragmatism and social interactionism. *American Sociological Review, 51*(1), 9–29.

Shapiro, G. (1973). Habit and meaning in Peirce's pragmatism. *Transactions of the Charles S. Peirce Society, 9*(1), 24–40.

Snipes, J. B., Bernard, T. J., & Gerould, A. L. (2019). *Vold's theoretical criminology* (8th ed.). New York: Oxford University Press.

Tant, E. (2004). An ocean of resistance: An interview with Howard Zinn. *Zmagazine.* Retrieved August 17, 2012 at www.zcommunications.org/an-ocean-of-resistance-by-ed-tant#

Treviño, A. J. (2012). *The social thought of C. Wright Mills.* Thousand Oaks, CA: Sage.

Ulmer, J. T. (2017). The extensive legacy of symbolic interactionism in criminology. In R. A. Triplett (ed.) *The*

*Wiley handbook of the history and philosophy of criminology* (pp. 103–122). Indianapolis, IN: Wiley.

West, C. (1989). *The American evasion of philosophy*. Madison, WI: The University of Wisconsin Press.

West, C., & Buschendorf, C. (2014). *Black prophetic fire*. Boston, MA: Beacon Press.

Wheeldon, J. (2015). Ontology, epistemology, and irony: Richard Rorty and re-imagining pragmatic criminology. *Theoretical Criminology, 19*(3), 396–415.

Wood, M. A. (2019). What is realist about ultra-realist criminology? A critical appraisal of the perspective. *Journal of Theoretical & Philosophical Criminology, 11*, 95–114.

Wood, M. A., Anderson, B., & Richards, I. (2020). Breaking down the pseudo-pacification process: Eight critiques of ultra-realist crime causation theory. *British Journal of Criminology, 60*, 642–661.

Young, J. (1975). Working-class criminology. In I. Taylor, P. Walton, & J. Young (eds.) *Critical criminology* (pp. 63–91). New York: Routledge.

# PART II

# A Realist Criminology of Computer Crime

PART II

A Realist Criminology
of Computer Crime

# 5

# TOWARD A REALIST CRIMINOLOGY OF COMPUTER CRIME

To date, realist criminology has yet to fully engage with computer crime and victimization. Of course, such an omission is understandable given that realist criminologists have largely been preoccupied with the very real problem of street violence—though the ultra-realists appear to target predatory behaviors more generally. Yet, as the internet becomes increasingly embedded in everyday life, it is getting harder to ignore the constellation of harms wrought by computer crimes. For this reason, there is a need for realist criminologists to broaden their horizons. This is not to say that an entirely new realist criminology is required. Instead, the perspective needs to be updated so that it can more adequately grapple with online and offline crimes (or anything in between).

This chapter begins this work by detailing five key challenges presented by the internet for realist criminology and, importantly, how we might go about addressing them. First, what are the kinds of harms of concern for the perspective? The harms of violence are often written in blood, offering a relatively uncontroversial problem for realist criminologists to tackle. While computer crimes

DOI: 10.4324/9781003277996-7

may cause significant pain and suffering, their damages are not always as apparent or recognized. Second, how do we address the problem of space and place in the context of computer crimes and the internet? Realist criminology—specifically left realism—has traditionally been a criminology of *place*, concerned with particular groups facing particular problems in particular locations. Locality, however, is complicated across the diffuse networks that comprise internet communications. The third challenge concerns the related problem of community or, specifically, the tracing of the "social relations of crime." How are realist criminologists to identify and chart the relationships between relevant actors (perpetrators, victims, bystanders, law enforcement, etc.) in the context of the internet? For the fourth challenge, we turn once again to the problem of class—should a realist criminology of the internet center its sights on class? Finally, this chapter revisits the tension between "reform" and "revolution" given the importance of policy and other solutions for realist criminology (Luxemburg, 1900/1999). The answers to these questions are important to establish a criminology dedicated to generating theoretically and empirically sound explanations of the crimes and harms in question while developing means of harm reduction.

## The Problem of "Harm"

There has long been a recognition in criminology that legal definitions of crime are an insufficient basis for a social scientific enterprise. One reason is that the law is a notoriously political construct. Though there are certain kinds of behaviors prohibited under law that most reasonable people agree should be prohibited like murder and armed assault (so-called *mala in se* crimes), there are also many acts criminalized with far less consensus.

including drug use and sex work (*mala prohibita*). Deciding what counts as crime or which groups constitute criminals can be the result of processes whereby the less powerful are subject to the interests of more powerful groups— that the law can be a weapon (Becker, 1963; Turk, 1976). Criminologists have therefore long sought a definition of crime decoupled from the politics of the state. Several alternatives have been entertained over the years, though no generally agreed-upon definition has arisen (Beirne & Messerschmidt, 2015, pp. 19–26). One popular approach has been the idea of crime as *social harm*.

The social harm approach can be traced back to the 1930s and 1940s when criminologists like Edwin Sutherland grappled with malfeasances of professionals, elites, corporations, and other figures with status and power—misdeeds often not explicitly criminalized under law but harmful all the same (Pemberton, 2015). Since then, many criminologists have embraced the social harm-perspective as a more inclusive and holistic foundation for criminological inquiry as it allows criminologists to focus on a wide array of acts including violence, deprivation, inequality, predation, exploitation, neglect, and others malign actions (or failures to act) that may or may not be circumscribed under law. Such an approach more readily facilitates examinations of "crimes of the powerful," which may not be adequately regulated, if they are regulated at all, as well as the damages wrought by social structural conditions (Canning & Tombs, 2021; Pearce, 1976).

Recent efforts have been made to establish the study of social harm as a separate discipline from criminology, to decouple the analysis of harm from the political baggage endemic to criminology and its uneasy relationship with criminalization and crime control (Canning & Tombs, 2021; Tombs, 2018). This "zemiology" has gained traction in recent years, particularly among British scholars. Though it is beyond the scope of this book to wade into the disciplinary politics of the matter, a realist criminology of the internet should be zemiological as, like Matthew's critical realist criminology and ultra-realism, this enterprise is more concerned with studying the production, experience, and amelioration of harm than the violation of law per se.

Here too, however, we encounter definitional issues. There currently exists no agreed-upon definition of social harm. Hillyard and Tombs (2004, pp. 19–20) argue that the social harm approach should consider "physical," "financial/economic," "emotional and psychological," and "cultural safety" harms. Pemberton (2015, pp. 10, 30) adds two "relational harms" including "harms resulting from enforced exclusion from social relationships, and harms of misrecognition" examples of which include "poverty, child poverty, financial insecurity, long working hours, youth unemployment and social isolation" created by nation-state actors. More recently, Canning and Tombs (2021, pp. 51–52) explain that "harm occurs when people are prevented by either the social structures or individual actions to meet their needs [citation omitted]." It thus seems that any kind of pain, suffering, indignity, or even inconvenience may be framed as social harm, depending on the definition adopted, and the sources of harm can seemingly come from anything and everything (Hillyard & Tombs, 2007, p. 17). Some zemiologists argue that such a broadness is perhaps a strength given the many ways that human flourishing can be stifled and the many direct and indirect causal pathways through which harms can manifest (ibid).

Majid Yar (2012) provides one approach to the notion of harm compatible with the pragmatic sensibilities charted in the previous chapter. Drawing from the work of Axel

Honneth (1995), Yar grounds harm in the social relations of *recognition*. The notion of "recognition" is based on the symbolic interactionist idea that for a person to achieve identity or personhood, it is necessary for them to be recognized as such by others. Honneth (1995) articulates three key forms of recognition rooted in "love," "rights," and "esteem," which Yar (2012, p. 59), quoting Honneth (1995, pp. 131–139), summarizes as:

> Love satisfies the demand for "emotional support" and a "basic self-confidence" that one will be cared for by others; "rights" mediate a demand for dignity and moral equality as an individual person amongst others; and "esteem" grants a sense of one's value as a person with *particular* social and cultural traits and abilities.

From this view, harm is the deprivation of recognition or "disrespect" along any of these three axes. The deprivation of love stems from encroachment on a person's body and bodily autonomy; the " 'denial of rights' amounts to a refusal to accord one basic human dignity and equality"; and the deprivation of esteem is to erode, suppress, eliminate, or otherwise deny an individual's culture or identity (Yar, 2012, p. 59). This perspective is not unlike the view of Dewey, who articulates harm as the suppression of individual potential for self-realization and civic participation. A limitation, however, is that this perspective generally limits harm to the realm of the human, omitting harms to the natural environment.

There is significant value in the harm-perspective. It allows for criminologists, victimologists, and zemiologists to consider a much wider array of detrimental actions, institutions, or structures than would be allowed under legal definitions of crime. The lack of conceptual consensus, however, frustrates. For present purposes, Hall (2012, p. 15) provides a useful working definition of harm:

> The meaning of this term relates directly, through exploitation and irresponsibility towards the fate of others and their environments, to practices of domination in social, economic, cultural and technological practices, all of which leave some others in conditions worse than those in which they are found.

Like the other definitions given, this also allows for consideration of a wide assortment of harms that cut across social strata both horizontally and vertically.

But what does any of this mean for the study of the harms associated with the internet? From my view, there should be an open season on any harms to human life and flourishing, as well as those against non-humans, that can be tied to online behavior and computer technologies. I am uninterested in limiting our analytic horizons in this regard. What follows is a brief exploration of just some of the kinds of harms that realist criminologists can (and should) consider.

One way of approaching harm is to consider the familiar rogue's gallery of computer crimes—the kinds of crimes that spring to mind for most when terms like "cybercrime" are invoked and the kinds that populate the pages of computer crime textbooks. While competing definitions exist, generally such crimes can be understood as the use of computers to commit an offense of some sort or the direct targeting of such systems by perpetrators for malicious purposes—sometimes distinguished as "computer-assisted" and "computer-focused" crimes, respectively (Furnell, 2002). Such definitions tend to be mired in the politics of criminalization endemic to legal definitions of crime (Steinmetz, 2016; Yar & Steinmetz,

2019). Yet, this does not mean they are all harmless acts of mischief or censored acts of rebellion. In fact, many of these crimes can produce significant financial, emotional, psychological, and even physical harms for their victims.

For instance, one of the most prevalent cybercrimes are technology-mediated or technology-facilitated forms of fraud like advanced fee frauds, romance scams, investment frauds, and the like. Financial damages from such frauds can be enormous. The Internet Crime Complaint Center (IC3, 2022, p. 23) reported that financial losses from investment frauds in 2021 alone amounted to more than $1.4 million. Romance frauds nearly reached $1 million. Individual losses for frauds can be in the tens of thousands of dollars lost on average. (Harms associated with fraud will be revisited in Chapter 8.) Beyond financial damages, victims of fraud may suffer significant emotional and psychological harms like anxiety, sadness, anger, shame, grief, post-traumatic stress, and even suicidal ideation (Cross, 2018; Cross, Richards, & Smith, 2016; Whitty & Buchanan, 2016). Their sense of self-worth and confidence may be compromised (Whitty & Buchanan, 2016). Physiological consequences may result including sleep troubles, nausea, and weight loss (Cross, 2018; Cross, Richards, & Smith, 2016). They may suffer lifestyle and livelihood consequences such as homelessness, unemployment, strains on their relationships with family and friends, and struggles to find support (Cross, 2018; Cross, Richards, & Smith, 2016; Whitty & Buchanan, 2016). Similar harms to mind, body, lifestyle, and livelihood are created by other computer crimes like the production, distribution, and consumption of online child sexual exploitation material (e.g. Domhardt, Münzer, Fegertz, & Goldbeck, 2015, p. 476; Gewirtz-Meydan, Walsh, Wolak, & Finkelhor, 2018), cyberstalking and harassment (e.g. Dreβing, Bailer, Anders, Wagner, & Gallas, 2014; Marganski, 2018), and others.

Realist criminologists should also consider the environmental toll of internet technologies both in terms of how such technologies directly impact the natural environment and how pollution of said environment impacts human health and well-being. For instance, the production of computer technologies often requires the use of many heavy metals and other toxic substances whose extraction, processing, and disposal can have deleterious effects on the natural environment, laborers, consumers, and bystanders (Department of Labor, 2018, pp. 8–14; Stretesky, Long, & Lynch, 2014). For instance, in 2015, the BBC published a report on the Baogang Steel and Rare Earth complex in Baotou, Mongolia, which processes rare earth metals like cerium and neodymium—materials frequently used in the production of consumer electronics (Maughan, 2015). The town is mired in pollution and home to a large "artificial lake filled with a black, barely-liquid, toxic sludge," which has poisoned the landscape (ibid). Cobalt, a metal frequently used in the production of lithium-ion batteries, presents a similar problem. Much of the world's cobalt is found in the Congo and, as a result, has led to the development of mines "where cobalt is extracted from the ground by hand, often using child labour, without protective equipment" (Katwala, 2018). In addition, cobalt mining has been linked to toxic exposure for local communities and associated with health issues like "breathing problems and birth defects" (Frankel, 2016). Recently, attention has been drawn to the environmental impact of cryptocurrencies, which require massive amounts of energy to be "mined" as computers work to solve increasingly complex equations, contributing significantly to greenhouse gas emissions as a result (Bogna, 2022; Chow, 2022).

A realist approach to online crimes should consider the harms caused by surveillance regimes (Kinsey, Lea, & Young, 1986, pp. 137–160; Snowden, 2019; Zuboff, 2015). In 2013, Edward Snowden (2019), an employee for the U.S. National Security Agency (NSA), leaked the details of a massive surveillance apparatus operated by the U.S. government involving the harvesting of massive troves of data on both citizens and foreign nationals. Revealed was the largest and most invasive surveillance program ever known up to that point. Of course, the U.S. government has been building powerful surveillance capabilities for decades involving systems with names that sound like they could be pulled directly from science fiction novels including ECHELON, Carnivore (later renamed DSC 1000 and followed by DSC 3000), PRISM, and XKeyscore. Countries around the world operate their own surveillance programs as well. Corporations are also involved in the surveillance game. A massive multi-billion-dollar industry exists dedicated to capturing, cataloging, analyzing, and selling data on individuals (Zuboff, 2015). Tech companies like Facebook and Google generate most of their revenue through advertising and a significant portion of their business model involved gathering and analyzing user data to engage in targeted advertising. So-called data brokers or information brokers have proliferated over the past two decades. These firms specialize in creating datasets of information about individuals, often from a variety of sources, which can then be sold or licensed to other companies. The scope and scale of these datasets can be staggering. For instance, a 2014 report by the U.S. Federal Trade Commission examined nine major data brokerage firms and found that "one of the nine data brokers has 3,000 data segments for nearly every US consumer" (Ramirez, Brill, Ohlhausen, Wright, & McSweeny, 2014, p. iv). It is likely that the current state of data brokerage far exceeds such figures. At this point, it is safe to assume that any use of an internet-connected device is tracked in some capacity.

It would be easy to conclude that such surveillance technologies generate harm exclusively through the erosion of privacy, but the secondary harms of such intrusions can be much worse. For instance, in late 2022, the U.S. Federal Trade Commission (FTC) sued the Kochava company, a data broker, for selling the geo-location data culled from millions of mobile devices (*The Guardian*, 2022). According to the FTC, there are concerns that such data can be used to track the movements of individuals to places like "reproductive health clinics, places of worship, homeless and domestic violence shelters, and addiction recovery services" as well as their home addresses— data which, until recently, was available to purchase by the public (ibid). The potential for the abuse of such information is significant. Yet, the possible harms of such surveillance are not wholly speculative. In Chapter 1, it was mentioned that spyware developed by the NSO Group and licensed out to government agencies has been used to track journalists, activists, and political opponents (Rueckert, 2021; Slater & Masih, 2021). Reports strongly suggest that the software may have been used against the journalist Jamal Khashoggi who was murdered in 2018, likely at the behest of the Saudi crown prince, Mohammed bin Salman. Such surveillance systems are utilized by repressive regimes the world over to control political oppositions and activism. Harms are therefore evident against democratic participation, privacy, and even life-and-limb.

Governments and corporations may generate harm in other ways. Censorship and content moderation systems may have significant effects on political activism and freedom of speech more generally. The "Great Firewall of China"—a complex system used by the Chinese government to regulate internet use and restrict access to certain platforms and materials—is perhaps the most notorious example. Sometimes authoritarian regimes will suppress political resistance by simply cutting off access to the internet. The internet can be used to communicate and coordinate political resistance and, as a result, there have been many instances where governments have shut off the internet to reduce the effectiveness of opposition activity (Bergin & Lim, 2022). The organization Access Now reported that over 180 shutdowns occurred in 2021 in 34 countries (Hernández, Anthonio, Cheng, & Skok, 2022). Such shutdowns constitute and clear and present threat to free speech and political activity while also allowing the underlying problems which generated such resistance to continue.

Relatedly, realist criminologists should also grapple with the harms that result from the increasing monopolization or even colonization of the internet by corporations and other business interests, most notably the "Big Tech" companies like Apple, Google, Microsoft, Facebook, and Amazon (Lingel, 2021; Zuboff, 2015). Such harms include invasions of privacy, behavioral and market manipulation, the proliferation of problematic speech on their platforms (hate speech, misinformation, etc.), the exposure of users to security risks, and others. There is nary a single facet of everyday life in the contemporary internet age that is not in some way monitored and shaped by these companies, and often not for the better.

And of course, a realist approach to harm reduction is (or should be) guided by a desire to avoid collateral consequences wrought by online crime control efforts. There is always a risk that efforts to protect victims can fuel punitive attitudes and policies. Recent critiques of "carceral feminism" provide a useful parallel to consider. Phillips and Chagnon (2020, p. 50) describe carceral feminism as "a view that promotes state-based responses to sexual violence (and gender violence more generally), primarily through the traditional criminal justice system and other appendages of the carceral state" (see also: Bernstein, 2012; Bumiller, 2008; Law, 2014). These scholars argue that punitive solutions of violence against women, as well-intended as they might be, contribute to penal expansion and encourage a reliance on state control and coercion as the corrective. Considering the myriad social problems attributed to mass incarceration, the expansion of "community corrections," and the increased policing of poor communities and communities of color, efforts to curtail crime that rely on state coercion may not reduce net social harm but may instead displace or redirect that harm (Cohen, 1979; Hough, 2014; Matthews, 2014; Meares, 2015; Young, 2007). After all, contemporary government surveillance programs have largely been justified on the grounds that they are necessary to prevent and detect crime and terrorism. Realist criminologists should bear such possible collateral consequences in mind as they work toward grounded solutions of computer-related crime and victimization.

Again, this is not intended to be a definitive list of the potential harms considered fair game for a realist criminology of the internet. We haven't considered, for example, the role of artificial intelligence (AI) systems in crime (Hayward & Maas, 2021). For this reason, the approach to harm taken here is necessarily broad. Any erosion of human and environmental flourishing should be targeted by realist criminologists. What is important is the realist criminologists remain *realist* about harm. In other words, it is necessary to assess harm claims and recognize their validity, even if they conflict with preconceived notions or political prejudices. Required is a nuanced and holistic view of social problems.

## Locality

As explained in Chapter 1, though often not explicit, realist criminology is a criminology of place. Likely because of its general focus on street crime and violence, its analyses and policies tend to focus on particular communities in particular locations (e.g. DeKeseredy & Schwartz, 1991, p. 256; Matthews, 2014, p. 4). At the same time, realist criminology works to transcend locality as "the forces that shape local crime problems are never just local in provenance" (Hogg, 2016, p. 72). As Donnermeyer (2016, p. 36) explains, place "represents a micro-expression or microcosm of all the inequalities found in the larger society." He adds that "within a specific locality... are multiple forms of collective efficacy, buttressed by overlapping networks or forms of social capital" (ibid). Place is a nexus point where the structural and the situational collide. It also provides a starting point for mapping the social relations of crime (a point to which we will return momentarily). For many crimes, particularly street crimes, victims, offenders, police, community leaders, and other relevant parties tend to be geographically concentrated. This proximity facilitates interaction and cooperation to create social democratic solutions. In this manner, location acts as a lynchpin for the structural and relational analyses central to realist criminology.

Place presents a challenge for the handling of online crimes. In the words of Gertrude Stein, "there is no there there." It is possible, however, to reconceptualize space and place to render the concepts compatible with internet technologies. Scholars have devoted significant time to understanding how place manifests in the digital realm. For instance, Castells (2010, p. xxxii) describes the internet as the "space of flows" or,

> The material support of simultaneous social practices communicated at a distance. This involves the

production, transmission and processing of flows of information. It also relies on the development of localities as nodes of these communication networks, and the connectivity of activities located in these nodes by fast transportation networks operated by information flows.

For Castells, space is rooted in the experience of rapid information transit and presentation. Individuals experience the internet as an amalgamation of conceptual spaces formed by the rapid transmission and presentation of information—"places" to meet others, share information, watch content, etc. The idiosyncracies of internet communications shape user experiences and, vicariously, the kinds of spaces that form online.

Like Castells, Hayward (2012) conceives of virtual spaces as rooted user experiences shaped by online communications and interaction with digital "things." From this view, space is a "process" or "phenomena in constant dialogue and transformation with other phenonena/technologies" (Hayward, 2012, p. 455). He traces four characteristics of the spatiality of online networks and interfaces.

The first is *convergence* or the intersection between technological change and regulatory processes—that new technologies may create situations that may test current regulations or create strange and contradictory legal situations. Spatially, convergence becomes a problem when such technological changes facilitate near-instantaneous interactions across vast distances while regulations are typically limited within a geographic jurisdiction based on boundaries drawn in the physical world (Yar & Steinmetz, 2019). Though international agreements have attempted to reconcile such regulatory tensions, there is little avoiding the fact that regulation and enforcement remains largely geographically constrained while offenders are relatively free to transcend terrestrial boundaries through online spaces.

Convergence is further complicated by *virtuality*—the creation of electronic, artificial, or simulated persons and environments in the digital realm. In online video games like *World of Warcraft,* for example, players create their own avatars (a stand-in for the player in the digital space through which their experiences will be mediated) which interact with other players, non-player characters (NPCs), enemies, and environmental fixtures like trees, rocks, and furniture. None of these items have physical dimensions but players still interpret and interact with objects in these environments like they would in physical spaces. Similar experiences of space can be found in other online platforms. Social media, for example, has spatial dimensions as users "navigate" the various links in search of content (news stories, videos, the pages of specific people) or interact with the interfaces of the platforms. There is a "thinginess" to these online spaces—code rendered as objects in a digital topography.

Hayward (2012) highlights and how the "virtual" may blur and intersect with "the actual" rendering the distinction between online and offline increasingly tenuous (see also: Brown, 2006). For instance, in 2014, Zoë Quinn (2017) was subjected to a massive campaign of abuse because of a slanderous and mendacious online post by their former romantic partner accusing them of sexual infidelity and quid pro quo to gain favorable reviews of their video game *Depression Quest* (accusations that are unfounded by most reputable accounts). The abuse continued for years. They were threatened with physical violence and sexual assault, subjected to public shaming, "doxxed" (the non-consensual disclosure of private information), and attempts were made to sabotage their career and relationships.

As Quinn's abusers and their enablers were given public platforms, Quinn found little support or protection from escalating attacks, which extended to their family, friends, acquaintances, and even people unaffiliated with them. Their case clearly demonstrates how online abuses can have significant effects in the offline world through emotional strains, fear of life and limb, relationship damages, and other consequences (Salter, 2018).

Recent research on criminal networks and syndicates similarly shows how computer crimes may actually involve significant offline components including locally situated social networks (Cross, 2019; Lusthaus & Varese, 2017). Consider, for instance, money mules—individuals used to move illicitly gotten gains in a manner that disrupts the ability of authorities to follow the money from origin to destination (Bekkers & Leukfeldt, 2022; Leukfeldt & Jansen, 2015). A fraudster may gain illicit access to a bank account and transfer funds to a new account. Because that transaction might be easily traced and the funds recovered, the fraudster may hire a money mule to pull the funds from the account—either as physical currency, a cashier's check, or some related method—and then deposit that money in a new account elsewhere, thereby frustrating any subsequent recovery attempts. In this manner, the criminal activity drifts between online and offline spaces.

Relatedly, *telepresence* refers to the ability of telecommunications technologies to "alter the way we experience the sense of *being* in an environment" (Hayward, 2012, p. 456). Phenomenologically, humans may exist in virtual and physical environments simultaneously and thus the experiences of these spaces are inseparable. Back when I used to play *World of Warcraft*, for instance, the physical experience of the game involved sitting in a chair in a semi-darkened room with one hand on a mouse and another on the WASD keys of my keyboard. My attention, however, was on my avatar running around in the world of Azeroth, casting spells, slaying monsters, and completing quests. Intense moments in the game would narrow my attention to the point that I was oblivious to the physical space around me. A full bladder or empty stomach, on the other hand, would quickly pull my focus from the in-game world back to meatspace. The gameplay loop of run, select enemy, cast spells, loot body, repeat was inseparable from the tactile sensations of repetitive keyboard commands and mouse clicks.

The point is that online, the physical and the virtual cannot be phenomenologically disentangled. There is a "blurring" that makes it increasingly difficult to sustain a dualism between "offline" and "online" (Powell, Stratton, & Cameron, 2018). Hayward (2012, p. 457) explains that "digital technology creates what one might describe as porous *spaces of subjectivity* in which moves made via the rhizomic, hyperlinked internet appear materially or spatially insignificant but, in reality, have tangible consequences." For instance, a person may be unable to engage in certain expressive acts in physical spaces—either due to normative constraints or fear of reprisal—and, instead, may find freedom online to engage in forms of expression "that would never be tolerated in physical space" like hate speech or calls for vigilantism (Hayward, 2012, p. 457). This is not unlike Goldsmith and Brewer's (2015) notion of "digital drift." Building on Matza's (1964) *Delinquency and Drift,* they argue that the internet facilitates the pursuit of illicit activity, and enables "tentative, even timid, encounters which may or may not lead to crime" through the provision of anonymity, a wealth of easy-to-access information, chances for social encounters, and criminal opportunities (Goldsmith & Brewer, 2015, p. 126). In other words, the internet makes it easier for folks to drift between deviance and conformity.

*Presence*, on the other hand, speaks to the ability of an identity to endure and exist in the form of scattered fragments across online profiles, account registrations, blogs, social media posts, and other interactional markers that create a "quasi-private disembodied virtual 'persona' that exists at various points across the spatial architecture of the internet" (Hayward, 2012, p. 457). In this sense, our online selves are fragmentary objects dispersed across the digital nether. A fraudster may gather information through various online platforms about their target to customize their deceptions (Steinmetz, Pimentel & Goe, 2021). A person's social security number and related information may be stolen from a company's database and used to apply for a bank loan. A politician's or celebrity's social media posts may come back to haunt them. The archival nature of the internet means that we need not be sitting in front of a computer to "exist" in online spaces.

These concepts, and others, speak to the complexities of space and place when dealing with the internet and related technologies. Technology can change the known terrain and create new interactional environments. The actual and the virtual become increasingly inseparable (Cross, 2019). People can occupy the virtual and actual realms simultaneously. Identities may persist in virtual spaces long after people have left (Powell, Stratton, & Cameron, 2018). Each of these dimensions may need to be considered when generating realist explanations and solutions for online crime and victimization problems. Spaces are sites of social encounters thus if we want to understand the nature of online offending or victimization, then we need to come to terms with the spaces in or through which such interactions occur.

## Mapping the Social Relations of Crime Control

Related to the problem of locality is the problem of community. Early left realists tended to approach the concept through "square of crime" or the "social relations of crime" (Lea, 2016; see Chapter 2). Involved is a consideration of the complex relationships between and among offenders, victims, state actors, and members of the public—an "act of deconstruction" that,

> Takes the phenomenon of crime apart, breaking it down to its component pieces and sequences... Realism places together these fragments of the shape of crime in their social context over time—to capture the real forces behind the one-dimensional time-frozen images of conventional accounts.
>
> *(Young, 1987, p. 337)*

While the square of crime is a robust conceptual tool for helping making sense of the multitude of actors, perspectives, interests, conflicts, and harms surrounding a given crime issue, it tends to situate these community relations in the context of location. For instance, Lea (2016, p. 55) explains that "the starting point of Left Realism was *local* democracy [emphasis added]." The emphasis on the local makes sense when examining violence and other kinds of street crimes—crimes with rates that can vary significantly between locations (i.e. neighborhoods, cities, states or provinces, countries, etc.). While crime may be underpinned by structural inequities and failing social policies, these causal elements are given life through day-to-day actions and their effects are felt by real people living in real places. Thus, addressing crime requires reconciling the local with the structural. Yet, focusing on local relations of crime makes less sense—or at least is insufficient—when considering computer-related crimes.

Just as the internet requires a reconceptualization of space, it also necessitates an expansion of the idea of community beyond locality. Online communities regularly include members from disparate geographic regions. This is not to say that physical ceases to matter in the formation of such communities. Locality is heavily correlated with one's native language, cultural norms, and other factors which may incentivize or prohibit involvement in certain communities. It makes little sense, for instance, that a non-English-speaking person would actively participate in an English-language message board (though it could happen). Yet, the geography-spanning character of the internet permits community building in a way that is far less reliant on physical space.

If locality no longer acts as the lynchpin holding together a community, then how do we define community in the context of the internet? One approach is to view communities as *networks* (Leighton, 1988). In the age of the internet, such an approach is useful given the role network communication technologies play in mediating relationships and interactions. Of course, the idea of social networks is an old one. Criminologists, sociologists, anthropologists, and other social scientists have long been interested in tracing relationships and interdependencies between individuals. The internet has introduced important changes to consider, however.

For instance, according to Raine and Wellman (2012, p. 8) the internet age is marked by "networked individualism." Before the rise of global telecommunications networks, they argue that "in generations past, people usually had small, tight social networks... where a few important family members, close friends, neighbors, leaders and community groups (churches and the like) constituted the safety net and support system for individuals" (ibid, p. 8). Today, people are increasingly embedded in multiple diffuse social networks mediated through communications technologies. These social networks give tremendous freedom to individuals to curate and expand their relationships. "Rather than investing in an maintaining strong ties in networks physically close to us," as Powell, Stratton, and Cameron (2018, p. 26) explain, "technology enables us to invest more in relationships with individuals far away, perhaps people we have never met face-to-face." On the other hand, they also create pressure for the individual to generate and maintain these relationships:

> They must actively network. They need to expend effort and sometimes money to maintain their ties near and far; choose whether to phone, visit, or electronically connect with others; remember which members of their network are useful for what sorts of things (including just hanging out); and forge useful alliances among network members who might not previously have known each other. In short, networked individualism is both socially liberating and socially taxing.
>
> *(Raine & Wellman, 2012, p. 9)*

Similarly, sociologist Zygmunt Bauman once reflected on the consequences wrought by networked individualism's erosion of locally based community networks:

> The question of identity has changed from being something you are born with to a task: you have to create your own community. But communities aren't created, and you either have one or you don't. What the social networks can create is a substitute. The difference between a community and a network is that you belong to a community, but a network belongs to you. You feel in control. You can add friends if you wish, you can delete them if you wish. You are in control of the

important people to whom you relate. People feel a little better as a result, because loneliness, abandonment, is the great fear in our individualist age.

*(Interview with De Querol, 2016)*

While Raine and Wellman warn that such networks require work and can be socially taxing, Bauman laments their tendency to promote social fragmentation. People can "cut themselves a comfort zone where the only sounds they hear are the echoes of their own voice, where the only things they see are the reflections of their own face." Such insights are certainly compelling considering contemporary political discourse mired in misinformation and polarization (Seymour, 2020). Individuals enmeshed in such networks—like those facilitated through social media—can comfortably engage in divisive argumentation with no intent of earnest dialog. Folks can easily retreat to their diffusely networked political tribes for support and reinforcement, be it QAnon conspiracy theory-spouting subreddits or keyboard warrior slacktivist social media communities. At the same time, many online community networks have been instrumental for members of marginalized and dispossessed communities. For instance, many LGBT youths find comfort and support in online networks while living in hostile local environments. Voices across the globe can reassure them that they deserve happiness—which is surely a good thing. As a result, the power of such networks in the internet age is to unify *and* fragment simultaneously.

These new networks bear significant implications for realist criminology. For instance, addressing crime problems through traditionally spatially bound concepts like social solidary, social capital, collective efficacy, or similar mechanisms may require a reimagination of what these concepts mean across these diffuse, selective, and exhausting new networks. To illustrate, Sampson, Raudenbush, and Earls (1997, p. 919) conceptualize collective efficacy as "the linkage of mutual trust and the willingness to intervene for the common good that defines the neighborhood context of collective efficacy." In the 'case of internet-mediated social networks, how does one generate "mutual trust" and "willingness to intervene for the common good?" Concepts like collective efficacy gain solidity when fixed in place but quickly disintegrate when we attempt to transplant them to internet communities. Potentially mass reconceptualization of core criminological concepts is necessary if we want to understand and intervene in the relationship between community and crime online.

Realist criminologists must also consider the complex interplay of multiple on- and offline networks. One useful perspective for this enterprise is Actor Network Theory (ANT) (Latour, 2005; Powell, Stratton, Cameron, 2018). Despite its name, ANT is best understood as a methodological orientation concerned with the "tracing of associations" among "actors" (Latour, 2005, p. 5). For ANT, human action is always shaped by relationships with other actors within an "actor network." Actors can be both human and non-human entities (objects, like technologies)—anything capable of acting or being acted upon. Networks are therefore dynamic entities constantly created and recreated through action. Further, an actor becomes more significant within a network when the volume and quality of attachments to other actors increases. ANT is useful for a realist criminology of the internet because it avoids common assumptions about non-human agency. Non-human entities like technologies, non-human animals, environmental features, law, policy, prior experience, and knowledge can become socially active players within a network, driving and being driven by other actors (Callon, 1984; Latour & Woolgar, 1986). Further, ANT encourages use to trace associations across actors both online and offline, allowing our social networks to transcend the technological networks involved in the internet.

Yet, an Actor Network Theory approach to mapping the social relations of crime control presents a problem for realist criminology—specifically in its view of social structure. As previously mentioned, Latour (2005, p. 165) argues that tracing associations within actor-networks requires the researcher to "keep the social flat" or resist the urge to project upward and rely on structural formations like "capitalism" and "patriarchy" to perform explanatory heavy lifting. Instead, the researcher should stick to what manifests within the context of the network—if capitalism, for instance, is a problem then it should manifest within the actions of the network, not as some esoteric spiritual force permeating its interstitial spaces. As Latour (2005, p. 64) explains, "power and domination have to be produced, made up, composed. Asymmetries exist, yes, but where do they come from and what are they made out of?" Realist criminology, on the other hand, mandates that the researcher remain sensitive to both the situational and the structural. Indeed, that consideration of the structural context is necessary to properly address crime and victimization (if you paid attention in Chapter 4, you likely see where this is heading). Speaking of structure...

**Whither Class?**

As noted in previous chapters, critical perspectives that draw on Marxist thought, like realist criminology, tend to be critiqued as economic reductionists, distilling myriad social harms to problems of class relations. While not diminishing the importance of class, a realism of the internet necessitates robust consideration of social stratification beyond the economic. In their criticism of cultural criminology, Hall and Winlow (2007, p. 83) claim that cultural criminology and other "liberal" criminologies had decided that "it was no longer hip to posit the capitalist economy and its relations of production as the bedrock of social life." Ferrell (2007, p. 92), however, retorted that it was not that "it was no longer hip" but, instead, "no longer sufficient." Chapter 4 notes that pragmatism encourages scholars to resist the urge to subsume all explanations within a class-based analytic—that way lies dogma. Though the material conditions and social relations of production undoubtedly play a significant role the creation of criminal contexts and motivations, like Ferrell we are unconvinced that crime and victimization are exclusively the products of or otherwise always reducible to the contradictions and consequences of capitalist class relations.

For instance, consider online harassment. One study by Lenhart and colleagues (2016, p. 4) indicate that while both men and women were equally likely to be harassed online, "women experience a wider variety of online abuse, including more serious violations." Such abuse includes "brigading," "dogpiling," or "virtual mobs," which involve offenders forming online mobs where they will heap abuse onto a victim, en masse, in a concentrated harassment campaign (Lenhart et al., 2016, p. 24; Quinn, 2017, p. 52). It would be difficult to explain the form and intensity of such abuse through pseudo-pacification or the exercise of special liberty, as might be argued by ultra-realists. Class may help explain the particular struggles triggering the abuse (e.g. the subject of "women in games"), the creation and maintenance of the vectors through which such abuse is transmitted (e.g. Twitter and Facebook), and even the underlying feelings of powerlessness or precariousness by male abusers misdirected toward women. Yet, a purely economic analysis may be insufficient to explain why gender becomes a lightning rod for such issues in the first place. Or why certain men hold so much ire for women online in general. This is not to say that there is no relationship between class and gender, only that gender cannot be reduced to an "epiphenomenon" of the political economy (Wood, Anderson, & Richards, 2020, p. 644).

The point is that the tendency of realist criminologists to attribute crime and victimization to the undulations of the political economy—either directly or indirectly—diminishes the importance of other variables of social stratification like gender, race, and sexuality. Yes, it bears repeating that realist criminologists have attempted to bridge the gaps between left realism, feminist criminology, and other perspectives to address this shortcoming (e.g. Schwartz & DeKeseredy, 2010; Hall & Winlow, 2015). Ultra-realists, in particular, have engaged in many robust studies of men and masculinity (e.g. Ellis, Winlow, & Hall, 2017; Winlow, 2001; Winlow & Hall, 2009). Still, a paucity remains (Renzetti, 2016). The underlying concern appears to be epistemological and ontological in nature—perhaps driven by some concern that a failure to explain other mechanisms of social stratification through political economic machinations will render the Marxist core of the perspective untenable. Yet, perhaps this anxiety is overstated. The world is complicated, after all. Perhaps there is room enough for Marxism and other perspectives to coexist.

In Chapter 3, I expressed concern that critical realism's insistence that social problems are caused by underlying structural mechanisms that exist in the realm of the real may lead to situations in which explanations are coerced into complying with such assumptions *and* that such explanations may never fail to be right given the unobservable nature of the real. Similarly, analyses which center class from the outset may always be able to find a way to make their explanations rooted in political economy. There exists the risk of tautology—that such scholars have arrived at their conclusions *a priori* and may bend observations accordingly. They will never fail to be wrong. If we are to develop sound, scientifically grounded, theories and research programs, there needs to be some mechanism by which theories can be validated or refuted. My worry is that, by insisting that all roads lead to capitalism in some form or fashion, we risk propagating circular reasoning. This is not to dismiss the value of Marxism and other class-based analytic frameworks (I have found much use for them myself—see Steinmetz, 2016), only to keep the explanatory field open to other possibilities.

In this manner, the explanatory significance of any given structure should not be assumed *a priori* as a causative factor. Realist criminologists need to be able to sustain a contradiction: be sensitive to the role of structure but only insofar as structure makes itself apparent. It is to engage in what Peirce (1960, p. 117) termed "abduction," the inferential development of a hypothesis to explain an observation using the following logic:

The surprising fact, C, is observed;
But if A were true, C would be a matter of course,
Hence, there is reason to suspect that A is true.

It is a good faith attempt to draw from what is known to create an appropriate explanation—one that we can gather further evidence upon to validate or refute. Misak (2013, p. 48) explains that "something very like this now gets called inference to the best explanation." In many ways, this is the fundamental logic of theory building. Regarding structural analyses, abduction means that the researcher makes observations and then makes use of appropriate structural explanations to pull pieces of the puzzle together to assemble a big picture view of the situation. It is a necessarily imperfect process but one that can be challenged and refined through subsequent analyses and, importantly, requires an openness of the researcher to alternative potentialities.

## Piecemeal Reform or Structural Change?

Traditionally, left and critical realist criminologists have embraced piecemeal reform as such strategies have more immediate potential for the alleviation of harm. The answer to the question "short- or long-term solutions?" or, in more Marxist terms, "reform or revolution?" is vital for the realist criminological problem, especially given the tension between left realists and critical criminologists with more revolutionary or anti-authoritarian proclivities. Of course, these questions are not limited to debates over realist criminology. Among Marxists or socialists more generally, there exists a long-standing debate between reformism and revolution. The nature of the debate often gives the impression that the choice is without compromise. It's one or the other. Meeting in the middle is to accept the worst of both worlds. Is an accord possible?

Marxists skeptical of reform often argue that reform is only palliative—that any short-term solutions will only result in the winning of small concessions while ultimately allowing for capitalism to prolong its existence or, worse yet, expand its power. Stalin (1907/2008), for instance, once stated that reformism "advocates not class struggle but class collaboration." Other Marxists, however, have embraced reformism. Eduard Bernstein (1899/2017) is perhaps the most prominent figure associated with this position. Though he was a friend of Marx and Engels during their lifetimes, he became critical of the thesis of the inevitability of violent revolution and instead advocated for peaceful political economic transitions. He argued for that the labor movement should seize opportunities to advance its interests, emphasizing the processes involved in the struggle rather than the "ultimate aims": "the movement, the series of processes, is everything, whilst every aim fixed beforehand in its details is immaterial to it" (ibid). Of course, Bernstein does not necessarily argue that the "ultimate aim" is useless, but only that any theories about the political economy and labor struggle,

> which try to determine the direction of the movement and its character without an ever-vigilant eye upon facts and experience, must necessarily always pass into Utopianism, and at some time or other stand in the way, and hinder the real theoretical and practical progress of the movement.
>
> *(ibid)*

In this manner, Bernstein advances a somewhat pragmatic position—that visions for a better society can be useful but should always be open to inquiry lest such visions become dogma.

In her critique of Bernstein entitled *Reform or Revolution*, Rosa Luxemburg (1900/1999) declared that "between social reforms and revolution there exists for the Social Democracy an indissoluble tie. The struggle for reforms is its means; the social revolution, its aim." In this work, she deconstructs Bernstein's arguments about embracing reformism *tout court* and, instead, emphasizes that such reforms should be pursued as part of a broader revolutionary project. In particular, she cautions that an overemphasis on reform may result in an emphasis on *only* reforms which loses sight of the big picture and, importantly, the potential consequences of any given reform—devolving into "class collaboration," in Stalin's words. Similarly, André Gorz (1967) argues that revolutionary reform will not out-pace capitalism's tendency to absorb change so long as the reform itself does not directly change the capitalist relationship between the worker and the mode of production. Gorz's resolution then is a slow progressive conquest of power for workers without excluding the possibility of revolutionary seizure. This will show that socialism is feasible and already at work—thus there will be an intermediate stage between the present and the idealized future.[1] Interestingly, these positions are not dissimilar to that of Dewey (1998c, p. 325) who cautioned against ad hoc reformism and, instead, advised that such efforts be guided by a "social goal based upon an inclusive plan," though Dewey was targeting overcoming the problems confronting liberalism while Luxemburg is concerned with the problem of capitalism and capitalists. Regardless, both embraced the need for a clear project and the use of reforms for the achievement of that goal—eschewing simple "opportunism" (Luxemburg, 1900/1999) or "piecemeal policies undertaken *ad hoc*" (Dewey, 1998c, p. 325).

Back in the realm of criminology, Madfis and Cohen (2016, p. 2) attempt to bridge the gap between left idealism and left realism and, as a result, advance a position like Luxemburg, Gorz, and Dewey:

> A left realist focus on short-term practical reform efforts represents a form of pragmatism that is necessary when attempting to bring about change in light of very real institutional barriers. This pragmatism must be directly informed and animated by the broader, more radical vision of structural change offered by left idealism.

Ultra-realists adopt a similar approach, asking us to consider what "what *must* be done" to create long-term harm reduction, thus embracing the revolutionary proclivities of other critical criminologists while also embracing the identification of concrete measures necessary to achieve those ends (Hall & Winlow, 2018, p. 51). A realist criminology of the internet recognizes that given the pervasive, persistent, and mercurial nature of capitalism and other structures of power, comprehensive societal changes must ultimately be made. Intermediate steps can be taken, however, to prove that crime control can be handled outside of the state apparatus (or in a more democratic fashion if accomplished through state institutions) and take steps toward a more just and equitable society. While this book does not provide a definitive list of measures can be taken to alleviate the harms associated with computer crimes and the internet more generally, Chapter 8 does demonstrate how realist criminologists can go about using research to identify potential points of intervention.

## Summary

This chapter presented what I view as key challenges confronting the development of a realist criminology dedicated to the explanation and amelioration of computer crimes and their harms. I do not pretend that these are the only issues at hand. My hope is that this work will encourage a broader conversation to bring a more fully realized perspective to fruition. Yet, the starting points presented here are sound. To review, a realist criminology of the internet:

1 Embraces a broad sweeping approach to the kinds of social harms related to computer technologies including "traditional" forms of cybercrime (i.e. illicit computer hacking, online child sexual exploitation, online stalking and harassment, etc.), environmental harms

caused by the development and proliferation of such technologies, the erosion of privacy and other harms associated with public and private surveillance regimes, government and corporate censorship, and the collateral consequences of punitive crime control policies.

2 Necessitates a reconceptualization of space. Hayward's (2012) conceptualization of virtual spaces was used to lay out one useful perspective on the matter. Other approaches may be used, however. The important point is that scholars must consider how humans form spaces of interaction through the transmission and representation of data over network technologies and how these spaces interact with one another and the physical world.

3 Traces the social relations of crime across multiple and diffuse networks of associations that comprise various computer crime-related problems.

4 Does not assume the primacy of class for analysis *a priori*. Class should be a significant component of the analysis, but the researcher should remain open to other elements of social stratification and oppression. One can generate new and grounded explanations of the subject at hand, rely on abductive reasoning, or some combination thereof.

5 Adopts a reformist view on social change, but one which involves the development of a plan for how short-term changes can build toward long-term objectives. The aim is to avoid devolving into the pursuit of reform for the sake of reform while also forgoing revolutionary window-gazing.

While these issues are important to consider, they exist primarily at the conceptual or theoretical level. It provides little guidance regarding what it looks like to *do* realist criminological research or to envision points of intervention in computer crime problems. Chapter 6 begins the methodological discussion by detailing what a computer-crime focused realist criminology research program does *not* look like, offering up a critique of the emergent area of *computational criminology*. Chapter 7 then goes into detail about the approach to research fitting for our enterprise. Finally, Chapter 8 considers how scholarly findings can be brought to bear to think about the "big picture" of computer crime and identifying points of intervention in a holistic manner.

## Note

1 Thanks to Adrienne McCarthy who first introduced me to Gorz, whose work she contributed to our initial book chapter exploring the idea of a realist criminology of the internet (see: Pratt and Turanovic's *Revitalizing Victimological Theory*, Routledge).

## References

Becker, H. (1963). *Outsiders: Studies in the sociology of deviance*. New York: Free Press.

Beirne, P., & Messerschmidt, J. W. (2015). *Criminology: A sociological approach* (6th ed.). New York: Oxford University Press.

Bekkers, L. M. J., & Leukfeldt, E. R. (2022). Recruiting money mules on Instagram: A qualitative examination of the online involvement mechanisms of cybercrime. *Deviant Behavior*. https://doi.org/10.1080/01639625.2022.2073298

Bergin, J., & Lim, L. (2022, August 28). Flicking the kill switch: Governments embrace internet shutdowns as a form of control. *The Guardian*. Retrieved August 29, 2022 at www.theguardian.com/technology/2022/aug/29/flick ing-the-kill-switch-governments-embrace-internet-shutdo wns-as-a-form-of-control?CMP=Share_AndroidApp_Other

Bernstein, E. (1899/2017). Conclusion: Ultimate aim and tendency—Kant against cant. In E. Bernstein (author) *Evolutionary socialism*. Independent Labour Party.

Republished on the Marxist Internet Archive. Retrieved October 24, 2022 at www.marxists.org/reference/archive/bernstein/works/1899/evsoc/ch04-conc.htm

Bernstein, E. (2012). Carceral politics as gender justice? The "traffic in women" and neoliberal circuits of crime, sex, and rights. *Theory and Society, 41,* 233–259.

Bogna, J. (2022). What is the environmental impact of cryptocurrency. *PCMag.* Retrieved August 29, 2022 from www.pcmag.com/how-to/what-is-the-environmental-impact-of-cryptocurrency

Brown, S. (2006). The criminology of hybrids: Rethinking crime and law in technosocial networks. *Theoretical Criminology, 18*(2), 176–197.

Bumiller, K. (2008). *In an abusive state: How neoliberalism appropriated the feminism movement against sexual violence.* Durham, NC: Duke University Press.

Callon, M. (1984). Some elements of a sociology of translation: Domestication of the scallops and the fishermen of St. Brieuc Bay. *The Sociological Review, 32*(1_suppl), 196–233.

Canning, V., & Tombs, S. (2021). *From social harm to zemiology: A critical introduction.* New York: Routledge.

Castells, M. (2010). *The rise of the network society* (2nd ed.). Malden, MA: Wiley-Blackwell.

Chow, A. R. (2022, July 1). Fact-checking 8 claims about crypto's climate impact. *Time.* Retrieved August 29, 2022 at https://time.com/6193004/crypto-climate-impact-facts/

Cohen, S. (1979). The punitive city: Notes on the dispersal of social control. *Contemporary Crises, 3,* 339–363.

Cross, C. (2018). (Mis)understanding the impact of online fraud: Implications for victim assistance schemes. *Victims & Offenders, 13*(6), 757–776.

Cross, C. (2019). Is online fraud just fraud? Examining the efficacy of the digital divide. *Journal of Criminological Research, Policy and Practice, 5*(2), 120–131.

Cross, C., Richards, K., & Smith, R. G. (2016). The reporting experiences and support needs of victims of online fraud. *Trends & Issues in Crime and Criminal Justice, 518,* 1–14.

DeKeseredy, W. S. & Schwartz, M. D. (1991). British and U.S. Left Realism: A critical comparison. *International Journal of Offender Therapy and Comparative Criminology, 35*(3), 248–262.

Department of Labor. (2018). *U.S. Department of Labor's 2018 list of goods produced by child labor or forced labor.* Washington, D.C. Retrieved November 26, 2018 at www.dol.gov/sites/dolgov/files/ILAB/ListofGoods.pdf

De Querol, R. (2016, January 25). Zygmunt Bauman: "Social media are a trap." *El País.* Retrieved September 20, 2022 at https://english.elpais.com/elpais/2016/01/19/inenglish/1453208692_424660.html#

Dewey, J. (1998c/1935). Renascent liberalism. In L. A. Hickman & T. M. Alexander (eds.) *The essential Dewey, Volume 1: Pragmatism, Education, Democracy* (pp. 323–336). Bloomington, IN: Indiana University Press.

Domhardt, M., Münzer, A., Fegert, J. M., & Goldbeck, L. (2015). Resilience in survivors of child sexual abuse: A systematic review of the literature. *Trauma, Violence, & Abuse, 16*(4), 476–493.

Donnermeyer, J. F. (2016). Without place, is it real? *International Journal for Crime, Justice and Social Democracy, 5*(3), 27–40.

Dreßring, H., Bailer, J., Anders, A., Wagner, H., & Gallas, C. (2014). Cyberstalking in a large sample of social network users: Prevalence, characteristics, and impact upon victims. *Cyberpsychology, Behavior, and Social Networking, 17*(2), 61–67.

Ellis, A., Winlow, S., & Hall, S. (2017). 'Throughout my life I've had people walk all over me': Trauma in the lives of violent men. *The Sociological Review, 65*(4), 699–713.

Ferrell, J. (2007). For a ruthless cultural criticism of everything existing. *Crime Media Culture, 3*(1), 91–100.

Frankel, T. C. (2016, September 30). The cobalt pipeline: Tracing the path from deadly hand-dug mines in Congo to consumers' phones and laptops. *The Washington Post.* Retrieved August 29, 2022 at www.washingtonpost.com/graphics/business/batteries/congo-cobalt-mining-for-lithium-ion-battery/

Furnell, S. (2002). *Cybercrime: Vandalizing the information society.* London: Addison-Wesley.

Gewirtz-Meydan, A., Walsh, W., Wolak, J., & Finkelhor, D. (2018). The complex experience of child pornography survivors. *Child Abuse & Neglect, 80*, 238–248.

Goldsmith, A., & Brewer, R. (2015). Digital drift and the criminal interaction order. *Theoretical Criminology, 19*(1), 112–130.

Gorz, A. (1967). *Strategy for labor: A radical proposal.* Boston, MA: Beacon Press.

Hall, S. (2012). *Theorizing crime and deviance: A new perspective.* Thousand Oaks, CA: Sage.

Hall, S., & Winlow, S. (2007). Cultural criminology and primitive accumulation: A formal introduction for two strangers who should really become more intimate. *Crime Media Culture, 3*(1), 82–90.

Hall, S., & Winlow, S. (2015). *Revitalizing criminological theory: Towards a new ultra-realism.* New York: Routledge.

Hall, S., & Winlow, S. (2018). Ultra-realism. In W. S. DeKeseredy & M. Dragiewicz (eds.) *Routledge handbook of critical criminology* (pp. 43–56). New York: Routledge.

Hayward, K. J. (2012). Five spaces of cultural criminology. *British Journal of Criminology, 52*(3), 441–462.

Hayward, K. J., & Maas, M. M. (2021). Artificial intelligence and crime: A primer for criminologists. *Crime Media Culture, 17*(2), 209–233.

Hernández, M. D., Anthonio, F., Cheng, S., & Skok, A. (2022). Internet shutdowns in 2021: The return of digital authoritarianism. *Access Now.* Retrieved August 29, 2022 at www.accessnow.org/internet-shutdowns-2021/

Hillyard, P., & Tombs, S. (2007). From 'crime' to social harm? *Crime, Law & Social Change, 48*: 9–25.

Hillyard, P., & Tombs, S. (2004). Beyond criminology? In P. Hillyard, C. Pantazis, S. Tombs, & D. Gordon (eds.) *Beyond criminology: Taking harm seriously.* London, England: Pluto Press.

Hogg, R. (2016). Left realism and social democratic renewal. *International Journal for Crime, Justice and Social Democracy, 5*(3), 66–79.

Honneth, A. (1995). *The struggle for recognition: The moral grammar of social conflicts.* Cambridge, MA: The MIT Press.

Hough, M. (2014). Confessions of a recovering 'administrative criminologist': Jock Young, quantitative research, and policy research. *Crime Media Culture, 10*, 215–226.

IC3 (Internet Crime Complaint Center). (2022). *Federal Bureau of Investigation Internet Crime Report 2021.* Retrieved August 29, 2022 at www.ic3.gov/Media/PDF/AnnualRep ort/2021_IC3Report.pdf

Katwala, A. (2018, , May 8). The spiralling environmental cost of our lithium battery addiction. *Wired.* Retrieved August 29, 2022 at www.wired.co.uk/article/lithium-batteries-environm ent-impact

Kinsey, R., Lea, J., & Young, J. (1986). *Losing the fight against crime.* New York: Basil Blackwell.

Latour, B. (2005). *Reassembling the social: An introduction to actor-network theory.* New York: Oxford University Press.

Latour, B., & Woolgar, S. (1986). *Laboratory life: The construction of scientific facts.* Princeton, NJ: Princeton University Press.

Law, V. (2014). Against carceral feminism. *Jacobin.* Retrieved November 26, 2019 at www.jacobinmag.com/2014/10/agai nst-carceral-feminism/

Lea, J. (2016). Left realism: A radical criminology for the current crisis. *International Journal for Crime, Justice and Social Democracy, 5*(3), 53–65.

Leighton, B. (1988). The community concept in criminology: Toward a social network approach. *Journal of Research in Crime and Delinquency, 25*(4): 351–374.

Lenhart, A., Ybarra, M., Zickuhr, K., & Price-Feney, M. (2016). *Online harassment, digital abuse, and cyberstalking in America.* Data & Society Research Institute. Retrieved January 1, 2020 at www.datasociety.net/pubs/oh/Online_ Harassment_2016.pdf

Leukfeldt, R., & Jansen, J. (2015). Cyber criminal networks and money mules: An analysis of low-tech and high-tech fraud attacks in the Netherlands. *International Journal of Cyber Criminology, 9*(2), 173–184.

Lingel, J. (2021). *The gentrification of the internet: How to reclaim our digital freedom.* Oakland, CA: University of California Press.

Lusthaus, J., & Varese, F. (2017). Offline and local: The hidden face of cybercrime. *Policing, 15*(1), 4–14.

Luxemburg, R. (1900/1999). *Reform or revolution.* London, England: Militant Publications. Republished on the Marxists Internet Archive. Retrieved October 24, 2022 at www.marxi sts.org/archive/luxemburg/1900/reform-revolution/intro.htm

Madfis, E. & Cohen, J. (2016). Critical criminologies of the present and future: Left realism, left idealism, and what's left in between. *Social Justice, 43*(4), 1–21.

Marganski, A. J. (2018). Feminist theory and technocrime. In K. F. Steinmetz & M. R. Nobles (eds.) *Technocrime and criminological theory* (pp. 11–34). New York: Routledge.

Matthews, R. (2014). *Realist criminology*. New York: Palgrave Macmillan.

Matza, D. (1964). *Delinquency and drift*. New York: Wiley.

Maughan, T. (2015, April 2). The dystopian lake filled by the world's tech lust. BBC.com. Retrieved August 29, 2022 at www. bbc.com/future/article/20150402-the-worst-place-on-earth

Meares, T. (2015). Broken windows, neighborhoods, and the legitimacy of law enforcement or why I fell in and out of love with Zimbardo. *Journal of Research in Crime and Delinquency, 52*(4), 609–625.

Misak, C. (2013). *The American pragmatists*. New York: Oxford University Press.

Pearce, F. (1976). *Crimes of the powerful: Marxism, crime, and deviance*. London: Pluto Press.

Peirce, C. S. (1960). Pragmatism and abduction. In C. Hartshorne & P. Weiss (eds.) *Collected papers of Charles Sanders Peirce—Volume V: Pragmatism and pragmaticism* (pp. 112–131). Cambridge, MA: Harvard University Press.

Pemberton, S. A. (2015). *Harmful societies: Understanding social harm*. Chicago, IL: Policy Press.

Phillips, N. D. & Chagnon, N. (2020). "Six months is a joke": Carceral feminism and penal populism in the wake of the Stanford sexual assault case. *Feminist Criminology, 15*(1), 47–69.

Powell, A., Stratton, G., & Cameron, R. (2018). *Digital criminology: Crime and justice in digital society*. New York: Routledge.

Quinn, Z. (2017). *Crash override: How GamerGate [nearly] destroyed my life and how we can win the fight against online hate*. New York: Public Affairs.

Raine, L. & Wellman, B. (2012). *Networked: The new social operating system*. Cambridge, MA: The MIT Press.

Ramirez, E., Brill, J., Ohlhausen, MK., Wright,. JD., & McSweeny, T. (2014). *Data brokers: A call for transparency and accountability* [report]. Washington, DC: Federal Trade

Commission. Retrieved July 23, 2018 at www.ftc.gov/system/ files/documents/reports/data-brokers-call-transparency-acc ountability-report-federal-trade-commission-may-2014/140 527databrokerreport.pdf

Renzetti, C. (2016). Critical realism and feminist criminology: Shall the twain ever meet? *International Journal for Crime, Justice and Social Democracy, 5*(3), 41–52.

Rueckert, P. (2021, July 18). Pegasus: The new global weapon for silencing journalists. *Forbidden Stories*. Retrieved July 19, 2021 at https://forbiddenstories.org/pegasus-the-new-glo bal-weapon-for-silencing-journalists/

Sampson, R., Raudenbush, S. W., & Earls, F. (1997). Neighborhoods and violent crime: A multilevel study of collective efficacy. *Science, 277*(5328), 918–924.

Schwartz, M. D. & DeKeseredy, W. S. (2010). The current health of left realist theory. *Crime, Law & Social Change, 54*, 107–110.

Seymour, R. (2020). *The twittering machine.* Brooklyn, NY: Verso.

Slater, J., & Masih, N. (2021, July 19). The spyware is sold to governments to fight terrorism. In India, it was used to hack journalists and others. *The Washington Post*. Retrieved July 19, 2021 at www.washingtonpost.com/world/2021/07/19/ india-nso-pegasus/

Snowden, E. (2019). *Permanent record.* New York: Metropolitan Books.

Stalin, J. V. (1907/2008). Anarchism or socialism? *Works, Vol. 1, November 1901–April 1907.* Moscow, Russia: Foreign Languages Publishing House. Republished on the Marxists Internet Archive. Retrieved October 24, 2022 at www. marxists.org/reference/archive/stalin/works/1906/12/ x01.htm

Steinmetz, K. F. (2016). *Hacked: A radical approach to hacker culture and crime.* New York: NYU Press.

Steinmetz, K. F., Pimentel, A., & Goe, W. R. (2021, Online First). Performing social engineering: A qualitative study of information security deceptions. *Computers in Human Behavior, 124*. https://doi.org/10.1016/j.chb.2021.106930

Stretesky, P. B., Long, M. A., & Lynch, M. J. (2014). *The treadmill of crime: Political economy and green criminology.* New York: Routledge.

*The Guardian*. (2022, August 29). Data company sued by US government amid fears of sensitive location tracking. *The Guardian*. Retrieved August 30, 2022 at www.theguardian. com/technology/2022/aug/29/ftc-sues-kochava-tracking-priv acy-data

Tombs, S. (2018). For pragmatism and politics: Crime, social harm and zemiology. In A. Boukli & J. Korzé (eds.), *Zemiology: Reconnecting crime and social harm* (pp. 11–31). Cham, Siwtzerland: Palgrave Macmillan.

Turk, A. T. (1976). Law as a weapon in social conflict. *Social Problems, 23*(3), 276–291.

Whitty, M. T., & Buchanan, T. (2016). The online dating romance scam: The psychological impact on victims–Both financial and non-financial. *Criminology & Criminal Justice 16*(2), 176–94.

Winlow, S. (2001). *Badfellas: Crime, tradition and new masculinities*. New York: Routledge.

Winlow, S., & Hall, S. (2009). Retaliate first: Memory, humiliation and male violence. *Crime Media Culture, 5*(3), 285–304.

Wood, M. A., Anderson, B., & Richards, I. (2020). Breaking down the pseudo-pacification process: Eight critiques of ultra-realist crime causation theory. *British Journal of Criminology, 60*, 642–661.

Yar, M. (2012). Critical criminology, critical theory and social harm. In S. Hall & S. Winlow (eds.) *New directions in critical criminological theory* (pp. 52–65). New York: Routledge.

Yar, M., & Steinmetz, K. F. (2019). *Cybercrime & Society* (3rd ed.). Thousand Oaks, CA: Sage.

Young, J. (1987). The tasks facing a realist criminology. *Contemporary Crises, 11*(4), 337–356.

Young, J. (2007). *The exclusive society: Social exclusive, crime and difference in late modernity*. Thousand Oaks, CA: Sage.

Zuboff, S. (2015). Big other: Surveillance capitalism and the prospects of an information civilization. *Journal of Information Technology, 30*, 75–89.

# 6

# THE MUNDANITY OF COMPUTATIONAL CRIMINOLOGY

In forging a realist criminology of the internet, it is vital to answer the question of method. What does realist criminology research *look like* in practice? This question is both empirical and political. To develop solutions to crime and victimization problems in a way that is mindful of state and corporate power requires methods that explore the lived experiences of crime and victimization and situate such issues in their proper context. An attunement to power (and powerlessness) is vital. What is therefore required is what C. Wright Mills (1959, p. 8) famously termed the "sociological imagination," a liberatory methodological orientation that addresses the "personal troubles of individuals" stemming from "the public issues of social structure" (Mills, 1959, p. 8). Involved is a holistic approach that situates individual circumstances into broader patterns of power. *The Sociological Imagination* is a natural fit into the realist criminology advanced in these pages. Mills' work, though undoubtedly in the genre of radical social study, was deeply influenced by American pragmatism (Aronowitz, 2012; Dunn. 2018). He viewed knowledge as inseparable from the context of

DOI: 10.4324/9781003277996-8

its production, was skeptical of absolute truth claims, and balked at pretenses of objectivity. As Aronowitz (2012, p. 53) explains, Mills remained "sympathetic to the open, undogmatic philosophy of its founders, particularly Peirce and, to a limited degree, Dewey as well" throughout his career, though he developed his radical approach by relying on social theorists like Weber, Veblen, and Marx to create an intensely skeptical, rigorous, and sweeping orientation to the study of power in society.[1]

The sociological imagination stands in juxtaposition to "abstracted empiricism" or methodologies which fetishize the technical details of method while treating both society and its actors as two-dimensional. Abstracted empiricism is bureaucratic—its agenda dictated by funding agencies and corporate sponsors. Under the guise of "science," researchers operate as technicians chasing data and processing statistical formulae. Control and administration are the objectives.

Though it was first published over 60 years ago, the sociological imagination is as relevant today as it was then. Many of the problems Mills attributed to abstracted empiricism endure. Corporate and government agencies still disproportionately dictate the research priorities of social scientists, awarding grant dollars accordingly. Stale quantitative methodologies proliferate and method is often treated as the default subject matter for social scientists (Ferrell, 2009). Criminology has not been immune from such trends. The late Jock Young (2011), a founding figure of Left Realism, lamented criminology's long-standing love affair with positivism—which he considered an epistemology of abstracted empiricism—and called for a critical intervention in his final book, appropriately named *The Criminological Imagination*. From its inception, realist criminology has been deeply skeptical of positivistic and abstracted empiricist approaches—a tradition unbroken in this analysis (e.g. Hall, 2012; Hall & Winlow, 2015; Matthews, 2014).

In an already unimaginative discipline, the criminology of computer-related crimes is perhaps the most unimaginative. A significant amount of research in the area consists of humdrum survey research or secondary data analyses looking for determinative causal relationships which come to mundane conclusions that do little to challenge the status quo. Self-control may be related to computer crimes perpetration. Routine activities or lifestyle patterns may be associated with victimization. So on and so forth. This is not to say that there is no value in such research—only that these studies have little to say about the lived experiences of crime and victimization and less to say about how to address these problems. Solutions, if stated at all, generally err toward generic calls for increased technological security, greater attention from law enforcement, content moderation by platforms, or less time spent online by potential victims (McGuire, 2018). There is little vision for something *more*. (I too have been guilty of this, though I hope to do better moving forward.)

Because of the challenges endemic to conducting criminological research on the internet—the anonymization of offenders, the increased scope and scale of offending, the transnational nature of certain kinds of cybercrimes, *et cetera* (Yar & Steinmetz, 2019)—some criminologists have called for the utilization of techniques derived from disciplines like computer science, engineering, mathematics, and data science. The use of such techniques is referred to as "computational criminology" (Berk, 2013). While social scientists have been relying extensively on computers to do research for decades, what differentiates computational approaches is the scope and scale of data examined, the complexity of processes involved, the processing power required for analysis, and the degree with which computer know-how is required to design and implement the methods. Though they do have utility, these techniques ultimately run afoul of the same problems that blight other forms of abstracted empiricism.

This chapter explores the abstracted empiricism of computational criminology, drawing primarily from the works of Mills (1959) and Young (2011). I argue that such methods fetishize numbers thereby advancing a false sense of objectivity while obscuring the various abstractions involved in producing and analyzing such data. These methods are also overly deterministic and dismiss the possibility of human agency. For these methods, given enough data and processing power, all human behavior can be modeled and predicted. Relatedly, there is a little room for subjectivity. Such methods also appear either incapable (or their users unwilling) to consider matters of social structure and they have difficulty with the role of history. While these methods may have their uses, they generally fall short of the promise of the sociological imagination. There are two major consequences detailed herein for these shortcomings. One is that the results produced by such research are obvious or trivial. The other is that these methods generally serve the interests of power and control, undermining the liberatory potential of social scientific research.

The purpose of this chapter, then, is to detail one possible trajectory for the study of computer crimes (and even crime more generally) as a point of juxtaposition for realist criminological research. It is sometimes easier to articulate what something *is* if you begin with what it is *not*. In setting forth my arguments I may appear unnecessarily harsh toward computational criminology. The reason for focusing on computational methods is to demonstrate that simply embracing the power of the computers will not alone solve the problems confronting the study of computer crimes. The intrepid social scientist should resist the temptation to believe the false promise of truth and objectivity offered by these techniques. One must keep humanity at the epistemic and moral center. Computers can be useful, but the heart and soul of social science, including realist criminology, is imagination. Thus, before embracing computational methods, criminologists should carefully inventory their limitations.

## Computational Criminology

"Computational criminology" is defined loosely as a "hybrid of computer science, applied mathematics, and criminology" (Berk, 2013, p. 1). Involved is the application of computer- and data-intensive statistical techniques to understanding criminal justice processes and crime, both traditional forms and computerized (Valentine, Hay, Beaver, & Blomberg, 2013). The application of computational approaches to study computer crime and security issues has been ongoing for years by computer scientists and engineers. Computational criminology generally refers to the use of such methods by criminologists (alone or within multidisciplinary research teams). For the sake of simplicity, it is this narrow field that will comprise the focus of this chapter, though many of the criticisms offered throughout are applicable to non-criminological uses of such techniques as well.

A notable computational approach involves the collection and analysis of "big data" (Lazer & Radford, 2017; Ozkan, 2019; Williams & Burnap, 2016; Williams, Burnap, & Sloan, 2017). Though competing definitions exist, Smith, Moses, and Chan (2017, p. 267) explain that "Big Data," in the context of criminology, refers to "the volume, variety and velocity of data that can be collected, stored and analysed" and "the diversity of data-capturing technologies that are applied to specific fields to generate novel insights on criminal behaviours and to initiate new forms of criminal justice practice." "Big data" thus refers to the gathering and structuring of massive datasets that can be analyzed in a variety of ways—some of which involve traditional social scientific research approaches (e.g. regression) and others which necessitate more computationally intensive tools from fields like data science (Lazer & Radford, 2017). Computational criminology may also involve using algorithmic modeling approaches (Banerjee, Swearingen, Shillair, Bauer, Holt, & Ross, 2021; Berk, 2013; Chan & Moses, 2016). These strategies assume there is an underlying structure within a dataset and use computers to identify a model of this latent structure that best fits the data. An example is "machine learning" (Berk, 2013; Chan & Moses, 2016, p. 30). In this approach, a dataset is curated, a sample is extracted from the dataset, and that sample is then set aside. An algorithm is then "trained" on the remaining data. The resulting predictive model is then tested against the extracted sample. The idea is that a good model will be equally good at predicting outcomes in the primary dataset *and* the sample. These are not the only computational techniques that have been applied to crime and criminal legal issue but they are notable examples (for an overview of other techniques, see: Campedelli, 2022).

At the extreme, certain computational techniques are said to threaten current disciplinary standards and practices as such technologies "are not constrained by preconceived theoretical or methodological disciplinary norms" (Hannah-Moffat, 2019, p. 459; see also: Mayer-Schönberger & Cukier, 2013). The vision for such techniques, particularly those based on big data and algorithmic approaches, is that the data will speak for themselves. Correlations can be found and applied to the real world with little need for the explanatory tools provided by criminological theory and research.

There are methodological and conceptual limitations facing these analyses, however, which many scholars have been quick to point out (e.g. Chan & Moses, 2016; Hannah-Moffat, 2019; Lynch, 2018; Ridgeway, 2013). For instance, such data is often curated by private or public actors with vested interests in particular uses and outcomes. Critics thus rightfully indicate that such techniques are not neutral in that they harbor latent assumptions about "society, individuals, social institutions and scientific practice" (Hannah-Moffat, 2019, p. 459). Further, problems of data quality exist which cannot be easily dismissed as such data is often not purpose-built for academic social science (Lynch, 2018). There is also a "black box" problem as the machinations of such techniques may be hidden from outside scrutiny for proprietary purposes or, if disclosed, may require a degree of expertise to fully understand beyond the capabilities of most social scientists—thus limiting the degree to which such analyses can be fully vetted through mechanisms like peer review (Brennan & Oliver, 2013; Bushway, 2013; Hannah-Moffat, 2019). Some evidence also exists that individuals involved in computer crimes develop methods to avoid having their data captured using big data techniques (Benjamin, Samtani, & Chen, 2017, p. 57; Hutchings, Pastrana, & Clayton, 2020).[2] Not to mention the variety of civil liberties and social inequity issues that may manifest from collecting and analyzing massive amounts of data (Hannah-Moffat, 2019, p. 465).

Regarding algorithmic techniques specifically, while these approaches may be able to generate surprisingly accurate predictions of outcomes within a given dataset, their predictive power may wane when applied to new datasets for which they are not trained (Ridgeway, 2013). Further, such strategies generally fail to yield *explanations* for the patterns in the data. In other words, although algorithmic approaches can be useful for uncovering connections and trends within a dataset on which they are trained, these approaches falter when applied beyond this narrow scope.

While these limitations are important to consider, this analysis contends that there are deeper problems confronting computational methodologies produced by their tendency toward abstracted empiricism. In fact, there exist striking parallels between Mills' descriptions of the sociological research that dominated during his time and contemporary advances in computational methods, including in the field of criminology. Meet the new boss, same as the old boss.

## Abstracted Empiricism and the Computational Epistemology

As an acute version of positivism, computational criminology and its correlates place faith in equations and computer processing to find order in the chaos of human life. A byproduct of the dependence on computer power for social scientific research is that social life is rendered *in computational terms*. Implicitly or explicitly, the social world and its actors are viewed as operating like machines subject to the whims of input and output under predictable operating parameters. Like the positivism said to blight criminology more generally, the computational epistemology is "denatured and desiccated,"

> Its actors inhabit an arid planet where they are either driven into crime by social or psychological deficits or make opportunistic choices in the marketplace of crime. They are either miserable or mundane: they are digital creatures of quantity, they obey probabilistic laws of

deviancy—they can be represented by the statistical symbolism of lambda, chi and sigma, their behaviour can be captured in the intricacies of regression analysis and equation.

*(Young, 2011, p. 84)*

This conception of humans as technical systems is not unique to computational criminology. Truitt (2015, p. 2) explains that "mechanism" or "using mechanical models to explain and understand the body, the universe, and the laws that govern both" is an idea that "stretches back to antiquity." Concepts such as artificial intelligence, automata, cybernetics, cyborgs, and robots, have, for centuries, presented curious philosophical dilemmas about the boundaries between humans and machines, life and death, sentience and non-sentience, and provided frames of reference for making sense of the world (Schaffer, 1999; Truitt, 2015). Though such ruminations on the boundaries between humans and machines make for interesting philosophy, the framing of human actors and social science in mechanical or computational terms is antithetical to the sociological imagination.

Computational methods suffer acutely from the "fetishism of numbers, the illusion of precision, the promise of science" (Young, 2011, p. 44). There is general sense that because these methods reduce everything to numerical calculation, that these methods are more objective—that the data is more *real*. Yet it is easy to forget that numbers are themselves abstractions produced by social actors under specific circumstances (Mills, 1959, p. 124). There is a slippage that might occur between human action and its quantification. For Young (2011), such an endeavor constitutes a kind of "madness," which believes that "human behavior can be encapsulated in a formula or captured in an equation" (Young, 2011,

p. 62). Like the positivistic methods both Mills and Young critique, computational methods require no interaction or observation of actual humans—only their digital traces are necessary. Humans are fractured along mathematical axes and processed through algorithmic black boxes.

In this manner, computational methods are highly deterministic. There exists little room for human agency—given sufficient data and computational power, all human thought and action can be modelled and predicted. This approach is the business model of many Big Tech companies like Google and Facebook, which gather the "data exhaust" of people to create and market targeted advertising solutions to vendors (Zuboff, 2015). Humans are not decision makers—at least not in the traditional sense—but are purely reactive creatures, behaving in predictable ways given sufficient data exists for making such predeterminations. In his 1921 play *Rossum's Universal Robots,* Czech playwright Karel Čapek coined the term "robots" to describe engineered soulless humanoids purpose-built for subservient labor. And like Dr. Hallemaier, the head of Rossum's Institute for Psychological Training of Robots, computational methods view humans act having "no will of their own. No soul. No passion." They are slaves of input, process, and output.

As agency disappears, so too does subjectivity and meaning. Computational approaches are steeped in what Young (2011, p. 73) refers to as the "nomothetic impulse" or "the search for generalization which is independent of nation or of locality."[3] While such research can be useful, it also tends to eschew the role of subjectivity, culture, and subculture. One would, according to Young (2011, p. 74) "have to believe cultural influences are merely a thin patina over the hard core of basic human behavior." In this way, computational methods for the study of cybercrime are "drunk on syntax, blind to semantics"

(Mills, 1959, p. 34).[4] Similarly, McGuire (2018) argues that research on computer crime privileges syntax, the "correct use of symbols and their combinations," over semantics or "what a syntactically correct sequence of symbols *mean*" (McGuire, 2018, p. 137). The elevation of syntax, for him, stems from a deference to computer science and engineering, a condition which similarly afflicts computational criminology. Yet he contends that social scientists are uniquely poised to grapple with the complexities of semantics. While computer scientists and engineers have worked to making inroads on meaning with techniques like "semantic analysis," these generally fail to advance beyond "positive" and "negative" connotations for words—leaving a wide range of human meaning unconsidered. Techniques also exist such as natural language processing, but these are similarly limited. Social science, particularly an imaginative one, is more suited for examining human meaning and subjective experience (at least until there are suitable advances in artificial intelligence, which perhaps might be coming sooner than we think).

The epistemology of computational methods also generally fails to consider social structure. Such approaches tend to myopically focus on patterns and trends which appear endemic among the smallest possible units within a dataset. The focus becomes individual behavior and difference. There thus appears to be little interest among computational studies of crime in drawing connections between results and the "big picture." For instance, in 2013 Berk and Bleich published an article in *Criminology & Public Policy*, a flagship policy-oriented journal in criminology, argued for the application of machine learning approaches to criminal justice risk assessment. This article was followed by response essays that evaluated the merits of Berk and Blech's (2013) arguments (Bushway, 2013;

Rhodes, 2013; Ridgeway, 2013). Collectively, these articles ruminate on statistical nuance regarding the use of offender risk prediction tools for justice administration. Yet none appear to consider, for example, contexts by which risk occurs nor the structural circumstances which birthed our current "risk society" (Beck, 1986; Ericson & Haggerty, 1997). In fact, Berk and Bleich (2013, p. 515) explicitly state they are avoiding social structural considerations like race, stating that "these issues are difficult and real, but they are not addressed in this article."

Of course, it may be unfair to critique this omission as articles are often narrowly focused and not all relevant matters may be discussed in the scope of a single work. The point, however, is that even if the authors wanted to discuss these issues, they could do little more than grapple with the subject as point of discussion as most of these datasets are not developed with social context in mind. In this sense, risk assessment instruments are flat and sterile things. They do not contain measures at this level of analysis and can only approximate them through identity characteristics like race and gender or life circumstances like income or family support. The tools would have to be rewritten to include measures designed to tap into structural and cultural contexts (Goddard & Meyers, 2017). Further, biases are often cooked into the instruments themselves which may further replicate structural problems in criminal justice administration (for instance, racial disparities in sentencings and community supervision) (e.g. Prins & Reich, 2021, pp. 13–16).

The *C&PP* analyses are thus statistical exercises that say little about the actuality of crime and victimization. This is by design—risk prediction is a criminal justice administrative tool used for limited bureaucratic purposes. In effect, the researchers are simply technicians quibbling about the best way to facilitate this control apparatus, seemingly uninterested in the structural context of risk assessment, at least in the scope of these analyses. As will be discussed in greater detail later in this chapter, this shortcoming renders computational methods acutely vulnerable to becoming weapons of control rather than tools of liberation.

To date, few studies of computer crimes conducted by criminologists have used computational techniques (e.g. Banerjee et al., 2021; Caines et al., 2018; de Vries & Radford, 2022; Pastrana, Hutchings, Caines, & Buttery, 2018), despite multiple calls for such methodological adaptations (e.g. Bossler, 2017; Holt, 2017). Machine learning techniques, for instance, have been used to study website defacements (Banerjee et al., 2021) and to automate the classification of posts on a hacking-related online forum (Caines et al., 2018). Like the risk assessment analyses described previously, these studies appear mostly to be methodological exercises with little to say about the social context in which computer crime and victimization occurs.

An additional problem posed by computational approaches is one of history (Uprichard, 2012). Such datasets are typically cross-sectional in nature, examining online happenings within a brief snapshot in time, capturing a frame of time only insofar as digital interactions are asynchronously logged in the digital platform under question. Of course, this weakness is not one specific to computational approaches. Indeed, criminology is awash with cross-sectional research. Yet it is worth acknowledging that the findings of such studies—computational or not— can only be given life when situated in their economic, political, cultural, *and* historical contexts. Without such consideration, these studies "cannot in themselves provide an explanation for their findings; longitudinal methods alongside them are necessary" (Uprichard, 2012, p. 131).

As Uprichard (2012, p. 131) explains, "this is primarily why the new genre of ahistorical digital research is not in itself able to deliver the promise of the sociological imagination." These approaches tend to overemphasize the present and, in their more extreme forms, focus on predicting immediate behaviors or engaging in "now-casting" (Bollier, 2010, p. 20). The result is that as history disappears from the analysis. The analyses get "stuck in a series of perpetual presents without any recourse to either understand our pasts or affect the future" (Uprichard, 2012, p. 134).

In this manner, computational methods eschew agency, diminish subjectivity, and avoid cultural, structural, and historical contexts. Such computational studies mirror Mills' (1963b) descriptions of "the scientist" who "aspires to be the IBM symbol and to wear white coats and become 'higher statisticians', exuding a bureaucratization of the mind that opts for apolitical, safe studies" (Brewer, 2004, p. 326). Absent is a "form of self-consciousness capable of comprehending biography, history, world politics, and particular societies as intertwined totalities" (Denzin, 1990, p. 2).

## The Thinness of Computational Methods

Despite the various limitations confronting computational methods, such approaches are billed by some as a panacea for the problems confronting criminological research including internet-related criminal activities. Lazer and Radford (2017, p. 20), for instance, argue that these tools have "the potential for a transformation" of social sciences. Berk (2013, p. 1) similarly argues that computational methods can uncover "important but elusive structures in a dataset" that might otherwise go unnoticed through more traditional methodologies and that "the computational muscle has grown so rapidly over the past decade that the new applications have the look and feel of dramatic, qualitative advances." Arguments also exist that because private companies like Facebook and Google use such approaches to significant effect to make social predictions implies an "empirical crisis" whereby criminology will be rendered obsolete if it does not embrace similar methodologies (Williams & Burnap, 2016, p. 217). Yet, if these methods are so necessary for the future of criminological inquiry, one might expect studies using these methods to offer ground-shaking insights. Yet this does not appear to be the case. In fact, many computational criminology studies arrive at rather obvious or banal conclusions. This has not seemed to stop researchers from hyping the promise of these methods.

Young (2011) argues that positivist criminology is characterized by a willingness to "skate on thin ice"—to acknowledge the limitations of its methods and then states its conclusions boldly as if those limitations are irrelevant. As he explains,

> What is remarkable is that the knowledge of the tenuous nature of the statistics is widespread, yet it does not seem to stop the world-be social scientist for more than a minute. Somewhere tucked into the text the authors admit the precariousness of their arguments, their scientific vulnerability, and yet continue on. It is as if the skater hesitates, notes the thin ice, yet skates blithely on.
>
> *(Young, 2011, p. 41)*

Computational studies are blighted by a similar problem. There exist studies published in prominent criminological journals which employ interesting computational methodological techniques but, likely due to inherent limitations in the method, come to muted conclusions with seemingly little awareness of how little is being said. What is left is a soulless criminology that generates mundane and unimaginative findings where, as Mills (1959, p. 52) explains, "the thinness of the results is matched only by the elaboration of the methods and the care employed."

Consider, for instance, Williams and Burnap's (2016) study examining the propagation of hate speech on Twitter following the 2013 Woolwich, London terrorist attack. The authors scraped Twitter data for 15 days following the event, capturing data using trending hashtags associated with discourse about the attack. This data was then subjected to a battery of regression analyses and data visualization techniques. Despite the novel techniques used, the conclusions are tepid. The authors summarize their findings by stating that "we found evidence of cyberhate originating from individual Twitter users, in particular those identifying with right wing political groups, that was directly related to the trigger event" (Williams & Burnap, 2016, p. 232). In other words, hate speech propagates following an act of violence conducted by historically marginalized individuals. Not to be unkind, but this kind of result is not unexpected. In fact, the authors themselves acknowledge this fact. They insist then that the "novel" finding is that such spikes in hate speech correspond to spikes in "offline hate crimes and incidents" as well (ibid). Their analysis also found that "information flows containing cyberhate were significantly less likely to grow large and survive for long periods during the study window" (ibid). To put it another way, overtly hateful comments online do not proliferate as widely as those which are less overt. They also conclude that "the number of newspaper headlines was predictive of the production of cyberhate, evidencing that tweeters posting hateful content may be fueled by coverage in the press in the early impact stage" (Williams & Burnap, 2016, p. 233). The finding that press attention corresponds with subsequent social media attention is unsurprising—it would be eyebrow-raising if the proliferation of social media posts was independent of news media interest around such events. The primary contribution of the analysis thus appears to be methodological—that computational methods "affords criminologists with the opportunity to identify, monitor and trace social reactions to events to a second in real time" (Williams & Burnap, 2016, p. 234).

Banderjee and colleagues (2021) examined an impressive sample of 2.24 million defacements and 40,000 images posted on such sites through a "deep learning model" to examine the disparity between images used in defacements and the motivations of the offenders (self-professed or machine-derived). The objective of the study, as stated in the abstract, is to explore "the usefulness of machine learning techniques to better understand attacker strategies and motivations." The analysis of self-professed motivations in this study ultimately confirms prior qualitative studies, finding that hackers claim to conduct their activities largely to have fun or demonstrate technical prowess (e.g. Hutchings, 2013; Steinmetz, 2016). The takeaway of this analysis is that once self-professed motivations and image clustering-derived motivations are compared, there appears to be little relationship between self-professed motivations for website defacements and the images used in those defacements. The reader (or at least this reader) was left wondering, "what do I do with this information?" Again, the analysis appears to be primarily a methodological exercise.

The obviousness or lukewarm nature of the results generated by computational approaches echo Young's (2011, p. 15) description of the "datasaur,"

> A creature is a very small head, a long neck, a huge belly and a little tail. His head has only a smattering of theory, he knows that he must move constantly but is not sure where he is going, he rarely looks at any detail of the actual terrain on which he travels, his neck peers upwards as he moves from grant to grant, from database to database, his belly is huge and distended with the intricate intestine of regression analysis, he eats ravenously but rarely thinks about the actual process of statistical digestion, his tail is small, slight and inconclusive.

The datasaur, according to Young, is a corpulent monster whose body is bloated with data and statistical formulae. Its tiny head contains only a minimal amount of theory. It has a tiny tail which waggles impotently between conclusions.

As previously noted, the critiques offered here are perhaps callous and cruel. I should be clear that the previously described studies are given as examples *not* because they are bad computational studies. They were chosen precisely because they are on the cutting edge in this subfield, written by well-respected authors, and published in prestigious journals. They are therefore *exemplary* analyses in this area. Any problems they contain are not theirs alone. It is my contention that the tepidness of the results is not a fault of the intellectual capacities of the authors but *built into the methodology itself.*

In addition, I admit that the criticisms leveled herein are not only unkind but, to some degree, unfair. There are many studies that rely on standard social scientific research methods, which produce results that are as much if not more unsurprising or muted. The argument made here is that the application of computational methods, at least to date, appears to border more on methodological exercises rather than ones designed to shed substantive insights on crime or crime control. I argue that these studies may never evolve beyond methodological prestidigitation unless they incorporate a more *imaginative* orientation, which will be considered in greater detail in the following chapter.

## Oblivious to Power

As indicated before, computational methods seem inadequately equipped to examine problems of social power. By focusing on primarily on the individual and eschewing social context, these techniques favor prediction and control rather than resistance and liberation—key concerns for the sociological imagination (Hannah-Moffat, 2016; Sanders & Sheptycki, 2017). In this manner, computational criminology is an advancement of an orthodox criminology which has long established itself as a discipline of control in the service of the status quo (Agozino, 2003; Cohen, 1988; Young, 2011).

In fact, the primary use of these techniques has been predicting and controlling consumer behavior by Big Tech corporations (Zuboff, 2015). Though industry supporters argue that consumers benefit from the tailored online experience such strategies offer, the ultimate objective— to promote consumption—benefits corporations. Further, by quantifying nearly every facet of social life, the data systems created by Big Tech companies create a lopsided relationship where these companies gather absurd amounts of data on individual consumers to shape their behavior and determine their online experience in exchange for access to Big Tech services, which consumers neither own nor control. The result is that corporations and their analysts can inflict their methods upon individuals, but these analyses are seldom ever turned toward the activities and behaviors of these corporations. They are top-down analyses.

More specifically in the realm of the internet, algorithmic methods of data analysis and social prediction have become the norm as companies like Google, Facebook, Twitter, and others regularly collect and analyze consumer data for marketing purposes. The power of these algorithms to predict consumer desires, if reports are accurate, is eerie. For instance, many have wondered if Facebook is listening in on consumer conversations as advertisements related to items of recent discussion have appeared on user feeds (Martínez, 2017). This is unlikely. Instead, these uncanny coincidences are most likely a result of the robustness of their proprietary algorithms.[5]

Control of the internet and its experience has become increasingly concentrated into the hands of Big Tech companies and, as a result, marginalized populations are disproportionately surveilled or excluded altogether from online spaces, a phenomenon Lingel (2021) refers to as the "gentrification of the internet" and Noble (2018) terms "technological redlining" or "algorithmic oppression." For many people, their primary experiences with the internet are mediated through proprietary platforms like those owned by Google and Meta. Such monopolistic enterprises may heavily police communities at the margins. Groups celebrating alternative sexual lifestyles, for instance, may be censored or platforms' terms of services may circumscribe the types of expression allowed (Lingel, 2021). Algorithms designed to hook users and keep them engaged with platform content may encourage polarization and discord. For example, arguments exist that YouTube's content algorithms gradually introduce more extremist, sensational content to users because such content increases view time and, as a result, drives advertising views (Roose, 2020). Yet a consequence is that users are potentially pulled into content bubbles which normalize extremist views like white supremacy and fascism (ibid).

Ownership of these platforms is thus concentrated disproportionately into the hands of mostly wealthy, white, cisgendered men while largely upholding structures of inequality. In this manner, predictive algorithms have fundamentally changed most people's experiences of the internet and, in a broader sense, cultural engagement and political discourse. Further, it has done so in ways that serve the interests of the powerful at the expense of the powerless.

As indicated previously, similar criticisms have been leveled at the use of computational methods in the realm of criminology and criminal justice. For instance, one of the most prominent uses of computational methods has been in the fields of probation and parole to analyze risk of recidivism and revocation (Berk & Bleich, 2013; Bushway, 2013; Rhodes, 2013; Ridgeway, 2013). These approaches thus have been explicitly employed for the purposes of control of populations caught in the net of the carceral apparatus. And because these methods tend to eschew consideration of social power and structure, they risk replicating structural inequalities (Eubanks, 2018; van Eijk, 2016). For instance, some research indicates that correctional risk assessment tools designed to predict potential for rearrest may overclassify Black folks as "high risk" relative to actual rearrest outcomes when compared to other racial or ethnic groups (Eckhouse, Lum, Conti-Cook, & Ciccolini, 2019). Further, the data upon which such decisions are based are potentially biased along axes like gender and race (Hannah-Moffat, 2016). Arrest rates, for example, are shaped by differences in police surveillance and patrol that cannot be entirely attributed to actual differences in criminal involvement (Eckhouse et al., 2019; Goddard & Myers, 2017). Thus, the use of prior arrests as a predictive variable of future arrests takes on a racial character that likely biases models. As Eckhouse and colleagues (2019, p. 197) explain, "the model is not predicting individual behavior, but an event by police decision-making... both the prediction and outcome are the result of racially biased law enforcement." As the expression goes, "garbage in, garbage out."

In this manner, correctional risk assessment, according to Goddard and Meyers (2017, p. 154) has "the potential to be oppressive in that it tolerates unjust structural conditions while demanding obedience." They add that "the exclusion of structural considerations as suitable targets" from risk assessments and similar "evidence-based" approaches "leaves little room for programs that target root causes of crime" (Goddard & Myers, 2017, p. 159). One of the key arguments for the use of such models is that they will be less biased than decisions based on human discretion. This may or may not be true, but it does not mean such measures are unbiased. Further, the illusion of true objectivity offered by risk assessment approaches may give an unwarranted degree of legitimacy to any disparities that emerge in predictive data and outcomes.

In her 2017 book *Automating Inequality,* Virginia Eubank's explores the use of algorithms to automate or guide social welfare and public assistance decisions. She contends that these algorithms filter out the deserving from the undeserving, thus becoming mechanisms of social exclusion that replicate longstanding social inequities and political agendas. She explains that "automated decision-making in our current welfare system acts a lot like older, atavistic forms of punishment and containment. It filters and diverts. It is a gatekeeper, not a facilitator" (Eubanks, 2017, p. 82). In this way, the pursuit of computerized objectivity risks crystalizing the status quo, making the system a more efficient oppressor.

The computational perspective is haunted by Heidegger (1977, p. 32), who warned in *The Question of Technology* that the essence of technology is mired in a desire to control. As a result, it is ready-built for social engineering. The term, "social engineers," was first introduced in 1842 by John Gray in his book, *An Efficient Remedy for the Distress of Nations,* where he flippantly compared the "political and social engineers" of the time to mechanical engineers (Gray, 1842, p. 117; Hatfield, 2018, p. 103). Later in the 19th century, others began using the term more earnestly, such as J.C. Van Marken, who, in his 1894 essay, described a class of professionals dedicated to dealing with the "'human problems' of factories and plants" (Larsson, Letell, & Thörn, 2012, p. 12). During this period, so-called Progressives sought reform through social control efforts to curb the excesses of industrialization and the unrest of the downtrodden (Brownell, 1983; McClymer, 1980; Zinn, 2003, p. 349).[6] For Progressives, public service and social change were to be implemented by trained professionals, such as mental health clinicians, social psychologists, social workers, and others who understood the roles of organizations and institutions in managing populations (Brownell, 1983; Graebner, 1987; McClymer, 1980). Relatedly, this period also saw the rise of the engineering profession, which specialized in developing and implementing the technologies that were dramatically altering the economic landscape. Engineers who offered solutions to social problems were often hostile to what they perceived to be overly idealistic and haphazard ideas of the progressive reformers. Instead, they saw society as organized by "social laws" and that technology was a means to achieve social progress (Layton, 1971). This understanding meant that careful scientific manipulation of society could be the solution for social issues, and could be applied only by a trained "social engineer" (Layton, 1971).

Thus emerged the social engineer as a specialized professional dedicated to creating more efficient and effective institutions and organizations. For these professionals, humans could be viewed as machines to be calibrated and coordinated to maximize utility through processes like Tolman's (1909) "industrial betterment" or Taylor's (1914) "scientific management." In addition to focusing on improving production, social engineers tended to view certain populations, usually workers and the lower classes, as being, in some way, deficient and in need of correction (Alexander & Schmidt, 1996).

It is no accident that computational approaches have been advanced by Big Tech and various government institutions. These are techniques designed to find patterns and predict individual behavior, with sometimes alarming accuracy, allowing advertisers and other interests to capitalize on their findings. They are techniques which flatten the social world and make it manipulable. While the insights produced by social scientific research using computational methods may be obvious or mundane, the scope and scale at which they can operate means they are highly scalable means for addressing specific problems in precise ways. Without an imaginative moral compass, computational methodologies have become the new social engineering.

Despite these criticisms, some scholars argue that risk assessments and related algorithmic approaches are not wholly without emancipatory potential. For instance, some argue that such models can, in fact, be calibrated to focus on the structural and community antecedents to crime thus allowing for programmatic interventions and investments in afflicted populations to ameliorate such root causes and material conditions (Hannah-Moffat, 2016; Goddard & Myers, 2017). Relatedly, Hannah-Moffat (2019) argues that big data strategies can be used by activists to challenge government and corporate power and affect social change. The liberatory potential, however, hinges on the democratization of big data tools, the transparency of methods, and the availability of data. Wholly rejecting computational approaches may thus throw the figurative baby out with the bathwater. What makes for potentially liberatory computational methodologies, however, is an explicit attunement to structural conditions, historical impact, and their relationship with individual circumstances; in other words, the sociological imagination. Of course, as previously noted, there are certain elements of these methodologies which appear antithetical to this perspective. There is a kind of gravitational force of these methods that pull them toward abstracted empiricism, positivism, and a reification of the present. There is potential, but only in the sense that a person might swim to safety through shark-infested waters—possible, but risky. But like good pragmatists, we should never close off the possibility of inquiry. If these tools can be used to fruitfully develop liberatory knowledge, then let's have it.

## Concluding Thoughts: Computational Methods and Engineering Envy

One of the reasons why criminologists may find computational methods enticing is not methodological utility but, instead, a matter of disciplinary legitimacy. The urge to embrace the strategies of computer science and related fields may be because those fields are seen to have a bigger claim to objectivity and scientific prestige in the domain of technology than criminology. This would mirror Mills' (1959, pp. 56–57) claims that the abstracted empiricism of his time was rooted in a desire to approximate the physical and natural sciences, viewed as more prestigious due to their positions within universities and favor among funding agencies. Richard Sennett (1995) referred to this as a kind of "physics envy" that seems to permeate positivistic sociology. By this token, we might say that the impulse to employ computational methods suffers from a similar "engineering envy."

An envious person desires what another has and, in the process, fails to appreciate what they already possess. In the context of computational methods, in envying the prestige and legitimacy conferred upon computer science and engineering, criminologists may not appreciate alternative non-computational methodological tools and orientations that may be better suited for the subject matter. As a result, the range of acceptable epistemic positions will become narrowed to only those acceptable under a computational framework. Like a codependent relationship, there is a risk of social sciences allowing computer science and engineering to dictate their identity. Engineering envy risks blinding criminologists to their own strengths and potentialities. For this reason, the sociological imagination is vital for the future of criminological research including the study of computer crime.

## Notes

1 None of this is to say that Mills was not *uncritical* of pragmatists. He once described pragmatism as "the ideology of the liberal professional man, however much he may have thought about the disadvantaged" (Mills, 1963a, p. 167). Despite his criticisms, it was clear that pragmatism had a deep influence on his thinking. It was just insufficient on its own to grapple with the kinds of problems he was interested in. For instance, he found Dewey's dithering about certain ethical problems to be rather milquetoast, arguing that

> there comes a point when any solution of any "value problem" becomes: Who can kill whom? Or in peaceful civilized countries: Who can have whom put in jail? That's tough for the philosopher, but that's the way things really are. The rest seems a mixture of often weird conventions and sham. You may dress up the killing as you will but in the individual's real path of life there it has been and there it is..
>
> (Mills, 1963a, p. 168)

He was unsatisfied with the tepid conclusions of folks like Dewey, seeing the urgency and obviousness of social problems described by the likes of Marx, Veblen, and Fromm.

2   Interestingly, the use of avoidance strategies by such individuals mirrors Mills' (1959, p. 117) observation that "men are not inert objects," which means "they may become aware of predictions made about their activities, and that accordingly they can of often do re-direct themselves; they may falsify or fulfill the predictions."

3   Similarly, pragmatists would reject such nomothetic research as attempting to isolate transcendental or universal external truths (Baert, 2005; Misak, 2013; Putnam, 1997).

4   In *The Sociological Imagination*, Mills (1959, p. 34) invokes the problem of semantics and syntax when criticizing what he referred to as "grand theory," which, while related to abstracted empiricism, refers to the tendency of some social scientists to revel in obscure abstraction with little regard for the lived realities of human subjects and their various problems.

5   It is worth noting that while social scientific uses of computational methods often result in obvious or tepid conclusions, that they can still generate predictive accuracy which can have massive utility for parties interested in tailoring services at the individual level. It is thus a kind of mundane science useful within the context of the status quo.

6   Care should be taken to disentangle the term "social engineering" in this historical sense to contemporary uses of the term among hackers and information security professionals to describe the use of deception to circumvent information security measures (Hatfield, 2018; Steinmetz, Pimentel, & Goe, 2020).

## References

Agozino, B. (2003). *Counter-colonial criminology: A critique of imperialist reason*. Sterling, VA: Pluto.

Alexander, J., & Schmidt, J.K.H. (1996). Social engineering. In A. Podgorecki, J. Alexander, & R. Shields (Eds.) *Social engineering* (pp. 1–19). Ottawa: Carleton University Press.

Aronowitz, S. (2012). *Taking it big: C. Wright Mills and the making of political intellectuals*. New York: Columbia University Press.

Baert, P. (2003). Pragmatism, realism and hermeneutics. *Foundations of Science, 8*, 89–106.

Baert, P. (2005). *Philosophy of the social sciences: Towards pragmatism*. Malden, MA: Polity Press.

Banerjee, S., Swearingen, T., Shillair, R., Bauer, J. M., Holt, T., & Ross, A. (2021, Online First). Using machine learning to examine cyberattack motivations on web defacement data. *Social Science Computer Review*. https://doi.org/10.1177/0894439321994234.

Beck, U. (1986). *Risk society: Towards a new modernity*. Thousand Oaks, CA: Sage.

Benjamin, V., Samtani, S., & Chen, H. (2017). Conducting large-scale analyses of underground hacker communities. In T. J. Holt (ed.) *Cybercrime through an interdisciplinary lens* (pp. 56–75). New York: Routledge.

Berk, R. A. (2013). Algorithmic criminology. *Security Informatics, 2*(5), 1–14 .

Berk, R. A., & Bleich, J. (2013). Statistical procedures for forecasting criminal behavior: A comparative assessment. *Criminology & Public Policy, 12*(3), 513–544.

Bollier, D. (2010). *The promise and peril of big data*. Washington, DC: The Aspen Institute.

Bossler, A. M. (2017). Cybercrime research at the crossroads: Where the field currently stands and innovative strategies to move forward. In T. J. Holt (ed.) *Cybercrime through an interdisciplinary lens* (pp. 37–55). New York: Routledge.

Brennan, T., & Oliver, W. L. (2013). Emergence of machine learning techniques in criminology: Implications of complexity in our data and in research questions. *Criminology & Public Policy, 12*(3), 551–562.

Brewer, J. D. (2004). Imagining *The Sociological Imagination*: The biographical context of a sociological class. *The British Journal of Sociology, 55*(3), 317–333.

Brownell, B.A. (1983). Interpretations of twentieth-century urban progressive reform. In D.R. Colburn & G.E. Pozzetta (Eds.) *Reform and reformers in the Progressive Era* (pp. 3–23). Westport, CT: Greenwood Press.

Bushway, S. D. (2013). Is there any logic to using logit: Finding the right tool for the increasingly important job of risk prediction. *Criminology & Public Policy, 12*(3), 563–568.

Caines, A., Pastrana, S., Hutchings, A., & Buttery, P. J. (2018). Automatically identifying the function and intent of posts in underground forums. *Crime Science, 7*(19). https://doi.org/10.1186/s40163-018-0094-4

Campedelli, G. M. (2022). *Machine learning for criminology and crime research: At the crossroads*. New York: Routledge.

Chan, J., & Moses, L. B. (2016). Is Big Data challenging criminology? *Theoretical Criminology, 20*(1), 21–39.

Cohen, S. (1988). *Against criminology*. New York: Routledge.

Denzin, N. K. (1990). Presidential address on 'The Sociological Imagination' revisited. *The Sociological Quarterly, 31*(1), 1–22.

De Vries, I., & Radford, J. (2022). Identifying online risk markers of hard-to-observe crimes through semi-inductive triangulation: The case of human trafficking in the United States. *The British Journal of Criminology, 62*, 639–658.

Dunn, R. G. (2018). *Toward a pragmatist sociology: John Dewey and the legacy of C. Wright Mills*. Philadelphia, PA: Temple University Press.

Eckhouse, L., Lum, K., Conti-Cook, C., & Ciccolini, J. (2019). Layers of bias: A unified approach for understanding problems with risk assessment. *Criminal Justice and Behavior, 46*(2), 185–209.

Ericson, R. V., & Haggerty, K. D. (1997). *Policing the risk society*. Toronto, ON: University of Toronto Press.

Eubanks, V. (2017). *Automating inequality: How high-tech tools profile, police, and punish the poor*. New York: St. Martin's Press.

Goddard, T., & Myers, R. R. (2017). Against evidence-based oppression: Marginalized youth and the politics of risk-based assessment and intervention. *Theoretical Criminology, 21*(2), 151–167.

Graebner, W. (1987). *The engineering of consent*. Madison, WI: The University of Wisconsin Press.

Gray, J. (1842). *An efficient remedy for the distress of nations*. Edinburg: Adam and Charles Black.

Hall, S. (2012). *Theorizing crime and deviance: A new perspective*. Thousand Oaks, CA: Sage.

Hall, S., & Winlow, S. (2015). *Revitalizing criminological theory: Towards a new ultra-realism*. New York: Routledge.

Hannah-Moffat, K. (2016). A conceptual kaleidoscope: Contemplating "dynamic structural risk" and an uncoupling of risk from need. *Psychology, Crime & Law, 22*(1–2), 33–46.

Hannah-Moffat, K. (2019). Algorithmic risk governance: Big data analytics, race and information activism in criminal justice debates. *Theoretical Criminology, 23*(4), 453–470.

Hatfield, J.M. (2018). Social engineering in cybersecurity: The evolution of a concept. *Computers & Security, 73*, 102–113.

Heidegger, M. (1977). *The question concerning technology and other essays*. New York: Harper Perennial.

Holt, T. J. (2017). Situating the problem of cybercrime in a multidisciplinary context. In T. J. Holt (ed.) *Cybercrime through an interdisciplinary lens* (pp. 1–14). New York: Routledge.

Hutchings, A. (2013). Hacking and fraud: Qualitative analysis of online offending and victimization. In K. Jaishankar & N. Ronel (eds.) *Global criminology: Crime and victimization in a globalized era* (pp. 93–114). Boca Raton, FL: CRC Press.

Hutchings, A., Pastrana, S., & Clayton, R. (2020). Displacing big data: How criminals cheat the system. In R. Leukfeldt & T. J. Holt (eds.) *The human factor of cybercrime* (pp. 408–424). New York: Routledge.

Larsson, B., Letell, M., & Thörn, H. (2012). Transformations of the Swedish welfare state. In B. Larsson, M. Letell, & H. Thörn (Eds.) *Transformations of the Swedish Welfare State: From Social Engineering to Social Governance?* (pp. 3–22). New York: Palgrave Macmillan.

Layton, E.T. (1971). *The revolt of the engineers*. Cleveland, OH: The Press of Case Western Reserve University.

Lazer, D., & Radford, J. (2017). Data ex machina: Introduction to big data. *Annual Review of Sociology, 43*, 19–39.

Lingel, J. (2021). *The gentrification of the internet: How to reclaim our digital freedom.* Oakland, CA: University of California Press.

Lynch, J. (2018). 2017 presidential address to the American Society of Criminology: Not even our own facts: Criminology in the era of big data. *Criminology, 56*(4), 437–454.

Marcum, C.D., Higgins, G.E., & Ricketts, M.L. (2014). Juveniles and cyber stalking in the United States: An analysis of theoretical predictors of patterns of online perpetration. *International Journal of Cyber Criminology, 8*(1), 47–56.

Martínez, A. G. (2017, November 10). Facebook's not listening through your phone. It doesn't have to. *Wired.* Retrieved July 2, 2021 at www.wired.com/story/facebooks-listening-smartphone-microphone/

Matthews, R. (2014). *Realist criminology.* New York: Palgrave Macmillan.

Mayer-Schönberger, V., & Cukier, K. (2013) *Big data: A revolution that will transform how we live, work, and think.* Boston, MA: Houghton Mifflin Harcourt.

McClymer, J.F. (1980). *War and welfare: Social engineering in America, 1890–1925.* Westport, CT: Greenwood Press.

McGuire, M. R. (2018). CONs, CONstructs, and misCONceptions of computer related crime: From a digital syntax to a social semantics. *Journal of Qualitative Criminal Justice & Criminology* 6(2): 1–27. Retrieved November 19, 2020 at https://assets.pubpub.org/s81gxv4r/037a9ec8-b393-4768-a613-0d5d6b502909.pdf

Mills, C. W. (1959). *The sociological imagination.* New York: Oxford University Press.

Mills, C. W. (1963a). Pragmatism, politics and religion. In I. Horowitz (ed.) *Power, politics and people: The collected essays of C. Wright Mills* (pp. 159–169). New York: Oxford University Press.

Mills, C. W. (1963b). Two styles of social science research. In I. Horowitz (ed.) *Power, politics and people: The collected essays of C. Wright Mills* (pp. 553–567). New York: Oxford University Press.

Misak, C. (2013). *The American pragmatists*. New York: Oxford University Press.

Noble, S. U. (2018). *Algorithms of oppression: How search engines reinforce racism*. New York: NYU Press.

Ozkan, T. (2019). Criminology in the age of data explosion: New directions. *The Social Science Journal, 56*(2), 208–219.

Pastrana, S., Hutchings, A., Caines, A., & Buttery, P. (2018). Characterizing Eve: Analysing cybercrime actors in a large underground forum. *Proceedings of the 21st International Symposium on Research in Attacks, Intrusions and Defenses* (RAID), Heraklion. Retrieved June 18, 2021 at www.cl.cam. ac.uk/~sp849/files/RAID_2018.pdf

Prins, S. J., & Reich, A. (2021, Online First). Criminogenic risk assessment: A meta-review and critical analysis. *Punishment & Society*. DOI: 10.1177/14624745211025751.

Putnam, H. (1997). Fact and value. In L. Menand (ed.) *Pragmatism: A reader* (pp. 338–362). New York: Vintage Books.

Rhodes, W. (2013). Machine learning approaches as tool for effective offender risk prediction. *Criminology & Public Policy, 12*(3), 507–510.

Ridgeway, G. (2013). Linking prediction and prevention. *Criminology & Public Policy, 12*(3), 545–550.

Roose, K. (2020). Rabbit hole [podcast]. *New York Times*. Retrieved July 7, 2021 at www.nytimes.com/column/rab bit-hole

Sanders, C. B., & Scheptycki, J. (2017). Policing, crime and "big data": Towards a critique of the moral economy of stochastic governance. *Crime, Law and Social Change, 68*, 1–15.

Schaffer, S. (1999). Enlightened automata. In W. Clark, J. Golinski, & S. Schaffer (Eds.) *The sciences in Enlightened Europe* (pp. 126–165). Chicago, IL: University of Chicago Press.

Sennett, R. (1995, May 25). Letter to the editors. *New York Review of Books*. Retrieved July 8, 2021 at www.nybooks.com/artic les/1995/05/25/sex-lies-and-social-science-an-exchange/

Smith, G. J., Moses, L. B., & Chan, J. (2017). The challenges of doing criminology in the big data era: Towards a digital and data-driven approach. *British Journal of Criminology, 57*, 259–274.

Steinmetz, K. F., Pimentel, A., & Goe, W. R. (2020). Decrypting social engineering: An analysis of conceptual ambiguity. *Critical Criminology, 28*(4), 631–650.

Taylor, F.W. (1914). *The principles of scientific management.* New York: Harper & Brothers Publishers.

Tolman, W. H. (1909). *Social engineering: A record of things done by American industrialists employing upwards of one and one-half million of people.* New York: McGraw Publishing Company.

Truitt, E.R. (2015). *Medieval robots.* Philadelphia, PA: University of Pennsylvania Press.

Uprichard, E. (2012). Being stuck in (live) time: The sticky sociological imagination. *The Sociological Review, 60*(1), 124–38.

Valentine, C. L., Hay, C., Beaver, K. M., & Blomberg, T. G. (2013). Through a computational lens: Using dual computer-criminology degree programs to advance the study of criminology and criminal justice practice. *Security Informatics, 2*(1), 1–7.

Van Eijk, G. (2016). Socioeconomic marginality in sentencing: The built-in bias in risk assessment tools and the reproduction of social inequality. *Punishment & Society, 19*(4), 463–481.

Williams, M. L., & Burnap, P. (2016). Cyberhate on social media in the aftermath of Woolwich: A case study in computational criminology and big data. *British Journal of Criminology, 56*, 211–238.

Williams, M. L., Burnap, P., & Sloan, L. (2017). Crime sensing with big data: The affordances and limitations of using open-source communications to estimate crime patterns. *British Journal of Criminology, 57*, 320–340.

Yar, M., & Steinmetz, K. F. (2019). *Cybercrime & Society* (3rd ed.). Thousand Oaks, CA: Sage.

Young, J. (2011). *The criminological imagination.* Malden, MA: Polity Press.

Zinn, H. (2003). *A people's history of the United States.* New York: HarperCollins.

Zuboff, S. (2015). Big other: Surveillance capitalism and the prospects of an information civilization. *Journal of Information Technology, 30*, 75–89.

# 7

# REALIST CRIMINOLOGICAL METHODS

The previous chapter offered a series of critiques of positivistic approaches to the study of computer crimes, particularly computational criminology. It explored the kinds of research methods that realist criminologists should be cautious about or skeptical of. Yet a vital question remains unanswered: how does one *do* realist criminology research? If the sociological imagination requires situating individuals in history and structure in a process connecting personal troubles to social problems, how can this be implemented in the study of the internet, crime, and harm? For our purposes, implementation of the sociological imagination in realist criminology involves a recognition of the importance of values in designing and interpreting research, an attentiveness to structural and historical contexts, a focus on solutions, and an ability to understand the subjective experiences and circumstances of others. After briefly detailing what might be called a realist criminological imagination, this chapter considers specific kinds of methods useful for realist criminological research. Like other realist criminologists (Hall & Winlow, 2015; Matthews 2014), the importance of both established

DOI: 10.4324/9781003277996-9

and emergent qualitative methodologies are emphasized. These approaches focus on human meaning, relationships, and action in ways often obscured through quantification. This does not mean, however, that quantification should be rejected outright, as will be explained.

The discussion contained herein is not a definitive statement on the methodological approach of a realist criminology of computer crimes. Detailing the methods that should be involved in solution-focused research attuned to social context, history, and power is not easy and I do not pretend to have all the answers. Further, considering the need for methodological pluralism, detailing all the procedures and tools fit-for-use is beyond the scope of a single chapter (or even book). This chapter is thus a single contribution on the matter, gesturing to the overall orientation of the realist criminological imagination and the general kinds of methods suitable for analysis. It is therefore intended to be part of an ongoing dialog of research on computers, the internet, and crime.

## The Realist Criminological Imagination

Building from the work of Mills (1959) and Young (2011), there is a need to establish what the sociological imagination means for realist criminological research—to articulate not just a criminological imagination, but a *realist* criminological imagination. Involved is the detailing of an epistemological position informed by pragmatic sensibilities and a radical desire for advancing the human condition. To accomplish this goal, we will necessarily have to revisit points explored in previous chapters. I hope the reader will forgive the repetition in the service of thoroughness.

The first step is to recognize that the act of research is value laden (Putnam, 1997). Choices about who or what to study, the gathering and analysis of data, presentation of findings, theories or frameworks to utilize, funding sources to pursue, and others are all "moral and political decisions" as well as intellectual ones (Mills, 1959, p. 76; see also: Ferrell, 1997). As Mills (1959, p. 78) explains,

> Values are involved in the selection of the problems we study; values are also involved in certain of the key conceptions we use in our formulation of these problems, and values affect the course of their solution. So far as conceptions are concerned, the aim ought to be to use as many "value-neutral" terms as possible and to become aware of and to make explicit the value implications that remain. So far as problems are concerned, the aim out to be, again, to be clear about the values in terms of which they are selected, and then to avoid as best one can evaluative bias in their solution, no matter where that solution takes one and no matter what its moral or political implications may be.

The matter of values raised here breaches the question of objectivity in research—how can a social scientist be objective in the research if they are making value choices? This question, however, ignores the fact that all social research in one capacity or another makes value choices.[1] What Mills (1959, p. 77) advocates is for social scientists to be both honest and earnest in their convictions. They must wrestle with their values and make them plain (Mills, 1959, p. 77; Tunnell, 1998). In this spirit, Flyvbjerg (2001, p. 60) presents a useful arrangement of questions that social scientists should ask before and during the research process, which include:

- "Where are we going?"
- "Is this desirable?"

- "What should be done?"
- "Who gains and who loses; by which mechanisms of power?"

Consistent with the pragmatist maxim that social inquiry should be rooted in experience and consequences, these questions force the researcher to confront possible outcomes from their research and assess whether those outcomes are desired.[2]

Related to values is the issue of structure. For Mills (1959, pp. 78–79), the social scientist should not concentrate so specifically on the "local milieux" of their research that they lose sight of the various political interests and conflicts of the time and how those might shape the phenomenon in question. Like a grazing animal, the researcher should periodically pull their head out of the grass to survey the landscape. Yet they should also be careful not to simply assume the nature of a structure in question. There is sometimes a tendency of social scientists, including criminologists, to formulaically approach the matter of structure, offhandedly claiming that capitalism, patriarchy, white supremacy, and the like are to blame. Such an approach runs afoul of pragmatism's skepticism toward universal laws and transcendental truths (Baert, 2003; Misak, 2013). Sufficient evidence exists that these structures are useful concepts, but the researcher should take caution and be open to (1) the possibility of alternative mechanisms at play and (2) the different ways that structures can manifest within a social field. Further, such abuse of structural ideas is lazy in that it relies on a massive concept to do the heavily lifting of the analysis without clearly specifying how such structures operate within the context of the social problem at hand.[3]

In this manner, the realist criminologist should behave, to at least some degree, like an actor network theorist.

Actor Network Theory (ANT) is concerned with the "tracing of associations" among "actors" (Latour, 2005, p. 5). It conceives of human action as always shaped by relationships with other actors that constitute an "actor network." As previously explained, actors include not only humans but also technologies, non-human animals, environmental features, law, policy, previous experience, and knowledge (Callon 1984; Latour & Woolgar, 1986). According to Latour (2005, p. 71), an actor can be identified in a network by asking the following question: "does it make a difference in the course of some other agent's action or not?" In this fashion, the human and non-human are mutually interdependent within networks. An actor becomes more significant within a network when the volume and quality of attachments to other actors increases (Latour, 2005).

For realist criminology, ANT is useful in that it asks the social scientist to focus on what is relevant in the network and resist the temptation to insert an explanation that may not fit the data. A researcher cannot recline in their armchair and simply proclaim that "capitalism did it!" Instead, they must do the work of showing how a situation or phenomenon came about by carefully tracing the associations between actors. Indeed, the mapping of the "square of crime" or "social relations of crime control" advocated for by left realists demands this sort of meticulous work (Jones, MacLean, & Young, 1986; Lea, 2002, p. 144; Lea, 2016, p. 56).

As previously explained, however, ANT is notoriously antagonistic to the idea of structure, which presents a problem for both realist criminology and the sociological imagination (Latour, 2005). Latour (2005) argues that if one has sufficiently mapped out a network of actors then explanations for a phenomenon will be evident within the network—there is little need to retreat to structure or social forces to explain matters. Reliance on such devices, according to him, renders the scientific enterprise as "conspiracy theory, not social theory," a belief in hidden hands manipulating actors and leaving no trace of their machinations in the network (Latour, 2005, p. 53). Latour (2005) thus argues for keeping the social "flat," focusing only on actors and associations that make themselves known during study in the most direct manner possible.

Actor Network Theory is thus useful in its demand that we remain attuned to meticulously detailing the relationships between actors in a social setting of concern, but we do not have to accept its conclusion that structure is unnecessary (Ingold, 2008; Sayes, 2017).[4] After all, humans *can* be influenced by matters that they take for granted or are otherwise oblivious to and disparate pieces can coalesce together into broader patterns beyond the immediate context. Mills (1959, p. 86) addresses this very point and argues

> If we break a society into tiny "factors," naturally we shall then need quite a few of them to account for something and then need quote a few of them to account for something and we can never be sure that we have hold of them all. A merely formal emphasis upon "the organic whole," plus a failure to consider the adequate causes—which are usually structural—plus a compulsion to examine only one situation at a time—such ideas do make it difficult to understand the structure of the *status quo*.

In this manner, realist criminologists must behave like actor network theorists in that they should resist the urge to *assume* the relevance of social forces and structures for a given social problem. They should "play dumb" and allow the social problem and its data to guide the researcher to conclusions. Without this willful ignorance, the researcher may not uncover surprising, counterintuitive, or contradictory results in their analysis. But they should also avoid reinventing the wheel—if structural concepts are the best suited for making sense of a given situation (and allow that situation to be connected to the bigger picture) then they should be utilized. The researcher, however, must be diligent to demonstrate why the concept is appropriate and to be transparent with its limitations.

An imaginative orientation underpinning a realist criminology additionally requires an attunement to history. Social problems seldom emerge from a vacuum—they often are the developments of prior processes and problems that superseded them. As Mills (1959, p. 143) explains, "without the use of history, and without an historical sense of psychological matters, the social scientist cannot adequately state the kinds of problems that ought now to be the orienting points of his studies." For him, history provides a robust foundation for comparison—to examine the current situation by contrasting it with prior states (ibid, pp. 146–147). Further, telescoping outward across historical periods allows for the role of structure to become more visible (ibid, p. 149). From the perspective of pragmatism, consideration of history allows the researcher to understand how contemporary knowledge, including their own, is embedded in language systems and concepts which are in a continual state of development and flux (Baert, 2005). In addition, pragmatism urges us to avoid adopting a determinative view of history where we are trapped by the sequencing of prior events (Rorty, 1998b). With apologies to Shakespeare, the past is not always prologue.

In an academic talk given at the 2010 International Crime, Media, and Popular Culture Studies conference, my friend Vic Kappeler offered a cautionary tale about ahistorical analyses of cultural phenomenon.[5] He used the Cueca, the national dance of Chile, to describe the perils of interpretation without context.

> The dance is said to resemble the courting ritual of a rooster and a hen. The male displays a quite enthusiastic and at times even aggressive attitude while attempting to court the female, who is elusive, defensive and demure. It is said to have Spanish and African influences and is thought to have originated in the early 19th century bordellos of South America. We could go into great detail and description of the dance—the gendered nature of the performance the movements, posture of the dancers, the difference between this dance and other Latin American or popular dances. We could attempt to understand the semiotics or symbolism in the dance. Eventually we could have a rather complete cultural understanding of the Cueca.

Yet, he contended that such an interpretation of the dance would lead the observer to focus on the gendered dynamics of the dance, potentially reinforcing patriarchal norms within the culture. The history of the dance, however, adds vital context.

> In 1970, a Marxist physician was democratically elected the President of Chile... Responding to this political turn, Richard Nixon organized and inserted CIA secret operatives in Chile, to quickly destabilize the government. In addition, American financial pressure restricted international economic credit to Chile. Simultaneously, opposition media, politicians, and other organizations, helped to accelerate a campaign of domestic destabilization. Finally, a military coup overthrew the President in 1973 with armed forces

bombarding the presidential palace. Allende reportedly committed suicide. A military junta, led by General Pinochet took over control of the country. The first years of the regime were marked by human rights violations. In October 1973, at least 72 people were murdered by the Caravan of Death, at least 2,115 were killed, and at least 27,265 were tortured (including 88 children younger than 12 years old). A new Constitution was approved on September 11, 1980, and General Pinochet became president of the republic for an 8-year term. *The Cueca was a dance used as a form of protest by women whose husbands and sons disappeared during the Pinochet years in Chile—it is a dance of protest and resistance, not just a dance, a unit of culture, a gendered cultural artifact about roosters and hens.*

*(emphasis added)*

In this manner, through consideration of the historical context, one can see how the individual action of dancing is mired in resistance against authoritarianism and political economic conflicts. History helps put action in context.

In the same way, it is difficult to understand contemporary issues of technology and crime without also considering history. My assertion, with no small degree of disappointment, is that the study of computer crimes is among the most ahistorical enterprises in criminology. There is a tendency to focus on the novelty of such crimes and lose sight of their position within the arch of human affairs, though few exceptions exist (e.g. Wall, 2008; 2012). Yet, there is much the study of history can contribute to our studies of computer crimes. For instance, historian David Churchill (2016) describes the rise of the security industry and its contributions to perceptions of criminality in Victorian and Edwardian Britain. Contained is a riveting account of how the security industry advanced an image of the criminal as a technology-savvy professional, which just happened to be conducive to the marketing of security products to the public. Importantly, he draws a parallel between this "scientific burglar" with contemporary images of the computer hacker. The two are similar in that their social construction is mired in "reflections upon the dark side of progress," garnering a "mix of fear and admiration," presenting a "new, sophisticated form of criminal activity which brings forth calls for control measures reaching beyond the conventional bounds of criminal justice" (Churchill, 2016, p. 870). He also adds that both are portrayed as highly skilled and sophisticated offenders. He thus highlights the role of economic interests and technological change in shaping public perceptions of crime and demands for security provisions. It gives us pause to consider contemporary framings of computer crime issues, how those images can be shaped by various interests, and the role such images might play in crime control and public discourse. The contemporary state of securitization is not an aberration of our contemporary historical epoch but the latest development in a drawn-out story.[6]

Subjective meaning is also a key intellectual tool useful for imaginative research. Though this argument is perhaps cliché by this point, the researcher needs an ability to entertain alternative viewpoints and to envision the experiences of others (Dewey, 1971/2008, p. 251). Weber (1968) referred to this as *verstehen*, which translates into "understanding." Involved is the "a grasp of the complex of meaning in which an actual course of understandable action thus interpreted belongs" (Weber, 1968, p. 9). It is to understand the battery of objective circumstances and subjective experiences that may shape an individual's interpretation of their situation. Cultural criminologists have advocated for such subjective attunement as a mechanism for grappling with the lived experience of crime and victimization and for drawing connections between situations and structure (Ferrell, 1997; Ferrell, Hayward, & Young, 2015). Feminist criminologists have also been instrumental in demonstrating the value of subjective understanding and empathy in crime and victimization research (Chesney-Lind & Morash, 2013; Comack, 1999; Renzetti, 1997; 2016). In fact, feminist criminologists have likely been the most successful in using engaged and empathetic research to affect substantive change in the lives of both victims and those caught in the web of the carceral state (e.g. Britton, 2000; Deegan, 2003), though its impacts have not been without controversy, including among feminist scholars, as some variants of feminist thought have contributed to penal expansion (e.g. Bumiller, 2008; Gruber, 2020; Law, 2014; Phillips & Chagnon, 2020).[7]

This subjective interpretation is another intellectual tool that allows researchers to connect situational contexts with structural circumstances. Consider, for instance, the following hypothetical scenario amalgamated from research on hacking and carding—the illicit procurement and trade of credit card information (Banks, 2018; Dupont & Lusthaus, 2021; Glenny, 2011; Holt, 2007; 2013; Holt & Lampke, 2010; Lusthaus, 2018; Steinmetz, 2016; Yip, Webber, & Shadbolt, 2013). A hacker is attending university and struggles to make ends meet. Balancing school and employment are difficult. They feel alone—making friends IRL ("in real life") has always been difficult.[8] Fortunately, they have friends online and are actively involved in various communities. Their experiences with the internet and its social spaces have made them aware of carding forums— places where individuals may buy, sell, and trade stolen credit card information. The hacker just happens to have access to a credit card "dump" they got while exploring a corporate network. They venture into the forum and try to sell it. It does not go well at first. They have not established a reputation on the forums and gained trust. But they continue to advertise their wares and eventually find an interested buyer. The money is good—perhaps not as good as if they were an established member, but it is more than they are used to earning at their job at the university library. The money even lets them treat their few IRL friends to a night out. It feels good. After this, they continue to go back. It's easy for them and they feel powerful—their skills are paying off. They develop a reputation on the forum and accumulate no small amount of respect as they continue to deliver quality credit card dumps. The extra money is nice as is the luxury it affords.

In this hypothetical case, it is easy to see how someone might get involved in illicit activities. They are under some degree of stress as they work to maintain their material well-being and secure their future (Agnew, 1992; Merton, 1938). Their social relationships make them keenly aware of the various criminal opportunities available to them and their experiences with technology give them the skills necessary to seize such opportunities (Cloward & Ohlin, 1961; Sutherland, 1937). Opportunity, ability, and motivation collide, and criminal involvement begins (Blumstein, Cohen, & Farrington, 1988; Cohen & Felson, 1979). The enterprise provides reinforcements through monetary rewards and subcultural status (Burgess & Akers, 1966; Cohen, 1955). The situation on its own is intrinsically understandable. The researcher, however, can expand the scope of analysis and note how the circumstances of this hacker are shaped by larger social processes and structural impediments. Education is expensive because of drastic increases in tuition and related cuts in educational funding while, at the same time, employers increasingly demand that applicants have college degrees (Carlson & Gardner,

2020; Paquette, 2021). The availability of credit card information online is specifically tied to the emergence of e-commerce including the long-term storage of sensitive financial information. The availability of this data coincides with global telecommunications technologies, namely the internet, which allows individuals to access sensitive data—with the right skillsets—remotely, making it easy to cover one's tracks and avoid detection or prosecution (Yar & Steinmetz, 2019). Using this research-informed hypothetical, one can see how structure and history work their tendrils into the subjective experiences of this carder. Conversely, the performative actions of this carder feed back into structure (Giddens, 1990).[9] They create the circumstances which legitimize (wrongly or rightly) a security industry which uses the figure of the hacker and digital thief to peddle their wares (Banks, 2018; Churchill, 2016; Steinmetz, 2016). Their participation in the competitive atmosphere of online sales may perpetuate gendered inequities in the online carding and hacker community (Steinmetz, Holt, & Holt, 2020; Turkle, 1984). The subjective experiences and meanings held by this one hacker thus are reciprocally and inextricably intertwined with the human collective (Ferrell, Hayward, & Young, 2015; Giddens, 1990; Messerschmidt, 1993). The job of the researcher is thus to trace these connections.[10]

Finally, as one might expect from a realist criminological approach, the researcher should endeavor that their analyses produce solutions of some kind. The matter of policy will be discussed in greater detail in Chapter 8, but it is worth commenting upon for a moment as an important component of the methodological orientation. The idea of selecting a *problem* to analyze necessarily implies that solutions will be derived. "Any adequate 'answer' to a problem," Mills (1959, p. 131) explains, "will contain a view of the strategic points of intervention—of the 'levers' by which the structure may be maintained or changed; and an assessment of those who are in a position to intervene but are not doing so." This is a necessary bridging between "basic" and "applied" forms of research which is intrinsic to the sociological imagination. Administrative criminology is a vacuous form of research which only focuses on "what works" to solve crime problems without considering collateral consequences or underlying mechanisms. Left idealism, on the other hand, is content to ignore ameliorative measures and solutions. Indeed, for such criminologists, all problems can only be addressed through revolution and activism (these are not bad things in and of themselves, only that they alone are insufficient to address suffering, particularly in the here-and-now). Thus, the methodological orientation must necessarily be grounded enough so that applied solutions become apparent, but not so myopic that one loses sight of the underlying and necessary causes of the problems in question.

In sum, imaginative realist criminological research requires an acknowledgment of the researcher's values in the enterprise, a willingness to examine structural and historical contexts, an eye toward solutions to the social problems under investigation, and a willingness to examine the subjective situation of the various actors involved. When considered *in toto,* these intellectual characteristics lend themselves to specific methodological tools. Qualitative methods designed to examine meaning and lived experience seem most appropriate.

## The Case for Qualitative Methods

Like other realist criminologists (Hall & Winlow, 2015; Matthews, 2014), I argue for the importance of qualitative methods for the research enterprise including well-established methods like interview research, ethnography, historiography, life history, content analysis, and others. As previously established, the methods used in criminological research should capture—to the best extent possible—meaning, interpretation, and context. Some of the most useful and important studies of computer crime have relied upon standard qualitative approaches—examinations which prioritize "semantics" over "syntax" (McGuire, 2018).

Consider, for instance, Jonathan Lusthaus' (2018) *Industry of Anonymity*. The book relies on over two hundred qualitative interviews with criminal justice officials, members of the cybersecurity industry, and former cybercrime perpetrators as well as legal documents gathered from a constellation of official sources. Despite utilizing what technological fetishists might consider primitive or rudimentary tools, Lusthaus shows how online criminal activity surrounding the buying and selling of illicit data like credit card information has transitioned overtime from being a largely informal, subcultural enterprise into an increasingly bureaucratic and professionalized industry. He traces the fundamental transformations that have occurred around the trade of financial data, including shifts in the social dynamics of participants, and their implications. In a sea of humdrum research on the subject, Lusthauss stands out.

Or take Monica Whitty's (2013) study of online dating romance scams, which involved interviews with 20 victims of these crimes. Through her analysis, she articulated the Scammers Persuasive Technique model, a framework for understanding the process of romance fraud. This model involves (1) the existence of a mark searching for an ideal romantic partner; (2) the curation and presentation of a false profile to match the desires of the mark; (3) a "grooming process" whereby the fraudster builds trust with the mark; (4) requests for money, either by starting with small requests and working toward bigger prizes or by manufacturing a financial crisis requiring the "assistance" of the mark; (5) persistence of the scam over time to elicit further funds from the victim; (6) possible sexual abuse and extortion of the mark; and (7) re-victimization where the victim may become aware of the scam but be enticed back into the original scam or fall for a new romance scam as they pursue their ideal partner. Drawing from twenty qualitative interviews, Whitty (2013), in my assessment, generated one of the most useful and insightful studies on the machinations of romance fraud to date.

Despite the excellent contributions made by such scholars, it is also important to avoid fetishizing method, including qualitative approaches. Mills (1959) explicitly cautions against methodological fetishism in any form, arguing that such research should "be defined by pressing empirical problems which then determine the methods and theories deployed to tackle them, rather than vice versa" (Gane & Back, 2012, p. 414). Similarly, Ferrell (2009, p. 1) rails against such fetishism in criminology, considering it as part of a "crisis" for criminology, arguing that "criminology first embraces methods wholly inadequate and inappropriate for the study of human affairs, and then makes these methods its message." Instead, what is needed is a kind of "kill method," an orientation that eschews methodology as pre-defined blueprints which the researcher obediently follows to be considered what one might call "good science" (Ferrell, 2009). For some, this blind subservience to methodological formulae is what makes research rigorous. Yet rigor is really an earnest and thorough engagement with the phenomenon in question. Rather than adhere to rigid methodologies, a kill method asks for research to engage participants on their own terms, taking whatever approach necessary.

In fact, a kill method or anti-method is perhaps best suited for capturing the sociological imagination and the pragmatist eschewal of "methodological unity" (Baert, 2005, pp. 147–151). Situating individuals in structure and history—connecting personal troubles to public issues—requires a methodological adaptability to grapple with the full range of possibilities and interlinkages that might be uncovered during research.

A realist criminology of the internet thus should embrace methodological innovation. In this way, the realist criminological approach here has much in common with cultural criminology, which has advocated a variety of novel qualitative methodological approaches designed to grapple with issues of structure, conflict, power, action, resistance, and meaning in the uncertain times of late modernity (Ferrell, Hayward, & Young, 2015; Young, 2011). Similarly, the study of computer crimes should be open to innovations in qualitative methods designed explicitly to grapple with the idiosyncrasies of technology and the information age. We have seen advancements in this regard in recent decades, including the development of methodologies designed to examine existing and emergent online data sources like virtual ethnography (Hine, 2000; 2015; Holt, 2015). As computers and the internet continue to change over time, realist criminologists and other social scientists should continue to explore methodological innovations.

## Open Season on Numbers?

Up to this point, I have considered computational methodologies and quantitative criminological analyses in general with no small degree of skepticism. The recalcitrance toward these approaches is in direct measure to the overall dominance of quantification and positivistic studies of crime and criminal justice in our discipline (Tewksbury, Dabney, & Copes, 2010; Young, 2011). None of this is to say, however, that there exists *no* place for quantification or even algorithmic analysis. Like Young (2004, p. 25), I am not proposing "an open season on numbers." Quantification has a role to play. Some measures are extraordinarily useful, for example, in understanding the scope and scale of social problems. Criminologists, mainstream and critical alike, refer to U.S. imprisonment rates to describe mass incarceration (the very problem itself is one of numbers). There are a variety of such metrics like those concerning arrests, sentencing, education achievement, infant mortality, and food insecurity which are invaluable for understanding social problems.

The problem, however, as Young (2004, p. 25) is in distinguishing between numbers which are reliable and precise and those which are suspect. As he explains,

> Precision must be constantly eyed with suspicion, decimal points with raised eyebrows. There are very many cases where statistical testing is inappropriate because the data is technical weak—it will simply not bear the weight of such analysis. There are many other instances where the data is blurred and contested and where such testing is simply wrong.
>
> *(ibid)*

Social scientists can thus use numbers, but they should be treated with extraordinary care regarding their limitations. Of course, this is standard advice given to all students taking research methods courses—treat data with care, be rigorous with conceptualization and operationalization, and only state what can be reliably derived from data. This lesson, however, seems to be often ignored as researchers seem all too willing to "skate on thin ice" and gloss over the weaknesses of their datasets and models (Young, 2011). For instance, in the realm of computers and the internet, there exist figures which can be useful like time spent online, content uploaded or downloaded, number of attacks launched against organizations, and financial losses experienced, to name only a few. These figures are often invoked to frame the scope and scale of a computer crime problem or as measures within statistical models. Though useful, there is often little acknowledgment of the fact that such numbers are often not produced in contexts independent of individual or business interests (Yar, 2008). They also may not be fully accurate measures of what they claim to measure, given the clandestine nature of certain kinds of online activity (Yar, 2008). Their provenance and quality, therefore, are often questionable and they should be approached with skepticism.

An unwillingness to jettison quantification entirely also stems from the fact that realist criminology has a long history of using survey methodologies to examine the prevalence and experience of crime and victimization (e.g. DeKeseredy, 2016, p. 15; Jones, MacLean, & Young, 1987). As Matthews (2014, p. 69) explains, "realists are methodological pluralists" who "advocate for the use of quantitative or qualitative methods or a combination of both, depending on whether the aim is to engage in intensive or extensive forms of research" (see also: Baert, 2005, pp. 150–151). Similarly, pragmatists are willing to employ a variety of methods to empirically assess the social world. There is thus no reason to think that such approaches may not be useful today still. The objection is to *stale* and *unreflexive* quantification that avoids context, ignores its limitations, and distances itself from lived experience (Young, 2011, p. 224).

Despite concerns about the abstracted empiricism of computational criminology and similar approaches, there is reason to think that computational approaches can be part of a robust methodological innovation for realist criminology. Savage and Burrows (2007; 2009) argue, for instance, that the standard approaches to sociological (and, vicariously, criminological) research like surveys and interviews—though useful—are increasingly dated in an era of networks and powerful computational methods. Under information capitalism, an enormous amount of data is produced and gathered, largely by private entities who can use various statistical and computational techniques to create powerful models for predicting human behavior—much more robust than any that most social scientific researchers in the academy have access to. In this manner, "a parallel and largely unknown (to academic sociologists) world of 'commercial sociology' was being revealed that certainly did not seem to lack sophistication" (Savage & Burrows, 2007, p. 887). Thus, the authors argue specifically that social scientific researchers should set aside their misgivings and grapple with the methods of generating social data that are proliferous in the contemporary technological context. Importantly, however, they argue that this strategy

Does not necessarily mean deference to the market research or consultancy community; a process of selling our souls to the devil. It means instead taking up the *cudgel of critical sociology*, armed with sophisticated theoretical resources, to challenge the right of private companies to use informational data as they will and how they will.

*(emphasis added; Savage & Burrows, 2009, p. 767)*

Their caution extends to sociologists and, realistically, academic social scientists more generally. Similarly,

Campedelli (2022, p. 169) advises that, "critical, mindful perspectives should guide the way in which we will decide to take advantage of the tools that we will have at our disposal. No algorithm is a shortcut to the long path ahead."

These arguments are particularly important for researchers tussling with computer crime and security issues. Because of the relatively anonymous, asynchronous, diffuse, and mediated nature of many computer crime activities, it can be tempting to turn entirely to computational and engineering techniques to make sense of these phenomenon—scraping meta data, tracking user connections, and reporting relatively superficial findings about user behavior and institutional outcomes. Yet the specific strength of criminology is its ability to place such findings in context—to view such activities as fundamentally concerned with humans situated in political, cultural, economic, and historical contexts. Such an orientation is necessary to avoid becoming a social science that dazzles in its methodological sophistication but produces findings that say little about the actual people involved in cybercrime and victimization, with utility that extends only to obvious or purely administrative solutions.

## Conclusion

As previously explained, the limitations imposed by the internet and computer-mediated communications generally create issues for mapping the social relations of crime (Lea, 2002; 2016). Identifying and locating the individuals and groups relevant for a given social problem and gaining reliable and valid data can be an extraordinarily difficult task. The researcher must do the best they can to overcome these limitations, be honest about the limitations, and interpret their findings accordingly. Regardless of the approach taken, the researcher must approach it with imagination and rigor.

It does bear mentioning, however, that trying to include every factor relevant for any single crime and victimization issue—as implied by the methodological proscriptions previously given—is difficult if not impossible. Add technology and media which diffuse connections between individuals over potentially vast distances and differentially reveal and obscure traits of the actors involved, and the task is overwhelming. It is certainly desirable for any single researcher to develop a mastery of their subject in such sufficient detail that they can describe all facets of a problem with confidence and derive definitive solutions, as Mills (1959) appears to demand. Science is an iterative process, however, mired in fits, spurts, leaps, setbacks, and disruptions (Kuhn, 1962). Knowledge production requires that we stand on the shoulders of giants. There is thus an inherent collaboration involved in the understanding of any given phenomenon. To most researchers, this point is obvious—it is the general ethos of the academy. Indeed, for this reason pragmatists emphasize the value of community in the production of scientific knowledge to ensure beliefs and truth claims are evaluated in a dialogic manner (Bruce & Bloch, 2013; Misak, 2013; Rorty, 1998b). The point is worth noting, however, because it highlights the difficulty of any single study stating anything—including the derivation of solutions—with certainty.

For this reason, one additional constellation of methodologies that realist criminologists should consider are those designed to evaluate the state of knowledge on any given subject or problem. There are a variety of methodologies on this subject including systematic literature reviews and meta-analyses (assessments of the totality of quantitative research on a subject) (Pratt & Cullen, 2019; Thorpe & Holt, 2008). This chapter will not go into the different methodological steps involved nor will it go into the various strengths and weaknesses of these approaches. It is worth highlighting, however, that these methods attempt to summarize what is known about a subject of interest. If we are interested in generating real, impactful solutions to crime problems, then such holistic approaches surely have a place on the criminological shelf.

## Notes

1 As Putnam (1997) articulates, all research, even studies of the natural world, are inseparable from the context of their production, including the values upon which the current research and it's predecessors are based. Importantly, just because values cannot be separated from research does not mean that such research is useless. From the position of pragmatism, the research can be considered useful in how it produces the desired objectives (which also means strong ethical engagement in what we *should* be striving for as scientists).

2 Misak's (2013, p. 131) reflections on the ethics of Dewey are useful in this regard. She comments that

> The Nazi or the child molester may find meaning or self-realization in vile and odious acts. Without some kind of check that goes beyond the individual and beyond the current, local, possibly homogenized community, there is nothing critical that can be said. Even in ethics, we need a thought like Peirce's; we must respond to something that is not extraneous to the facts.

In other words, we need some external criteria or circumstance against which we can make sense of our ethics and our experiences therein. She goes on to detail a constant state of (fallible) reflection that muddles through ethical problems despite the fact that it is "not appropriate to look for tidy answers" (Misak, 2013, p. 134). "Nonetheless," she explains, "we try to do ever better" and subject ethical perceptions to scrutiny. In the context of this study, the process of ethics can draw is initial positioning from the works of radical and critical scholars who have done considerable work showing the significant harms generated by abuses of power and criminologists and victimologists who clearly demonstrate the social harms created by criminal acts. These are the positions from which we can start our ethical deliberations and then subject them to the process of inquiry. In other words, in the assessment of outcomes of our research, we do not have to start from square one. Similarly, when discussing the work of Hilary Putnam, she remarks that

> the way that Putnam makes the attempt as a venerable pragmatist history: he tries to show how ethics is a kind of inquiry. We inherit values and then we question and criticize them. We take ethical disputes as matters to be settled by intelligent argument and inquiry, not by appeals to authority [citation omitted].
>
> (Misak, 2013, p. 243)

3 Here I must agree with Rorty (1998b, pp. 233–234) in his essay titled "The End of Leninism, Havel, and Social Hope" where he derides the use of the term capitalism as a catchall term that gets thrown around whenever convenient for Marxist analysis:

> We can no longer use the term "capitalism" to mean both "a market economy" and the "source of all contemporary injustice." We can no longer tolerate the ambiguity between capitalism as a way of financing industrial production and capitalist as the Great Bad Thing that accounts for most contemporary human misery.

I do not agree with Rorty's seeming willingness to throw out the baby with the bathwater and disregard Marxist analyses entirely. There remains tremendous utility in Marxist analyses of capitalism and I believe the historical and contemporary evidence has made it clear that the capitalist mode of production is a significant problem facing human existence, not just happiness. But I do agree with his sentiment that use of these terms and concepts can be abused—that too much can be attributed to the causal forces they supposedly represent and that such analyses may fail to consider adequately the shortcomings of purely anti-capitalist explanations of social problems.

4 Ingold (2008, p. 212) likens social context—including structure—to the air through which a butterfly flies or the water a fish swims in, the "material media in which living things are immerse, and are experienced by way of their currents, forces and pressure gradients." He ultimately argues that these things many are not conferred with agency as they are not consciously reflected upon as agentic—the fish may take the water for granted, for example, and not be conscious of it as an important component for its movement and, indeed, life. In this way, actors may be enmeshed in fields where they may not be aware of the subtle influences that structure their immediate surroundings. In the same manner, we may not be able to detect social structure in the flattened network of social actors but when viewed *in toto,* then the undulations of structure may become apparent, measurable in the holistic patterns and trends that percolate in the lived experiences of actors. From the perspective of pragmatism, it does not require a belief in structural metaphysics to develop and employ big-picture concepts to describe complex social dynamics occurring within a setting. From the perspective of critical realism, this means that we can excavate the empirical for evidence of the real and actual (though pragmatists resist the "transcendental" implications of this ontology, see Baert, 2005, pp. 92–93).

5 Direct quotes from this talk are pulled from the lecture notes provided by Vic Kappeler via email correspondence.

6 Importantly, there is a point of divergence to be found between the pragmatic realist criminology advanced here and the hardline stance of some Marxists regarding their understanding of the role of history in the present. For some Marxists, history is a powerful force that creates law-like circumstances under which we are bound in the present—that if one can isolate the dialectical mechanisms at play then one can look for similar circumstances in the present and possibly make predictions (e.g. Enfield, 1976). Pragmatists, however, generally contend that history is not determinative and there can be few law-like consistencies to be found there. History, in this sense, is not doomed to repeat itself but we can learn from the past and how it structures the present. Importantly, there are too many

ins, outs, and *whathaveyous*—to quote the Dude from *The Big Lebowski*—in open systems to make law-like generalizations and predictions (e.g. Baert, 2005; Putnam, 1997; Rorty, 1998b). Importantly, alternative interpretations of Marx exist, which are more compatible with American pragmatism by adopting a softer view regarding historical influence or causality. Take, for instance, Marxist historian Eric Hobsbawm's (1984, p. 113) description of the Marxist view of history, which reads as if it might have come from the pages of Peirce:

> Where debate is definitively concluded, science is at an end. That is why Marx can influence and has influenced non-Marxist research. *Both are concerned with an objectively existing reality, even though this reality is only visible through contemporary systems of understanding and models of thought—or even through the lenses of different ideologies.*
>
> (emphasis added)

7 Renzetti (2016) usefully details areas of compatibility between realist and feminist criminologies more generally. I suggest the reader check out her piece on the subject.

8 Evidence indicates that most hackers are boys and men (see Steinmetz, Holt, & Holt, 2020). This hypothetical, however, uses gender neutral pronouns for the purposes of inclusivity.

9 Some pragmatists take issue with theories like those posed by Anthony Giddens (1990). The objections seem to stem not from the insights generated by structuration theory and similar perspectives, but in how they are treated by academics—as something to be "applied" overtop a social problem. As Baert (2005, p. 143) explains,

> whereas research in the humanities should enhance our imaginative capacities, open up new futures, this form of "theory-inspired research" does precisely the opposite: it closes off new experiences. However risqué or avant-garde this research would like to present itself as being, it is in the end intellectually deeply conservative, using the object of study not to learn something new, but to reinforce what is already presupposed.

10 My use of a narrative to trace the connections between lived experience and structure in this case is indebted to Ferrell, Hayward, and Young's (2015) *Cultural Criminology: An Invitation*, which used a similar strategy.

## References

Agnew, R. (1992). Foundation for a general strain theory of crime and delinquency. *Criminology, 30*(1), 47–88.

Baert, P. (2003). Pragmatism, realism and hermeneutics. *Foundations of Science, 8,* 89–106.

Baert, P. (2005). *Philosophy of the social sciences: Towards pragmatism*. Malden, MA: Polity Press.

Banks, J. (2018). Radical criminology and the techno-security-capitalist complex. In K. F. Steinmetz & M. R. Nobles (eds.) *Technocrime and criminological theory* (pp. 102–115). New York: Routledge.

Blumstein, A., Cohen, J., & Farrington, D. P. (1988). Criminal career research: Its value for criminology. *Criminology, 26,* 1–35.

Britton, D. M. (2000). Feminism in criminology: Engendering the outlaw. *Annals of the American Academy of Political and Social Science, 571,* 57–76.

Bruce, B. C., & Bloch, N. (2013). Pragmatism and community inquiry: A case study of community-based learning. *Education and Culture, 29*(1), 27–45.

Bumiller, K. (2008). *In an abusive state: How neoliberalism appropriated the feminism movement against sexual violence*. Durham, NC: Duke University Press.

Burgess, R. L., & Akers, R. L. (1966). A differential association-reinforcement theory of criminal behavior. *Social Problems, 14*(2), 128–147.

Callon, M. (1984). Some elements of a sociology of translation: Domestication of the scallops and the fishermen of St. Brieuc Bay. *The Sociological Review, 32*(1_suppl), 196–233.

Campedelli, G. M. (2022). *Machine learning for criminology and crime research: At the crossroads*. New York: Routledge.

Carlson, S., & Gardner, L. (2020, December 19). The year that pushed higher ed to the edge. *The Chronicle of Higher*

*Education.* Retrieved July 14, 2021 at www.chronicle.com/article/the-year-that-pushed-higher-ed-to-the-edge

Chesney-Lind, M., & Morash, M. (2013). Transformative feminist criminology: A critical re-thinking of a discipline. *Critical Criminology, 21,* 287–304.

Churchill, D. (2016). Security and visions of the criminal: Technology, professional criminality and social change in Victorian and Edwardian Britain. *British Journal of Criminology, 56*(5), 857–876.

Cloward, R., & Ohlin, L. (1961). *Delinquency and opportunity: A theory of delinquent gangs.* New York: The Free Press.

Cohen, A. K. (1955). *Delinquent boys: The culture of the gang.* New York: Free Press.

Cohen, L. E., & Felson, M. (1979). Social change and crime rate trends: A routine activity approach. *American Sociological Review, 44*(4), 588–608.

Comack, E. (1999). Producing feminist knowledge: Lessons from women in trouble. *Theoretical Criminology, 3*(3), 287–306.

DeKeseredy, W. S. (2016). Contemporary issues in left realism. *International Journal for Crime, Justice and Social Democracy, 5*(3), 12–26.

Dewey, J. (1971/2008). Moral approbation, value and standard. In J. a. Boydston (ed.) *John Dewey–The early works, 1882–1898* (vol. 4) (pp. 247–291). Carbondale, IL: Southern Illinois University Press.

Dupont, B., & Lusthaus, J. (2021, Online First). Countering distrust in illicit online networks: The dispute resolution strategies of cybercriminals. *Social Science Computer Review.* https://doi.org/10.1177/0894439321994623

Enfield, R. (1976). Marx and historical laws. *History and Theory, 15*(3), 267–277.

Ferrell, J. (1997). Criminological *verstehen*: Inside the immediacy of crime. *Justice Quarterly, 14*(1), 3–23.

Ferrell, J. (2009). Kill method: A provocation. *Journal of Theoretical and Philosophical Criminology, 1*(1), 1–22.

Ferrell, J., Hayward, K., & Young, J. (2015). *Cultural criminology: An invitation* (2nd ed.). Thousand Oaks, CA: Sage.

Flyvbjerg, B. (2001). *Making social science matter: Why social inquiry fails and how it can succeed again.* Cambridge, MA: Cambridge University Press.

Gane, N. & Back, L. (2012). C. Wright Mills 50 years on: The promise and craft of sociology revisited. *Theory, Culture & Society, 29*(7/8), 399–421.

Giddens, A. (1990). *The consequences of modernity*. Stanford, CA: Stanford University Press.

Glenny, M. (2011). *Darkmarket: Cyberthieves, cybercops, and you*. New York: Alfred A. Knopf.

Gruber, A. (2020). *The feminist war on crime: The unexpected role of women's liberation in mass incarceration*. Berkeley, CA: University of California Press.

Hall, S., & Winlow, S. (2015). *Revitalizing criminological theory: Towards a new ultra-realism*. New York: Routledge.

Hine, C. (2000). *Virtual ethnography*. Thousand Oaks, CA: Sage.

Hobsbawm, E. J. (1984). Marx and history. *Diogenes, 32*(125), 103–114.

Holt, T. J. (2007). Subcultural evolution? Examining the influence of on- and off-line experiences on deviant subcultures. *Deviant Behavior, 28*(2), 171–198.

Holt, T. J. (2013). Exploring the social organization and structure of stolen data markets. *Global Crime, 14*(2–3), 155–174.

Holt, T. J. (2015). Qualitative criminology in online spaces. In H. Copes & J. M. Miller (eds.) *The Routledge handbook of qualitative criminology* (pp. 173–188). New York: Routledge.

Holt, T. J., & Lampke, E. (2010). Exploring stolen data markets online: Products and market forces. *Criminal Justice Studies, 23*(1), 33–50.

Ingold, T. (2008). When ANT meets SPIDER: Social theory for arthropods. In C. Knappett & L. Malafouris (eds.) *Material agency* (pp. 209–215). New York: Springer Sciences+Business Media, LLC.

Jones, T., MacLean, J., & Young, J. (1986). *The Islington crime survey*. Aldershot, England: Gower.

Kuhn, T. S. (1962). *The structure of scientific revolutions*. Chicago, IL: University of Chicago Press.

Latour, B. (2005). *Reassembling the social: An introduction to actor-network theory*. New York: Oxford University Press.

Latour, B., & Woolgar, S. (1986). *Laboratory life: The construction of scientific facts*. Princeton, NJ: Princeton University Press.

Law, V. (2014). Against carceral feminism. *Jacobin*. Retrieved November 26, 2019 at www.jacobinmag.com/2014/10/against-carceral-feminism/

Lea, J. (2002). *Crime and modernity*. London: Sage.

Lea, J. (2016). Left realism: A radical criminology for the current crisis. *International Journal for Crime, Justice and Social Democracy, 5*(3), 53–65.

Lusthaus, J. (2018). *Industry of anonymity: Inside the business of cybercrime*. Cambridge, MA: Harvard University Press.

Matthews, R. (2014). *Realist criminology*. New York: Palgrave Macmillan.

McGuire, M. R. (2018). CONs, CONstructs, and misCONceptions of computer related crime: From a digital syntax to a social semantics. *Journal of Qualitative Criminal Justice & Criminology 6*(2): 1–27. Retrieved November 19, 2020 at https://assets.pubpub.org/s81gxv4r/037a9ec8-b393-4768-a613-0d5d6b502909.pdf

Merton, R. K. (1938). Social structure and anomie. *American Sociological Review, 3*(5), 672–682.

Messerschmidt, J. W. (1993). *Masculinities and crime*. Lanham, MD: Rowman & Littlefield.

Mills, C. W. (1959). *The sociological imagination*. New York: Oxford University Press.

Misak, C. (2013). *The American pragmatists*. New York: Oxford University Press.

Paquette, G. (2021, March 4). Can higher ed save itself? *The Chronicle of Higher Education*. Retrieved July 14, 2021 at www.chronicle.com/article/can-higher-ed-save-itself

Phillips, N. D. & Chagnon, N. (2020). "Six months is a joke": Carceral feminism and penal populism in the wake of the Stanford sexual assault case. *Feminist Criminology, 15*(1), 47–69.

Pratt, T. C., & Cullen, F. T. (2019). Assessing macro-level predictors and theories of crime: A meta-analysis. *Crime and Justice, 32*, 373–450.

Putnam, H. (1997). Fact and value. In L. Menand (ed.) *Pragmatism: A reader* (pp. 338–362). New York: Vintage Books.

Renzetti, C. (1997). Confessions of a reformed positivist: Feminist participatory research as good social science. In M. D. Schwartz (ed.) *Researching sexual violence against women: Methodological and personal perspective* (pp. 131–143). Thousand Oaks, CA: Sage.

Renzetti, C. (2016). Critical realism and feminist criminology: Shall the twain ever meet? *International Journal for Crime, Justice and Social Democracy, 5*(3), 41–52.

Rorty, R. (1998b). The end of Leninism, Havel, and social hope. In R. Rorty (author) *Truth and progress: Philosophical papers, volume 3.* New York: Cambridge University Press.

Savage, M., & Burrows, R. (2007). The coming crisis of empirical sociology. *Sociology, 41*(5), 885–899.

Savage, M., & Burrows, R. (2009). Some further reflections on the coming crisis of empirical sociology. *Sociology, 43*(4), 762–772.

Sayes, E. (2017). Marx and the critique of actor-network theory: Mediation, translation, and explanation. *Distinktion: Journal of Social Theory, 18*(3), 294–313.

Steinmetz, K. F. (2016). *Hacked: A radical approach to hacker culture and crime.* New York: NYU Press.

Steinmetz, K. F., Holt, T. J., & Holt, K. M. (2020). Decoding the binary: Reconsidering the hacker subculture through a gendered lens. *Deviant Behavior, 41*(8), 936–948.

Sutherland, E. H. (1937). *The professional thief.* Chicago, IL: University of Chicago Press.

Tewksbury, R., Dabney, D. A., & Copes, H. (2010). The prominence of qualitative research in criminology and criminal justice scholarship. *Journal of Criminal Justice Education, 21*(4), 391–411.

Thorpe, R., & Holt, R. (2008). Systematic literature reviews. In R. Thorpe & R. Holt (ed.) *The SAGE Dictionary of qualitative management research.* Retrieved July 26, 2021 at https://methods.sagepub.com/reference/the-sage-diction ary-of-qualitative-management-research/n103.xml

Tunnell, K. D. (1998). Honesty, secrecy, and deception in the sociology of crime: Confessions and reflections from the backstage. In J. Ferrell & M. S. Hamm (eds.) *Ethnography at the Edge* (pp. 206–220). Boston, MA: Northeastern University Press.

Turkle, S. (1984). *The second self.* New York: Simon and Schuster.

Wall, D. S. (2008). Cybercrime, media, and insecurity: The shaping of public perceptions of cybercrime. *International Review of Law, Computers, and Technology, 22,* 45–63.

Wall, D. S. (2012). The Devil drives a Lada: The social construction of hackers as cybercriminals. In C. Gregorious (ed.) *Constructing crime: Discourse and cultural representations of crime and 'deviance'* (pp. 4–18). Basingstoke, UK: Palgrave MacMillan.

Weber, M. (1968/1978). *Economy and society.* Edited by G. Roth & C. Wittich. Berkeley, CA: University of California Press.

Whitty, M. T. (2013). The scammers persuasive techniques model. *British Journal of Criminology, 53,* 665–684.

Yar, M. (2008). Computer crime control as industry: virtual insecurity and the market for private policing. In K. F. Aas, H. O. Gundhus, & H. M. Lomell (eds), *Technologies of insecurity: The surveillance of everyday life* (pp. 189–204). New York: Routledge-Cavendish.

Yar, M., & Steinmetz, K. F. (2019). *Cybercrime & Society* (3rd ed.). Thousand Oaks, CA: Sage.

Yip, M., Webber, C., & Shadbolt, N. (2013). Trust among cybercriminals? Carding forums, uncertainty and implications for policing. *Policing and Society: An International Journal of Research and Policy, 23*(4), 516–539.

Young, J. (2004). Voodoo criminology and the numbers game. In J. Ferrell, K. Hayward, W. Morrison, & M. Presdee (eds.) *Cultural criminology unleashed* (pp. 13–27). Portland, OR: Glasshouse Press.

Young, J. (2011). *The criminological imagination.* Malden, MA: Polity Press.

# 8

# WHAT IS TO BE DONE ABOUT COMPUTER CRIME?

Previous chapters considered steps involved in developing a realist criminology of the internet. Curiously absent, however, is any substantive discussion of solutions or policies. Sure, I've banged the drum over and over that such considerations are important. But the follow-through has been lacking. The reader may thus wonder, "okay, smarty pants, how would *you* go about addressing computer crime?" Drawing from relevant literature and my own research experience, this chapter explores two relevant types of crime—computer hacking and online fraud—as case studies to demonstrate how realist criminologists might identify points of intervention and solutions in a manner attuned to the reality of perpetration and victimization.[1] Considered are interventions rooted in social policy, public awareness campaigns, and other non-technological or non-punitive means to prevent harm. The account provided is undoubtedly incomplete (these are complex problems, after all) but should give the reader some idea of what crime prevention and harm reduction programs might look like.

DOI: 10.4324/9781003277996-10

The various solutions presented throughout this chapter can be considered intermediary steps toward the kind of large-scale structural changes that would need to occur to address computer crime problems at their root. The ultimate objective is to challenge the relations of power in society—those that produce the generative conditions of criminality, criminal opportunity, and victimization—and the technologies that structure and mediate these relations. In other words, we endeavor to reduce the exploitation, abuse, and concentration of power in online spaces while maximizing the well-being and autonomy of all, especially the historically marginalized and downtrodden. This chapter can thus be considered a guide to how to "think like a realist criminologist."

## Addressing Perpetration—The Case of Computer Hacking

For many, the hacker is the "archetypal 'cybercriminal'" (Wall, 2008, p. 47). Today, the term is often associated with a bevy of computer-related offenses such as unauthorized computer intrusions, data theft, system sabotage, website defacement, denial of service attacks, malware production and distribution, and so on. Despite such usage, the term's definition is contested and has long a historical arch tracing back to the world of computer programming in the 1960s (Levy, 1984; Steinmetz, 2016; Yar & Steinmetz, 2019). It was originally used among self-described hackers and other computer enthusiasts to describe someone highly skilled in developing creative, elegant, and effective solutions to computing problems (Levy, 1984; Yar, 2005). Over time, the term entered the general lexicon and became linked to computer malfeasance in the public imagination (Steinmetz, 2016; Wall, 2008). Though the term has ossified in public usage, hacking is generally still understood among hackers as amalgamation of creativity, skill, passion, and willingness to subvert expectations or rules—subversions which may or may not be illegal (Holt, 2010; Steinmetz, 2016; Taylor, 1999; Turkle, 1984; Yar, 2005). In this sense, hacking is as much an identity as it is an activity (Yar, 2005). It is therefore important to note that the focus here is not on computer hacking *in general* but specifically the aforementioned battery of computer-based malfeasances.

A useful first step on the path toward solutions is to inventory the kinds of harms associated with malicious security hacking. Discussions of the matter tend to be veiled in the *possibility* of significant harm to not only individuals but society (Skibell, 2002; 2003; Steinmetz, 2016; Wall, 2008). For instance, consider the 1983 movie *War Games*, one of if not the earliest major pop culture portrayal of hackers. The movie centered around a young hacker, David Lightman (played by Matthew Broderick), who uses his home computer to unwittingly access a Department of Defense supercomputer through the telephone system. He interacts with an advanced artificial intelligence on the system, which he mistakenly believes is a video game, and nearly causes World War III as a result. Though obviously a work of fiction, the movie caused an uproar among U.S. legislators and contributed to the passing of the Computer Fraud and Abuse Act of 1984 (Skibell, 2002; 2003). Even today, there is a tendency for hacking-related computer crimes to be shrouded in myth and misconception as there is no shortage of portrayals of technological wizards wreaking widespread havoc (Steinmetz, 2016). Yet, the fact that that public understanding of hackers is distorted does not mean that such crimes cannot result in significant harms.

It is worth noting from the outset that it is likely that the biggest risks do not come from the stereotypical "lone wolf" hacker but, rather, computer security intrusion specialists working for nation-states (Follis & Fish, 2020a; Payton, 2020; Perlroth, 2021). Countries across the world have heavily invested into "cyberwarfare" capabilities for the purposes of espionage, sabotage, and propaganda (Follis & Fish, 2020a; Rid, 2013). These nations have the resources to support complicated, expensive, and time-consuming digital attacks on persons and infrastructure (Perlroth, 2021; Zetter, 2014a). While it may be a misnomer to refer to the use of these tactics as "warfare" as they lack the use of kinetic force that characterizes war (Rid, 2013), there is little denying that these strategies can significantly impact not only institutional targets, but civilians as well. For instance, in 2015, Ukraine's power grid was hit with a digital attack on their electrical grid that left hundreds of thousands without power for up to six hours—an attack most likely conducted by Russia (though attribution is always tricky) (Zetter, 2016).

Because of the potential harms that can be caused by state-propagated attacks on computer systems, critics have suggested the possibility of a "digital" or "cyber Geneva Convention"—an international agreement to limit the use of certain computer network-based strategies by nation-state actors and to protect human rights in the information age (Guay & Rudnick, 2017; Smith, 2017; Wheeler, 2018). Such an agreement would be an important benchmark for computer security. Of course, these conventions only have an effect if they are enforced. It is difficult enough to uphold Geneva Convention prohibitions such as those against war crimes on the battlefield (Mullins, Kauzlarich, & Rothe, 2004). It is another matter to regulate the more clandestine behaviors of nation-state actors. Regardless, a Digital Geneva Convention could be one fruitful step toward curbing the problem behaviors endemic to cyberwarfare. At the very least, it would clearly communicate an ethical standard against which such activities and actors should be judged.

While it seems likely that state-sponsored or state-employed hackers present the biggest contemporary problem for computer security, this is not to say that non-state-affiliated hackers are harmless. Computer security hackers, especially those affiliated with computer crime syndicates (Lusthaus, 2018), can damage systems, compromise sensitive or otherwise private information, and cause significant financial losses. Admittedly, I am less concerned with the harms to corporations or government agencies than those inflicted on individual users, consumers, or bystanders. For instance, The Home Depot, a home improvement retail chain, was breached in 2014, resulting in the exposure and theft of around 56 million consumers' credit and debit card information (Zetter, 2014b). In 2017, one of the major credit reporting agencies—Equifax—was compromised due to a failure to properly patch critical systems (Newman, 2017). Over 145 million people in the United States—roughly half the population—had their information compromised including "birth dates, addresses, some driver's license numbers, about 209,000 credit card numbers, and Social Security numbers" (this breach may have been conducted by state actors, according to the U.S. Department of Justice) (Barrett, 2020; Newman, 2017). In 2021, the data of 48 million people was compromised in a breach of T-Mobile's systems. Involved was the exposure of the "full names, dates of birth, social security numbers, and driver's license information" of current, former, or prospective customers (Barrett, 2021). Because such data is used and exchanged clandestinely, it is difficult—if not impossible—to estimate damages to the individuals whose personal information was compromised. That said, it is equally difficult to overlook the significant risk of financial exploitation or other kinds of abuse created by such breaches. Additionally, the financial costs of these breaches (e.g. security remediation, lawsuits, fines) can have cascading economic impacts that may not only damage organizations but employees, customers, and related parties too.

Explaining illicit or malicious hacking is no simple feat. It requires consideration of individual proclivities and characteristics, group dynamics, and social structure. As previously stated, I cannot offer a complete account in these pages. For instance, I will not delve further into the political dynamics that propel nation-state hacking (and, anyway, that is likely best left for state crime researchers and political scientists). But the explanatory factors considered herein provide some indication of the complexity and nuance involved while noting potential interventions for demonstrative purposes. Importantly, the explanations and solutions explored herein are grounded in the research and guided by ethical principles to strike at the problems at a deeper level, albeit in an incremental fashion. In short, reduce the harm of crime, avoid unduly expanding the coercive power of corporate and state entities, and look to the interests of the public in all their diversity.

### Addressing Criminality

There exist various accounts which attribute criminal hacking to factors of individual difference—that there is something particular to hackers themselves that explains their involvement. For instance, researchers have explored connections between criminal hacking among juveniles and low self-control (Holt, Cale, Brewer, & Goldsmith, 2021; Marcum, Higgins, Ricketts, & Wolfe, 2014). Some scholars and journalists have pursued pathological explanations of hacking. In the early days of hacking, some laid blame on "internet addiction disorder"—a pseudo-diagnosis that carries less water in contemporary times filled with smartphones, social media, and video calls (Yar, 2005). Others have explored the role of autism spectrum disorder (ASD) in hacking involvement (Glenny, 2011; Schell & Holt, 2010; Schell & Melnychuk, 2010). From this perspective, ASD supposedly explains the intense interest endemic among hackers and a lack of regard for potential consequences or human collateral (Glenny, 2011). I am skeptical of such explanations as they cannot explain why hackers without ASD engage in such behaviors or why many folks with ASD do not engage in such acts. Further, without further research on the matter, such explanations are potentially discriminatory—casting folks with ASD as a "problem" with which to be dealt while "discrediting any meaning or motivations they offer for their actions" (Cohen, 1988, p. 51). Yet, it is difficult to deny that many hackers are *intensely* interested in computer technologies. They desire to learn more; to hone their skills to the level of mastery (Holt, 2010; Steinmetz, 2016; Turkle, 1984).

Rather than try to suppress the hackers technical and creative energies of hackers, various programs have emerged which attempt to channel these drives in licit directions, showing pathways to gainful employment, giving hackers a sense of purpose, and providing them with legal means to scratch their itch. These may include diversion programs and education workshops (Brewer et al., 2019). Workshops, for instance, bring together "groups of (potential) offenders in single or multiple sessions for the purposes of educating them about the nature of crime, and reinforcing prosocial values and behaviors" (Brewer et al., 2019, p.52). While few such programs exist dedicated to preventing computer crimes, the UK's National Crime Agency and Cyber Security Challenge UK operated one such program for a brief period in the late 2010s

(Brewer et al., 2019; Collins, 2018). It sought to divert teenagers apprehended for certain computer crimes into an educational program that encouraged ethical computer use and emphasized how such skills and interests could lead to lucrative careers (Collins, 2018). The program also disseminated cybercrime-related educational materials to teachers (Brewer et al., 2019, p. 53). A similar program, Hack_Right, was developed in the Netherlands (Zand, Matthijsse, Fischer, & Wagen, 2021). This program targets juvenile and young adult offenders and engages them in a modular program designed to encourage pro-social cognitive, social, and behavioral skills and outcomes while directing participants toward legitimate opportunities.

Of course, hackers possessing a distinctly anti-authoritarian streak may bristle at such programs. Others may not be so easily dissuaded from criminal activities given such opportunities can be significantly more lucrative than going straight (Glenny, 2011; Lusthaus, 2018). Those who celebrate hackers as a kind challenge to an increasingly state-surveilled and corporately owned technological age may also lament that such programs tend to steer hackers toward licit cybersecurity careers, thus encouraging them to become an industry cog. Though not to deny that hackers can be powerful and effective agents of resistance, such views tend toward romanticism, neglect the diversity found among hackers, and ignore the real harms that can be perpetuated against ordinary folks. Further, if our interest is in reducing the harms faced by individuals navigating the contemporary technological landscape, then diversion and education programs may constitute one promising prong of a hacking-related harm reduction agenda (but, importantly, such programs should not be the *only* prong). That said, more criminological research is needed on the effectiveness of such intervention strategies (Brewer et al., 2019, p. 51).

Scholars have also approached hacking as a subculture—utilizing theoretical tools familiar to many realist criminologists who have often turned to the role of subculture to understand criminal activity (e.g. Holt, 2010; Steinmetz, 2016; Steinmetz, Holt, & Holt, 2020; Yar, 2005). Subcultures offer members sets of rules governing their interactions, strategies for solving problems, and cognitive and linguistic tools for making sense of their position in the world (Cohen, 1955; Ferrell, 2013; Ferrell, Hayward, & Young, 2015; Miller, 1958). A word of caution: as indicated previously, it is inappropriate to speak of a singular hacker community or subculture. Rather, there exist many such communities (Levy, 1984; Söderberg, 2008; Steinmetz, 2016; Taylor, 1999; Thomas, 2002; Turkle, 1984). There are some general characteristics, however, that seem more-or-less consistent. For instance, the politics of hackers tend to orient around shades of liberalism, libertarianism, or anarchism (Fuchs, 2013; Jordan, 2001; Steinmetz, 2016). As a result, hacker cultures tend to emphasize the power of the individual and resist restrictions on freedom and autonomy. Hackers are also characterized by a sense of *technological utopianism*—that technology can solve our social problems (sometimes described as "techno-optimism") or that failures to implement and control technology properly will lead to dystopian outcomes (Hayward & Maas, 2021; Seymour, 2020; Steinmetz, 2016; Yar, 2014). Finally, there exists the aforementioned desire for mastery—for control over the technology, for self-development through the curation of skill, and to overcome challenges (Holt, 2010; Steinmetz, 2016; Taylor, 1999; Thomas, 2002; Turkle, 1984).

Subcultural theorists like Albert Cohen (1955) argue that subcultures appeal to potential members because they offer avenues toward status that may otherwise be denied in "mainstream" culture. This seems to be the case with hacking as these communities often award social status to those who demonstrate expertise and creativity in exposing or solving technical problems. Bonus points for successful hacks against noteworthy targets—for example, identifying major security vulnerabilities in prominent software systems. David Matza (1964), however, famously noted in *Delinquency and Drift* that subcultures are never completely separated from mainstream culture.[2] Rather, subcultural values are often alternative expressions of values or sensibilities found in mainstream culture. From this view, the subcultural features of hacking (or at least *Western* hacking) are reflections of American or Western societies characterized by individualism, deregulation, an elevation of STEM (science, technology, engineering, and mathematics) fields over other educational domains, and a belief that we can technologically innovate ourselves out of our problems (Barbrook & Cameron, 2001; Barlow, 2001; Joy, 2000; Matza, 1964).

What does all this mean for the possibility of interventions? In short, it signals that many of the problems we might ascribe to hackers are, at their root, problems of society at large. Thus, with an eye to the long term, addressing potentially criminogenic value systems necessitates sweeping institutional and cultural changes (Currie, 1985; 2007; 2020l; Hall & Winlow, 2015). But does this necessarily mean that the issue of values is one that cannot be addressed through short-term reforms? Potentially. But perhaps initial steps can be taken. These might include the proliferation of the aforementioned educational programs designed to encourage hackers to use their skills toward non-criminal ends. Such programs can be scaled-up to include major awareness campaigns to change public and political sensibilities—to demythologize and promote the potential benefits of hacking—while encouraging a sense of social responsibility among potential hackers. Of course, there is a fine line between "public awareness campaign" and "propaganda." The point is that perhaps we can do more to shape public values (Currie, 2007).

At this point, a momentary diversion is warranted. Unfortunately, there is a contingent of the contemporary academic left, which/that has largely abandoned the question of values—of who we, as a society, should be— and instead focus primarily on critique. While critique is useful, change requires a vision of the future and what we hope to achieve—it requires "agents" rather than "spectators" (Rorty, 1998a, p. 9). "Hopelessness," Rorty (1998a, p. 37) explains, "has become fashionable on the Left—principled, theorized, philosophical hopelessness." In this manner, some on the academic left seem to conclude that that our past and our values are things to be ashamed of and, importantly, things that cannot be moved beyond or overcome. Yet, this way lies fatalism. If we want to sustain a hope for the future, Rorty (1998a, p. 33)— drawing from Dewey—explains that,

> What makes us moral beings is the fact that, for each of us, there are some acts we believe we ought to die rather than commit. Which acts these are will differ from epoch to epoch, and from person to person, but to be a moral agent is to be unable to imagine living with oneself after committing these acts. But now suppose that one has in fact done one of the things that one could not have imagined doing, and finds that one is still alive. At that point, one's choices are suicide, a life of bottomless self-disgust, and an attempt to live so as never to do such a thing again. Dewey recommends the third choice. He thinks you should remain an agent, rather than either committing suicide or becoming a

horrified spectator of your own past. He regards self-loathing as a luxury which agents—either individuals or nations—cannot afford.

In this manner, we not only need to critique and be aware of our collective failings, but to actively work to be the kind of society that would not repeat those mistakes. Required is an active engagement in democratic processes to promote a vision of the kind of people we hope to be—one in which we can take pride in ourselves (Rorty, 1998a). It requires not only the identification of problems, but the active effort toward solutions (Currie, 2007). Solving cultural and value problems is difficult, for sure, and such matters are intractably intertwined with issues of structure (after all, why should someone embrace the idea of community-obligation in local communities fragmented by economic policies which divest resources, ship jobs overseas, reduce social safety net, and subject members to government scrutiny and harassment?) (Currie, 1985, p. 226; Ferrell, 2018). But considering the importance of values in shaping criminogenic attitudes and systems of oppression, winning hearts and minds should be part of a realist harm reduction agenda.

What is needed is a "public criminology" that not only endeavors to shape public views about crime and crime control as well as impact public policy, but one that does so in a way that reduces potentially criminogenic value systems—ones rooted in self-interested individualism, vulgar displays of wealth, etc. (Barak, 2007; Currie, 2007; Hall & Winlow, 2015; Loader & Sparks, 2010; Tunnell, 1995). Required is a "utopian realism" or a criminology that connects "issues of crime and social regulation with questions of ethics and politics" while also engaging "with the *realpolitik* of crime and criminal justice" to advanced "proposals that have some immanent purchase on the world" (Loader, 1998, p. 205). Discussions surrounding public criminology are typically concerned with the nature of the disciplinary apparatus of criminology and the strategies used by criminologists to shape public perceptions of crime and control as well as public policy. It should, however, also involve the advancing of proposals for programs and policies designed to shape the cultural value systems of society—not just the values of the discipline—in pro-social ways. Admittedly, this is a Herculean task in an age of social media, misinformation, and significant political division marred by waning trust in political institutions. Yet, it seems necessary if we are to strike at the underlying issues of crime and criminality. This may mean that significant structural change is ultimately required, but perhaps short-term solutions can get us part of the way there in the meantime. As such, the prospect of hope of what we can be or achieve as a society and the kinds of values that should be endemic to our collective democratic identity deserve more attention within not just realist criminology, but critical criminology more generally.

As indicated above, changing cultural values might mean relatively little if the structural conditions which gave rise to or sustain such values go unameliorated. In my prior book *Hacked,* I gesture toward the role of class in hacking—noting that many hackers tend to come from the ranks of the middle class, though this is certainly not always the case. That said, most of my work ruminated on American hacking. This insight may not hold true in other societies. It may also not be the case that hacking is class-limited as technology continues to become increasingly ubiquitous and inexpensive. While this chapter will consider below the economic and policy conditions which may give rise to criminal opportunities for illicit hacking, it does not consider possible political economic antecedents for hacking criminality (predispositions toward or motivations to engage in crime) because of a dearth of scholarship on this subject. As such, more research is necessary before interventions can be advanced on that front. What can be said is that evidence indicates that the political economy and class likely play a significant role in shaping the drives and motivations underlying illicit security hacking (Banks, 2018; Steinmetz, 2016; Söderberg, 2008).

Gender and masculinity are also important crimino-genic considerations when examining hacker subcultures. Research has established that hacking is largely—though not exclusively—a male activity, one characterized by a kind of "boy culture" accompanied by certain expressions of masculinity (Jordan & Taylor, 1998; Reagle, 2017; Steinmetz, 2016; Steinmetz, Holt, & Holt, 2020; Tanczer, 2015; Taylor, 1999; Thomas, 2002; Turkle, 1984; Yar, 2005). Like the problems of subculture, the exclusionary and potentially criminogenic masculinity among some hacker communities mirrors the problems of masculinity and chauvinism in tech or geek cultures more generally or, indeed, the whole of society (Alfrey & Twine, 2017; Huws, 2014; Salter & Blodgett, 2017). In this manner, we not only must consider the connections between contemporary capitalism and the values of individualism and competition but also how these values are connected to forms of masculinity. While such class and gender dynamics may be inseparable, it would be irresponsible to wholly conflate the two (Raymen & Kuldova, 2020; Wood, Anderson, & Richards, 2020, 2021).

For all this recognition, there exist—to my knowledge—surprisingly few organizations or programs dedicated to combating sexism and misogyny in tech circles directly. Instead, most efforts have been geared toward adjacent efforts, such as increasing the representation of women in these fields through, for instance, organizations like

Women in Cybersecurity (WiCyS) and Women and Information Security and Privacy (WISP). Other efforts include individual challenges to instances of sexism and misogyny (e.g. "callouts" or anti-discrimination/harassment lawsuits) as well as internal organizational attempts to promote diversity and inclusion. While these approaches are certainly important, more work is needed to address the problems associated with excessive or harmful masculinity-based behaviors and the associated values and status criteria which may encourage illicit computer feats. What is needed are perhaps programs which promote positive expressions of manhood and discourage their more toxic manifestations. There have been some efforts to create such programs to prevent gender-based or intimate-partner violence with some promising results, though more research is certainly needed (Pérez-Martínez et al., 2021). Perhaps these kinds of programs can be retooled for computer crimes?

### Addressing Criminal Opportunity

Of course, crime cannot occur without opportunity. This section explores just a few factors which structure the landscape of opportunities available for criminal security hacking starting with the existence of underground marketplaces which provide both opportunities and incentives for hackers to sell their skills and their ill-gotten gains. "White hat" hackers, those interested in findings bugs and other problems to improve security, can submit vulnerabilities directly to software or hardware vendors in the hope that these vendors will make necessary fixes (though this practice is legally questionable in many jurisdictions and some companies may sue hackers who find and report such vulnerabilities). These hackers may also submit discovered vulnerabilities to "bug bounty" programs—websites or databases designed to allow individuals to disclose discovered vulnerabilities in a relatively protected manner. Less scrupulous hackers, however, can sell knowledge of vulnerabilities on the black or gray markets. In fact, it appears far more lucrative to sell vulnerabilities in these marketplaces than to participate in legal vulnerability disclosure programs (Perlroth, 2021).

The most valuable vulnerabilities and exploits are known as "zero-days" or "0-days." These vulnerabilities are "attack holes that are still unknown to the software maker and to the antivirus vendors—which means there are no antivirus signatures yet to detect the exploits and no patches available to fix the holes they attack" (Zetter, 2014a, p. 6). In other words, zero days have transpired between the vendor becoming aware of a vulnerability and the release of a fix. Once knowledge of a zero day gets out, however, it quickly loses value as it is likely only a matter of time until the vulnerability is patched away.

Given their role in providing opportunities and incentives toward illicit and harmful activities, there is a need to disrupt these marketplaces. Law enforcement and intelligence agencies are already making efforts in this regard, so I won't waste additional time discussing the black markets. Instead, our attention may be better served describing what might be an even bigger problem—the secretive purchasing of software or hardware vulnerabilities by government law enforcement or intelligence agencies (Perlroth, 2021). These "gray markets" thrive on the trade of zero-day vulnerabilities and exploits which may net large returns for sellers. Critics have called for restrictions on this practice. The argument is that while knowledge of system vulnerabilities may provide government agencies with an advantage against an adversary, failure to disclose these vulnerabilities means leaving affected systems open to attack should someone else discover these weaknesses.

This, of course, raises the question "is it ethically just to purposefully withhold information that could prevent others from coming to harm?" (the answer, from my view, is likely "no"). More importantly, however, restricting such gray markets may be necessary to disincentivize the unscrupulous buying and selling of vulnerabilities and exploits. In other words, how can we hope to curb the illegal or malicious theft and selling of sensitive data if government institutions are themselves participating in these markets?

Though sub rosa economies are inevitable whenever certain goods or services are regulated under law, there are other factors to consider which feed into the economics of illicit security hacking. For instance, the damage from hacking is often a result of databases containing sensitive information being "breached" by systems intruders. While the knee-jerk reaction is to place the blame on the intruders, it also raises important questions about data collection and retention. Organizations regularly gather and store massive amounts of personal data for various purposes. Some data gathering is necessary—it makes sense, for instance, that banks would collect social security numbers and related personal identifying information to prevent fraud and manage financial accounts. Yet it is becoming increasingly routine for all manner of organizations to collect voluminous amounts of data on individuals. For instance, the internet platforms and services that govern most of our experiences of the internet routinely track user activity with granular detail. Google, Meta, Apple, Microsoft, and a host of other tech companies hoover up data on millions and millions of users daily for the purposes of advertising, product development, and behavioral modification (Zuboff, 2019). We also cannot forget the massive troves of data being gathered on individuals, foreign and domestic, through government surveillance programs. The point is that we have allowed all manner of organizations to gluttonously collected and retain enormous quantities of information about us and our activities.

While it is ultimately a normative question, the need to protect individual privacy should outweigh whatever limited administrative, intelligence, marketing, or advertising uses for such data. A key step in preventing the damages caused by computer data breaches should be to implement stricter regulations governing the kinds of data organizations can collect, how that data is stored, and how long such data can be retained. Many countries and international collectives have already created regulations designed to curb data hoarding and protect individual privacy. For instance, in the United States, the collection, protection, and divulgence of medical related data is regulated under the Health Insurance Portability and Accountability Act (HIPAA) of 1996. The European Union passed the General Data Protection Regulation (GDPR) in 2016 (implemented in 2018). This law is an ambitious and expansive attempt to regulate the use of personal information for commercial or professional activities. There also exist a variety of standards for developing, maintaining, and assessing information and computer security systems published by organizations like the International Organization for Standardization (ISO), the U.S. National Institute of Technology and Standards (NIST), and the Information Systems Audit and Control Association (ISACA). Unfortunately, these standards seldom carry the weight of law on their own (though they be used in assessing compliance with legal regulations or may become pertinent in civil litigation). Despite these strides, more robust and comprehensive regulations are necessary to hold organizations accountable for their data gathering, analysis, retention, and security practices. Of course, these regulations would need teeth—they would need to significantly curb the ability of these companies to monetize personal data at the expense of personal privacy and security while also providing meaningful punishments for violations (while I previously said I wanted to avoid punitive approaches, they may be necessary to hold organizations accountable).

In addition to regulating data collection and retention, the organizational structures and processes which govern hardware and software development are also in need of correction. Contemporary computer systems can be extraordinarily complicated and the organizational apparatuses necessary to brings these systems to fruition can be equally complex, with various interests and factions vying for priority in product design and implementation. For instance, in the creation of a smartphone, hardware engineers may want to include more powerful hardware to give the device a performance edge over the competition while design teams may resist as more powerful phones may need larger components, rendering the device overly cumbersome for everyday use. Similarly, marketing personnel may protest at the inflated costs that would correspond to the use of more powerful components. In the fray, it is easy for security concerns to be overlooked and, as a result, vulnerabilities may be introduced into hardware and software along the way. For this reason, there is a push to make security a more central pillar of development—to reduce the total number of vulnerabilities present from the outset rather than something to be addressed after the fact. For instance, NIST (2022) recently finalized version 1.1 of its Secure Software Development Framework (SSDF), a "set of fundamental, sound, and secure software development practices" which "should help software producers reduce the number of vulnerabilities in released software, reduce the potential impact of the exploitation of undetected or unaddressed vulnerabilities, and address the root causes of vulnerabilities to prevent recurrences." While such measures will not stop security hacking entirely, if implemented in earnest, they should help reduce the total number of opportunities available while also increasing the skill and effort required to exploit available vulnerabilities.

By considering the overall topography of hacking, it is possible to determine potential points of intervention that do not rely exclusively on individualized punitivity, the erosion of privacy, and the undue expansion of state and corporate control. The strategies detailed above would target some of the factors involved in the production of criminal propensity and opportunity in the domain of illicit security hacking. Detailed above are only a few approaches that can be taken to reduce involvement in criminal hacking and the availability of opportunities for such offenses. Despite some noteworthy efforts made to date, more work is necessary. There are thus ample opportunities for realist criminologists to address the harms of illicit computer hacking while working toward a more just and equitable information age.

### Addressing Victimization—The Case of Online Fraud

Preventing and reducing the prevalence of crime is certainly important. Yet, a realist criminological harm reduction program must also consider the amelioration of harm once victimization has occurred. While this discussion could continue to explore criminal hacking, this section turns toward fraud for two reasons. First, many of the harms associated with illicit computer hacking—at least those inflicted on individuals—manifest through fraud. Breach data, for example, can be used to open lines of credit under victims' names and access other accounts associated victims' details. Second, fraud victimization has received considerably more attention by criminologists and victimologists alike compared to hacking victimization, thus providing a deeper well from which to draw. This section will consider difficulties faced by victims of fraud and strategies for addressing such harms. Before delving into such matters, we should first review fraud's various harms.

To begin, reporting data, flawed as they are, point toward significant monetary damages for victims. Of the 847,376 complaints received by the U.S. Internet Crime Complaint Center (IC3, 2022) in 2021, over 685,000 were for various forms of fraud with reported damages nearing $7 billion USD.[3] While the organization does not fully distinguished between online and offline fraud, the UK's Action Fraud received 875,622 reports of fraud amounting to over £2.35 billion in losses in 2021 (Action Fraud, 2021). Australia's Scamwatch (2022) received 286,608 reports of fraud in the same year with around 9 percent of these incidents including reported financial losses totalling over AU$323 million. Canadian Anti-Fraud Centre received 74,525 reports of fraud in 2020, amounting to CA$269 million lost (CAFC, 2022).

The harms associated with fraud are not limited to monetary damages, however. As Button and Cross (2017, pp. 93–94) explain, "fraud victimisation can extend to the deterioration of physical and emotional health and well-being, depression, relationship breakdown, homelessness, unemployment and in worst case scenarios, suicide." The consequences thus extend to emotional, psychological, physiological, relational, employment, and other quality-of-life domains (Button & Cross, 2017; Cross, Richards, & Smith, 2016; Cross, Smith, & Richards, 2014). Consider, for instance, romance fraud, a type of fraud where a perpetrator feigns romantic interest in their target and then exploits the victim's emotional investment in the "relationship" for monies and gifts. Research indicates that victims suffer significant emotional distress, feeling foolish and betrayed (Button & Cross, 2017; Whitty & Buchanan, 2016). While the relationship may have been based on deception, it often feels very real for the victims. They thus grieve its loss and struggle to cope, an experience which is compounded by the fact that family and friends often do not understand their trauma (Whitty & Buchanan, 2016).

So how can we help the victims of fraud? Preventing their victimization in the first place is an obvious starting point. Like hacking, fraud has proliferated in recent times because of the opportunities made available by the internet—specifically the growth of internet access, the rise of social networks, the use of such technologies to facilitate commerce and trade, and the accumulation of data for the purposes of surveillance and marketing (Button & Cross, 2017, pp. 20–22; Yar & Steinmetz, 2019). The internet age has made fraud relatively easy, inexpensive, fast, scalable, and low risk for perpetrators. Many of the same kinds of strategies previously suggested for preventing the harms associated with illicit computer hacking can apply here as well such as the regulation of data collection and retention and measures to reduce the introduction or persistence of vulnerabilities in computer software and hardware— problems that make it easier for perpetrators to access information that can be used in various forms of fraud.

But the objective here is not to think about fraud prevention but, rather, amelioration. A realist criminological approach to harm reduction demands that not only do we attempt to reduce the *occurrence* of such offenses but also the *degree* of harm experienced in the wake of crime. In this case, it means providing robust support systems for fraud victims. Unfortunately, there is a significant lack of support services for victims of fraud (Button & Cross, 2017; Cross, Richards, & Smith, 2016). This is at least partially attributable to a prevailing tendency to overlook or even dismiss the experiences of these victims. Even though anyone can be defrauded under the right circumstances, no matter how resilient they believe they are, victim-blaming is prevalent (Button & Cross, 2017; Cross, 2015). This further extends to self-blame—that many victims may experience intense shame or embarrassment because of their victimization and thus may refuse to seek help (Button & Cross, 2017). As Cross (2015, p. 189) explains,

> The popular discourse surrounding online fraud victimization is very much founded upon notions of blame and responsibility levelled toward the victims themselves for their failure to avoid victimization in the first place. It is also premised very strongly on a perception of greed and gullibility on the part of the victim.

She also argues that there exists a tendency to use humor to "trivialize" fraud and its corresponding damages. Of course, addressing victim-blaming is easier said than done. Required is a widespread effort to educate others on the nature of the offense and its harms. Like with hacking, there is a need to change hearts and minds. There have been some efforts in this regard. For instance, the AARP (2022) recently released a report titled "Blame and Shame in the Context of Financial Fraud" detailing their commitment to ending fraud victim blaming. More work is needed, however.

A more direct strategy of harm reduction is victim compensation. Certain types of fraud have become so commonplace that victim compensation has become part of the cost of doing business for many companies. Many credit card companies and banks may remove fraudulent charges made against customers if reported. Other kinds of fraud, however, can leave victims with significant financial burdens. For instance, the IC3 (2022, p. 22) received 24,000 reports of romance fraud in 2021 amounting to over $956 million in losses—an average of almost $40,000 per case assuming each report includes claims of monetary damages. Of course, these figures are restricted only to *reported* losses—many victims of fraud do not report their experiences, and some may be unaware that they have been defrauded at all (Button & Cross, 2017; Yar & Steinmetz, 2019). Regardless, the point is that such losses can be debilitating for individuals.

Some countries provide compensation for crime victims. Unfortunately, these resources may not be available to fraud victims in many jurisdictions. In 1984, the United States passed the Victims of Crime Act, which, in addition to other provisions, created the Crime Victims Fund to support victims' services and provide victim compensation. Many jurisdictions, however, reserve these funds for the victims of violent crime—a tendency evident in other countries as well (Button & Cross, 2017, p. 138; Cross, 2018b). As such, many fraud victims may only be able to seek financial redress if an offender is caught and compelled by courts to provide compensation (Button & Cross, 2017, p. 142).

There is a push in some countries to legally compel companies to compensate victims defrauded through their platforms and services. For instance, the UK House of Commons Treasury Committee (HCTC, 2022, p. 31) recently published a report which recommends that "the Government seriously consider whether online companies should be required to contribute compensation when fraud is conducted using their platforms." In 2017, the U.S. Department of Justice, the Federal Trade Commission, and other agencies compelled Western Union to forfeit $586 million as punishment for failing to "maintain an effective anti-money laundering program and aiding and abetting wire fraud" (FTC, 2017). Forfeited funds were used by the Department of Justice to compensate victims of fraud facilitated through Western Union transactions between 2004 and 2016 (DoJ, 2022). Such efforts could encourage platforms to take fraud more seriously and implement more protections for users.

There are significant challenges confronting the compensation of fraud victims. Because of public perceptions regarding fraud victims, making these funds available depends upon changing prevailing narratives surrounding fraud victimization—to overcome the aforementioned problem of victim blaming to generate a consensus that such victims deserve due consideration (Cross, 2018a; 2018b). Given the amount of fraud that occurs—billions of dollars annually in the United States (IC3, 2022; FTC, 2022)—compensation may admittedly become an extraordinarily expensive affair. Policymakers and the public will have to decide how such compensation funds will be procured. They might, for instance, consider funding victim through fines issued against companies for non-compliance with computer security and fraud prevention regulations. Further, some might beg the question, "should all victims of fraud be compensated fully or equally?" If two people are defrauded for the same amount and one makes $500,000 USD a year and the other $40,000, the impact of the loss will most likely be felt more acutely by the lower-income individual. In an ideal world, all victims would be made whole after a crime has occurred. But if there are limits on the funds available, decisions will have to be made regarding equitable and fair distribution of compensation. In addition, some may argue that there exists a distinct possibility that making funds available for fraud victims may itself be an endeavor vulnerable to fraud. What might stop a perpetrator—alone or conspiring with others—from engineering a scenario where it appears they had been defrauded to gain access to crime victims compensation funds? All these present obstacles for implementing a fraud victim compensation effort, but addressing such matters is necessary to alleviate the duress experienced by many victims.

Another problem confronting the victims of fraud is a potentially bewildering array of channels they must go through to seek help. Assuming they decide to report the crime (and many fraud victims elect not to, for various reasons), it may be unclear to whom they should report (Button & Cross, 2017). Should they contact their local police department? State police? Federal? In the United States, some police departments may be unwilling to accept reports of online fraud and may direct individuals to the FBI's Internet Crime Complaint Center. The U.S. Secret Service, while known for providing protection services for government officials, is also tasked with conducting fraud investigations—a fact seemingly unknown to many. Regardless of whether they file a report, victims may need to report the fraud to relevant vendors, financial institutions, credit monitoring agencies, and related organizations to recover losses, stop further damages from occurring, or acquire guidance. They may have to contact consumer credit counseling services to work out new payment plans, consolidate debt, or otherwise reduce monthly payments or interest owed. They may have to contact credit reporting agencies, credit card companies, or banks to have their assets or credit records frozen. Many victims are thus forced to navigate the "fraud justice network," an oft byzantine web of bureaucracy, to get any kind of relief (Button, Tapley & Lewis, 2012). Navigating this Kafka-esque nightmare is itself a kind of secondary victimization—an additional battery of harms above and beyond those directly caused by the initial offense (Williams, 1984). Though resources do exist that attempt to help victims work through these channels, if we are to reduce the harms experienced by fraud victims, then we need to streamline and consolidate the various processes that victims must navigate as they seek amelioration or redress.

In addition, given the various emotional and psychological consequences that fraud might bring— including depression, anxiety, shame, self-hatred, and suicidal ideation—there is a need to provide counseling services to victims (Button & Cross, 2017, p. 143; Cross, 2018b). Such counseling can also help victims navigate the potential relational problems that may result from fraud including managing unsupportive friends and family members, discussing their victimization experiences with loved ones, or navigating the potential collateral consequences such fraud might bring (e.g. losing savings, inheritance, retirement funds). These services should be made free or at least affordable for victims of all sorts, including those affected by fraud.

Victims of crime often want to see perpetrators brought to justice. This fact is no less true for many victims of fraud (Button & Cross, 2017; Cross, Richards, & Smith, 2016). For victims, justice is—for the most part—a combination of four separate albeit interrelated desires: to have their victimization taken seriously, to feel that others are sympathetic to their suffering, to see perpetrators held to account, and to be made whole again (Button, Tapley, & Lewis, 2012; Cross, Richards, & Smith, 2016).[4] The various measures described above may help address these different facets of justice for victims with the exception of holding perpetrators accountable. If we can provide some measure of relief or reassurance across the other fronts, perhaps there will be less of a need to rely on the punitive logics of the criminal legal system to give victims a sense that justice has been served.

## Conclusion

The objective of this chapter was not to provide a complete account of potential policies or points of intervention that can or should be brought to bear in dealing with computer crime offenses. Instead, the point was to demonstrate how realist criminologists can approach solutions in a way that is sensitive to the nuances of crime and victimization while actively avoiding overly punitive or intrusive means. It also is a demonstration of how seemingly patchwork or piecemeal reforms can be a part of a more comprehensive vision for harm reduction. The strategies advanced in this chapter are intended to reduce criminal propensity and opportunity in a manner that challenges a status quo where corporations and governments increasingly exercise their dominion over not just the internet but our everyday lives. In this sense, these solutions generally punch upward while acknowledging the real harms produced by computer crime activity. Additionally, this chapter deliberately considered the needs of victims as an important component of an overall realist criminology harm reduction project. But let's not lose sight of the big picture. Many of these reforms will amount to little if they are not accompanied by constant pushes toward sweeping economic, cultural, and political changes that will fundamentally reconfigure our collective relationship to technology, information, privacy, trade, and other factors. We cannot settle for just these reforms. They are steps in a plan—not an end in-and-of themselves.

## Notes

1   My work on hacking primarily arose from my dissertation research and related projects, culminating in my first book *Hacked: A Radical Approach to Hacker Culture and Crime* (2016). My work on fraud stems mostly from a National Science Foundation–funded study of social engineering—the use of deception to circumvent information security protocols—I conducted with my colleagues, Richard Goe and Alexandra Pimentel (Award #1616804).

2   Matza's argument here was more specifically oriented toward *juvenile* subcultures as he was doubtful that juveniles could ever really create a subculture separate from mainstream culture. That said, I would argue his argument holds for non-juvenile subcultures as well. Cultural habits and traditions are so pervasive that escaping them entirely would be nigh impossible.

3   Estimates of fraud reporting from the IC3 were calculated by adding together the reported figures for the following crime categories: Phishing/vishing/smishing/pharming, non-payment/non-delivery, extortion, identity theft, spoofing, misrepresentation, confidence fraud/romance, BEC/EAC, credit card fraud, employment, tech support, real estate/rental, advanced fee, government impersonation, overpayment, investment, lottery/sweepstates/inheritance, civil matter, health care related, re-shipping, and charity. These figures may not include forms of fraud coinciding with categories like malware/scareware/virus, ransomware, or other as it is impossible to disaggregate fraudulent from non-fraudulent cases in these figures. Thus, the estimates presented in the text are likely underestimates of fraud incidence within the IC3 data.

4   The research on the matter informs my argument here, but I am also making selective choices based on which wants and needs stated by victims are most directly related to achieving justice in an institutional setting. This is by no means a definitive list, however.

## References

AARP (2022). Blame and shame in the context of financial fraud. Retrieved October 7, 2022 at www.aarp.org/content/dam/aarp/money/scams_fraud/2022/07/aarp-fraud-victim-blaming-report-06-07-22.pdf

Action Fraud (2021). Fraud crime trends. London, England: National Fraud & Cyber Crime Reporting Centre. Retrieved October 10, 2022 at https://data.actionfraud.police.uk/cms/wp-content/uploads/2021/07/2020-21-Annual-Assessment-Fraud-Crime-Trends.pdf

Alfrey, L. & Twine, F. W. (2017). Gender-fluid geek girls: Negotiating inequality regimes in the tech industry. *Gender & Society, 31*(1): 28–50.

Banks, J. (2018). Radical criminology and the techno-security-capitalist complex. In K. F. Steinmetz & M. R. Nobles (eds.) *Technocrime and criminological theory* (pp. 102–115). New York: Routledge.

Barak, G. (2007). Doing newsmaking criminology from within the academy. *Theoretical Criminology, 11*(2), 197–207.

Barbrook, R. & Cameron, A. (2001). Californian ideology. In P. Ludlow (ed.) *Crypto anarchy, cyberstates, and pirate utopias* (pp. 363–388). Cambridge, MA: MIT Press.

Barlow, J. P. (2001). A declaration of the independence of cyberspace. In P. Ludlow (ed.) *Crypto anarchy, cyberstates, and pirate utopias* (pp. 28–30). Cambridge, MA: MIT Press.

Barrett, B. (2020, February 10). How 4 Chinese hackers allegedly took down Equifax. *Wired.* Retrieved September 27, 2022 at www.wired.com/story/equifax-hack-china/

Barrett. B. (2021, August 18). The T-Mobile breach is much worse than it had to be. *Wired.* Retrieved February 3, 2022 at www.wired.com/story/t-mobile-breach-much-worse-than-it-had-to-be/

Brewer, R., Vel-Palumbo, M., Hutchings, A., Holt, T., Goldsmith, A., & Maimon, D. (2019). *Cybercrime prevention: Theory and applications.* Cham, Switzerland: Palgrave Pilot.

Button, M., & Cross, C. (2017). *Cyberfrauds, scams and their victims.* New York: Routledge.

Button, M., Tapley, J., & Lewis, C. (2012). The 'fraud justice network' and the infra-structure of support for individual fraud victims in England and Wales. *Criminology & Criminal Justice, 13*(1), 37–61.

CAFC. (Canadian Anti-Fraud Centre). (2022). The impact of fraud so far this year. Retrieved February 15, 2022 at www. antifraudcentre-centreantifraude.ca/index-eng.htm

Cohen, A. K. (1955). *Delinquent boys: The culture of the gang.* New York: Free Press.

Cohen, S. (1988). *Against criminology.* New York: Routledge.

Collins, K. (2018, August 6). Inside the bootcamp reforming teenage hackers. *Cnet.* Retrieved September 27, 2022 at www.cnet.com/news/privacy/inside-the-boot-camp-reform ing-teenage-hackers/

Cross, C. (2015). No laughing matter: Blaming the victim of online fraud. *International Review of Victimology, 21*(2), 187–204.

Cross, C. (2018a). Denying victim status to online fraud victims: The challenges of being a 'non-ideal victim.' In M. Duggan (ed.) *Revisiting the "ideal victim": Developments in critical victimology* (pp. 243–262). Bristol, England: Bristol University Press.

Cross, C. (2018b). (Mis)understanding the impact of online fraud: Implications for victim assistance schemes. *Victims & Offenders, 13*(6), 757–776.

Cross, C., Richards, K., & Smith, R. G. (2016). The reporting experiences and support needs of victims of online fraud. *Trends & Issues in Crime and Criminal Justice, 518*, 1–14.

Cross, C., Smith, R. G., & Richards, K. (2014). Challenges of responding to online fraud victimisation in Australia. *Trends & Issues in Crime and Criminal Justice, 174.* Canberra, Australia: Australian Institute of Criminology. Retrieved October 6, 2022 at www.aic.gov.au/sites/default/ files/2020-05/tandi474.pdf

Currie, E. (1985). *Confronting crime: An American challenge.* New York: Pantheon Books.

Currie, E. (2007). Against marginality: Arguments for a public criminology. *Theoretical Criminology, 11*(2), 175–190.

Currie, E. (2020). *Peculiar indifference: The neglected toll of violence on Black America.* New York: Metropolitan Books.

DoJ (Department of Justice). (2022, July 6). Justice Department announces phase two of compensation process for Western

Union fraud victims. Washington, D.C.: U.S. Department of Justice. Retrieved October 7, 2022 at www.justice.gov/opa/pr/justice-department-announces-phase-two-compensation-process-western-union-fraud-victims

Ferrell, J. (2013). Cultural criminology and the politics of meaning. *Critical Criminology, 21*, 257–271.

Ferrell, J. (2018). *Drift: Illicit mobility and uncertain knowledge.* Berkeley, CA: University of California Press.

Ferrell, J., Hayward, K., & Young, J. (2015). *Cultural criminology: An invitation* (2nd ed.). Thousand Oaks, CA: Sage.

Follis, L., & Fish, A. (2020a). Hacker states. Cambridge, MA: MIT Press.

FTC (Federal Trade Commission). (2017, January 19). Western Union admits anti-money laundering violations and settles consumer fraud charges, forfeits $586 million in settlement with FTC and Justice Department. Washington, DC: Federal Trade Commission. Retrieved October 7, 2022 at www.ftc.gov/news-events/news/press-releases/2017/01/western-union-admits-anti-money-laundering-violations-settles-consumer-fraud-charges-forfeits-586

Fuchs, C. (2013). The Anonymous movement in the context of liberalism and socialism. *Interface: A Journal for and About Social Movements, 5*(2), 345–376.

Glenny, M. (2011). *Darkmarket: Cyberthieves, cybercops, and you.* New York: Alfred A. Knopf.

Guay, J., & Rudnick, L. (2017, June 25). What the Digital Geneva Convention means for the future of humanitarian action. *UNHCR The Policy Lab.* Retrieved September 22, 2022 at www.unhcr.org/innovation/digital-geneva-convention-mean-future-humanitarian-action/

Hall, S., & Winlow, S. (2015). *Revitalizing criminological theory: Towards a new ultra-realism.* New York: Routledge.

Hayward, K. J., & Maas, M. M. (2021). Artificial intelligence and crime: A primer for criminologists. *Crime Media Culture, 17*(2), 209–233.

HCTC (House of Commons Treasury Committee). (2022). Economic crime—Eleventh report of Session 2021–22. London, England: House of Commons. Retrieved October 7, 2022 at https://committees.parliament.uk/publications/8691/documents/88242/default/

Holt, T. J. (2010). Becoming a computer hacker. Examining the enculturation and development of computer deviants. In P. Cromwell (ed.) *In their own words: Criminals on crime* (pp. 109–123). New York: Oxford University Press.

Holt, T. J., Cale, J., Brewer, R., & Goldsmith, A. (2021). Assessing the role of opportunity and low self-control in juvenile hacking. *Crime & Delinquency, 67*(5), 662–688.

Huws, U. (2014). Shifting boundaries. Gender, labor, and new information and communication technology. In C. Carter, L. Steiner, & L. McLaughlin (eds.) *The Routledge companion to media and gender* (pp. 147–156). New York: Routledge.

IC3 (Internet Crime Complaint Center). (2022). *Federal Bureau of Investigation Internet Crime Report 2021.* Retrieved August 29, 2022 at www.ic3.gov/Media/PDF/AnnualRep ort/2021_IC3Report.pdf

Jordan, T. (2001). Language and libertarianism: The politics of cyberculture and the culture of cyberpolitics. *The Sociological Review, 49*(1), 1–17.

Jordan, T., & Taylor, P. (1998). A sociology of hackers. *The Sociological Review, 46*(4), 757–780.

Joy, B. (2000). Why the future doesn't need us. *Wired.* Retrieved from www.wired.com/2000/04/joy-2/

Levy, S. (1984). *Hackers: Heroes of the computer revolution.* New York: Penguin.

Loader, I. (1998). Criminology and the public sphere: Arguments for utopian realism. In P. Walton & J. Young (eds.) *The New Criminology revisited* (pp. 190–212). New York: Palgrave.

Loader, I., & Sparks, R. (2010). *Public criminology?* New York: Routledge.

Lusthaus, J. (2018). *Industry of anonymity: Inside the business of cybercrime.* Cambridge, MA: Harvard University Press.

Marcum, C. D., Higgins, G. E., Ricketts, M. L., & Wolfe, S. E. (2014). Hacking in high school: Cybercrime perpetration by juveniles. *Deviant Behavior, 35*(7), 581–591.

Matza, D. (1964). *Delinquency and drift.* New York: John Wiley & Sons, Inc.

Miller, W. B. (1958). Lower class culture as a generating milieu of gang delinquency. *Journal of Social Issues, 14*(3), 5–19.

Mullins, C. W., Kauzlarich, D., & Rothe, D. (2004). The international criminal court and the control of state crime: Prospects and problems. *Critical Criminology, 12*, 285–308.

Newman, L.H. (2017, December 31). The worst hacks of 2017. *Wired*. Retrieved September 27, 2022 at www.wired.com/story/worst-hacks-2017/

NIST (U.S. National Institute of Standards and Technology). (2022). Secure Software Development Framework. Retrieved September 29, 2022 at https://csrc.nist.gov/Projects/ssdf

Payton, T. (2020). *Manipulated: Inside the cyberwar to hijack elections and distort the truth*. Lanham, MD: Rowman & Littlefield.

Pérez-Martínez, V., Marcos-Marcos, J., Cerdán-Torregrosa, A., Briones-Vozmediano, E., Sanz-Barbero, B., Davó-Blanes, M., Daoud, N., Edwards, C., Salazard, M., la Parra-Casado, C., & Vives-Cases, C. (2021, Online First). Positive masculinities and gender-based violence educational interventions among young people: A systematic review. *Trauma, Violence, & Abuse*. https://doi.org/10.1177/15248380211030242

Perlroth, N. (2021). *This is how they tell me the world ends: The cyberweapons arms race*. New York: Bloomsbury Publishing.

Raymen, T., & Kuldova, T.O. (2020). Clarifying ultra-realism: A response to Wood et al. *Continental Thought & Theory: A Journal of Intellectual Freedom, 3*(2): 242–263.

Reagle, J. (2017). Naïve meritocracy and the meanings of myth. *Ada*, (11). Retrieved September 22, 2017 from http://adanewmedia.org/2017/05/issue11-reagle/

Rid, T. (2013). *Cyber war will not take place*. Cambridge, MA: Oxford University Press.

Rorty, R. (1998a). *Achieving our country: Leftist thought in twentieth century America*. Cambridge, MA: Harvard University Press.

Salter, A., & Blodgett, B. (2017). *Toxic geek masculinity in media: Sexism, trolling, and identity policing*. London: Palgrave Macmillan.

Schell, B. H., & Holt, T. J. (2010). A profile of the demographics, psychological predispositions, and social/behavioral patterns of computer hacker insiders and outsiders. In T. J. Holt & B. H. Schell (eds.) *Corporate hacking and technology-driven crime: Social dynamics and implications* (pp. 190–213). Hershey, PA: IGI Global.

Schell, B. H., & Melnychuk, J. (2010). Female and male hacker conference attendees: Their autism-spectrum quotient (AQ)

scores and self-reported adulthood experiences. In T. J. Holt & B. H. Schell (eds.) *Corporate hacking and technology-driven crime: Social dynamics and implications* (pp. 144–168). Hershey, PA: IGI Global.

Seymour, R. (2020). *The twittering machine.* Brooklyn, NY: Verso.

Skibell, R. (2002). The myth of the computer hacker. *Information, Communication, and Society, 5*, 336–356.

Skibell, R. (2003). Cybercrime and misdemeanors: A reevaluation of the Computer Fraud and Abuse Act. *Berkeley Technology Law Journal, 18*, 909–944.

Smith, B. (2017, February 14). The need for a Digital Geneva Convention. *Microsoft.* Retrieved September 22, 2022 at https://blogs.microsoft.com/on-the-issues/2017/02/14/need-digital-geneva-convention/#sm.0001hkfw5aob5evwum620jqwsabzv

Söderberg, J. (2008). *Hacking capitalism: The free and open source software movement.* New York: Routledge.

Steinmetz, K. F. (2016). *Hacked: A radical approach to hacker culture and crime.* New York: NYU Press.

Steinmetz, K. F., Holt, T. J., & Holt, K. M. (2020). Decoding the binary: Reconsidering the hacker subculture through a gendered lens. *Deviant Behavior, 41*(8), 936–948.

Tanczer, L. (2015). Hacking the label: Hactivism, race, and gender. *Ada: A Journal of Gender, New Media, & Technology*, (6). Accessed January 26, 2022 at https://adanewmedia.org/2015/01/issue6-tanczer/

Taylor, P. A. (1999). *Hackers: Crime in the digital sublime.* New York: Routledge.

Thomas, D. (2002). *Hacker culture.* Minneapolis, MN: University of Minnesota Press.

Tunnell, K. (1995). Silence of the left: Reflections on critical criminology and criminologists. *Social Justice, 22*(1), 89–101.

Turkle, S. (1984). *The second self.* New York: Simon & Schuster.

Wall, D. S. (2008). Cybercrime, media, and insecurity: The shaping of public perceptions of cybercrime. *International Review of Law, Computers, and Technology, 22*, 45–63.

Wheeler, T. (2018, September 12). In cyberwar, there are no rules: Why the world desperately needs digital Geneva Conventions. *Foreign Policy.* Retrieved September 22, 2022 at https://foreignpolicy.com/2018/09/12/in-cyberwar-there-are-no-rules-cybersecurity-war-defense/

Whitty, M. T., & Buchanan, T. (2016). The online dating romance scam: The psychological impact on victims–Both financial and non-financial. *Criminology & Criminal Justice* 16(2), 176–194.

Williams, J. E. (1984). Secondary victimization: Confronting public attitudes about rape. *Victimology, 9*(1), 66–81.

Wood, M. A., Anderson, B., & Richards, I. (2020). Breaking down the pseudo-pacification process: Eight critiques of ultra-realist crime causation theory. *British Journal of Criminology, 60*, 642–661.

Wood, M. A., Anderson, B., & Richards, I. (2021). Notes on ultra-realism: A response to Raymen and Kuldova. *Continental Thought & Theory, 3*(2), 158–177. http://dx.doi.org/10.26021/10688

Yar, M. (2005). Computer hacking: Just another case of juvenile delinquency? *The Howard Journal of Criminal Justice, 44*(4), 387–399.

Yar, M. (2014). *The cultural imaginary of the internet.* New York: Palgrave Macmillan.

Yar, M., & Steinmetz, K. F. (2019). *Cybercrime & Society* (3rd ed.). Thousand Oaks, CA: Sage.

Zand, E. van 't, Matthijsse, S., Fischer, T., & Wagen, W. van der. (2021). Interventions for cyber offenders. In J. J. Oerlemans & M. W. Kranenbarg (eds.) *Essentials in cybercrime: A criminological overview for education and practice* (pp. 255–283). The Hague, The Netherlands: Eleven.

Zetter, K. (2014a). *Countdown to zero day: Stuxnet and the launch of the world's first digital weapon.* New York: Crown Publishers.

Zetter, K. (2014b, December 23) The year's worst hacks, from Sony to celebrity nude pics. *Wired*. Retrieved January 11, 2018 at: www.wired.com/2014/12/top-hacks-2014/

Zetter, K. (2016, March 3). Inside the cunning, unprecedented hack of Ukraine's power grid. *Wired*. Retrieved September 26, 2022 at www.wired.com/2016/03/inside-cunning-unprecedented-hack-ukraines-power-grid/

Zuboff, S. (2019). *The age of surveillance capitalism: The fight for a human future at the new frontier of power.* New York: Public Affairs.

# 9

# WHERE DO WE GO FROM HERE?

A problem with many books on criminological theory and method is that they violate the Cardinal Rule of Writing: "show, don't tell." The ideas contained therein might be compelling, but there is not much by way of a blueprint for implementation. I have often wondered "so how do I go about doing this?" after reading such works (maybe that says more about my intellect than anything else). In these pages, I have done my best to give a relatively clear roadmap for *doing* realist criminology research on computer crime issues. It isn't perfect, of course. There are many times where definitive answers are not provided and I am left gesturing toward possibilities. As research is advanced using the parameters advanced throughout, however, my hope is that a more cohesive realist criminology of computer crimes emerges. In sum, such a realist criminology involves:

- A pragmatic approach to inquiry, one attuned to power and context.
- A broad view toward the kinds of harms considered fair game for consideration—one primarily concerned with

DOI: 10.4324/9781003277996-11

damages of varying kinds against everyday folks, the natural environment, and other entities subject to the unjust exercise of power.

- A view toward space that decouples the concept from terrestrial geography and considers the multifaceted ways that spaces can form, propagate, interact, fragment, and disappear altogether online.
- The tracing of connections between the various actors involved in crime, victimization, and crime control—a network-based approach to the "social relations of crime."
- A consideration of many elements of power and structure—class, race, gender, sexuality, etc.—without giving one analytic primacy *a priori*.
- The pursuit of short-term changes guided by a plan to achieve long-term objectives.
- The embrace of imaginative approaches to social science which take a "big picture" perspective toward crime, victimization, and control issues.

Such a program is rather simple but that should not be a detraction. Simple gives us something to get our fingers around. Complicated things are prone to failure. And there is a distinction between simple and rudimentary. I hope that any shortcomings in this work inspire others to build a better mousetrap.

Related, an objective of this book was to provide criminologists a philosophical and methodological platform for theoretical synthesis and innovation. To their credit, there have been significant advancements offered by contemporary realist criminologists. Ultra-realism's concepts of "undertakers," "special liberty," and "pseudo-pacification," for instance, are novel and do much to reinvigorate a Marxist or Marxist-adjacent understanding of crime and other predatory behaviors (Hall, 2012; Hall

& Winlow, 2015). Yet, there is room to grow by building bridges between realist criminology and other critical criminologies—even those which realist criminologists have previously chided as "liberal" or otherwise not sufficiently radical enough (Winlow & Hall, 2019). Of course, such criticisms offered by realist criminologists are not without merit. For instance, while I had previously critiqued realist criminologies of the past for insisting that class be central to all analyses, other critical criminologies err by eschewing the concepts of class or the utility offered by Marxist analyses (Hall & Winlow, 2007; Lynch, 2015; Matthews, 2014; Winlow & Hall, 2019). I am not trying to advance a kind of "both-sides-ism" (though perhaps I can fairly be accused of doing so). Rather, my contention is that we should earnestly grapple with nuance, complexity, and ambiguity in our research and theorizing. There may be cases—many, in fact—where the political economy is a primary driver of a given crime or control problem. But it would be a mistake to assume so in all cases, all the time. It would also be a mistake to neglect such factors. As Young (1998, p. 33) once explained,

> the causes of crime cannot conceivably be of a blanket nature; that is, all crime cannot be caused by poverty, unemployment or market individualism, and so on. Conversely, to say that all crime is not caused by poverty is not to eliminate poverty as a cause of some crime.

To this end, realist criminologists should consider absorbing the best points from other critical criminological perspectives, especially cultural criminology, as originally suggested in Chapter 4. When I began writing this book, I did not originally set out to argue for a synthesis between realist criminology and cultural criminology. Yet, in the process of advancing a realist criminology of computer crimes, I have come to see significant potential in such a marriage. For the uninitiated, cultural criminology is "an orientation designed especially for critically engagement with the politics of meaning surrounding crime and crime control, and for critical intervention into those politics" (Ferrell, 2013, p. 258). To grossly oversimplify, cultural criminology examines meaning as an intermediary between structure and agency, which informs and is informed by action, reaction, interpretation, and reinterpretation. It is chiefly, though not exclusively, interested in media, subculture, popular culture, experience, control, and resistance as objects of study. For cultural criminologists, "cultural forces… are those threads of collective meaning and understanding that wind around the everyday troubles of social actors, animating the situations and circumstances in which their troubles play out" (Ferrell, Hayward, & Young, 2015, p. 3). The perspective is chiefly concerned with the undulations of meaning in the context of "late modernity" or "a globalized world always in flux, awash in marginality and exclusion, but also in the ambiguous potential for creativity, transcendence, transgression and recuperation" (ibid, p. 9).

Hall and Winlow (2007, p. 83) once accused cultural criminology of retreating into "the less than intellectually taxing realm of subjectivist-culturalism" and romanticizing crime as a form of resistance. Their withering critique mirrored those made by the original left realists against left idealism so long ago. Ferrell (2007, p. 92), one of the architects of cultural criminology, responded that the "materialist analysis of capitalism" was "no longer sufficient." Instead, cultural criminology embraces a "fuller analysis of power, domination, and crime" (ibid). He elaborates that

I moved beyond Marxist materialism because *it wasn't sufficiently radical;* it wasn't equipped to get at the root of the problem, to provide a ruthless and thoroughgoing critique, to conceptualize crime in relation to the many complexities of structured inequality and injustice.

*(ibid)*

There is a pragmatic thread in Ferrell's defense of cultural criminology—a wariness of a dogmatic intellectual approach which demands that answers be reduced to those readily supplied under a Marxist or neo-Marxist framework. Obviously, such approaches have been indispensable in the development of both realist and cultural criminology. But this is not without its limitations. I will continue to bang this drum: Critical criminologists (realist criminologists included) should be open to the possibility that there are situations in which a Marxist approach is insufficient. Though cultural criminology is perhaps best considered a "loose federation of outlaw intellectual critiques" rather than a complete theoretical approach (Ferrell, 2007, p. 99), one of its pronounced strengths is its willingness to incorporate diverse perspectives and ideas—a fundamentally *pragmatic* characteristic.

Despite such disagreements, some scholars have suggested that the two may be brought together fruitfully. For instance, Mooney (2022) explains that prior to his death, Jock Young "was returning to a more left realist position: he expressed unease with how little contemporary criminology, including cultural criminology, evidence commitment to a notion of praxis and the concerns of ordinary working people." He argued, for instance, that "there is much that cultural criminology and realism can learn from each other" and that "both fit together like pieces of a jigsaw puzzle: one depicts the form of social interaction that we call crime, while the second breathes human life into it" (Young, 2013, pp. xxxiv, xxxxvi). Matthews (2014a), for his part, similarly gestured toward the possibility of synthesis and reconciliation in his work titled "Cultural Realism?," though he argued that there exist conflicts and contradictions which would need to be addressed first.

My intent is not to detail such a "cultural realism" here. Instead, I argue for the need for such theoretical synthesis given the utility offered by cultural criminology for a realist criminology of the internet. Unlike realist criminologists of the past, cultural criminologists have earnestly grappled with the new media, telecommunications, and computer network technologies (e.g. Ferrell, Hayward, & Young, 2015; Hallsworth & Kaspersson, 2017; Hayward, 2012; Hayward & Maas, 2021; Yar, 2018). This is a criminology which considers how "political economies of contemporary culture regularly set meaning in motion and, at least initially, set the terms and parameters of its movement" and "emerging technologies invent new channels through which mediated perceptions can move or be confronted" (Ferrell, Hayward, & Young, 2015, p. 154). In Chapter 5, I argued that criminologists interested in taking computer crimes seriously must address how online criminal opportunities manifest, the social relations of crime form, the way that technologies generate and shape online spaces, and the variegated ways that harms can manifest through and around computer technologies. These are questions that cultural criminology—with its emphasis on mediation and meaning—can help answer. It is precisely for these reasons that perspectives like "digital criminology"—an approach centers the role of digital technologies in the shaping of crime and control—incorporate insights from cultural criminology (Powell, Stratton, & Cameron, 2018).[1]

Perhaps most importantly, I hope that this book invigorates imaginative research into the study of computer crimes and fosters innovation in technological harm reduction. Compared to other areas of criminology, there are relatively few theoretical advancements in the study of "cybercrime" apart from the aforementioned—and, unfortunately, relatively marginal—digital criminology. This is not to say that there are not intelligent and earnest folks working in the area—far from it. I have many dear friends and colleagues doing outstanding research and policy work. My complaint is chiefly one of unrealized potential stemming from a relative paucity of historically situated, structurally aware, and politically minded work informed by robust theory and philosophy. As previously noted, much of the work is largely descriptive or couched in humdrum "mainstream" criminological theories. When innovation is sought, it is largely in the realm of computational data gathering and analytic methods and seldom in conceptual and theoretical domains.

In short, my ambition is that computer crimes research will give up its engineering envy and, instead, embrace its potential as a social science to become a criminology that is analytical, rigorous, willing to make value commitments, and honest about those ethical subscriptions. Such work is earnest, unafraid of politics, willing to take big swings (and sometimes fail), and committed to solving major social problems. The alternative is not only useless in achieving the kinds of major social changes necessary to address the harms of computer crime—or crime more generally—but it is also rather boring. And that is a problem academically, professionally, and personally. Jock Young once stated that,

> When you get to certain points in your life, you get into your head that you're not going to bore yourself. You haven't got an interminable amount of time. There's a very strong feeling on my part that I don't want to spend hours doing things I don't want to do. So trying to bring zest back into your work is important.
>
> *(quoted in Ferrell & Hayward, 2014, p. 187)*

In this spirit, we should avoid doing work that doesn't interest us or, more importantly, doesn't challenge anyone or anything.

Sometimes boring is good, however. Life is boring and if we are interested in describing and explaining the social world, then our work will occasionally be boring. Further, boredom can be a catalyst for change. It "creates opportunities for our imaginations to come alive and propels us toward other experiential possibilities" (Steinmetz, Schaefer, & Green, 2017, p. 344). Rather than eschew boring work entirely, perhaps a better mantra for the study of computer crimes, or criminology in general, is "avoid *bullshit*." In *Bullshit Jobs: A Theory,* David Graeber (2018) describes the proliferation of jobs under capitalism that don't seem to do much of anything including a litany of white-collar, professional work (if you have seen shows like *The Office*, then you have an idea; see: Wisecrack, 2019). Similarly, I would argue that scholarship which never reaches beyond the superficial, fails to escape the descriptive, or treads familiar turf with no new insights constitutes "bullshit research." I fear that a lot of criminology, especially work in the realm of computer crime, veers into such territory. This work elevates itself through the perceived novelty of its subject matter rather than the novelty of its ideas. If we want to escape such academic manure, it is vital that we turn our attention to the "big picture" and set forth a plan to shape social policy and transform institutions.

### Note

1  The reader may wonder why this book is not couched as a form of "digital criminology." While I think digital criminology is a significant advancement for the field, I am uncomfortable with the degree to which it elevates the role of digital technologies in the criminological enterprise. My read

is that digital criminology seeks to draw our attention to the role of the digital—which is all well and good. My objective is to update existing forms of criminology to better grapple with the digital while also still being capable of tackling the non-digital realms (as much as that distinction is possible anymore in our increasingly digital world). In addition—and I'd be happy to be proven otherwise—the perspective does not grapple much with solutions to crime.

## References

Ferrell, J. (2007). For a ruthless cultural criticism of everything existing. *Crime Media Culture, 3*(1), 91–100.

Ferrell, J. (2013). Cultural criminology and the politics of meaning. *Critical Criminology, 21,* 257–271.

Ferrell, J., & Hayward, K. J. (2014). Never boring: Jock Young as cultural criminologist. *Crime Media Culture, 10*(3), 179–190.

Ferrell, J., Hayward, K., & Young, J. (2015). *Cultural criminology: An invitation* (2nd ed.). Thousand Oaks, CA: Sage.

Graeber, D. (2018). *Bullshit jobs: A theory.* New York: Simon & Schuster.

Hall, S. (2012). *Theorizing crime and deviance: A new perspective.* Thousand Oaks, CA: Sage.

Hall, S., & Winlow, S. (2007). Cultural criminology and primitive accumulation: A formal introduction for two strangers who should really become more intimate. *Crime Media Culture, 3*(1), 82–90.

Hall, S., & Winlow, S. (2015). *Revitalizing criminological theory: Towards a new ultra-realism.* New York: Routledge.

Hallsworth, S., & Kaspersson, M. (2017). Punitivity and technology. In M. R. McGuire & T. J. Holt (eds.) *The Routledge handbook of technology, crime and justice* (pp. 565–576). New York: Routledge.

Hayward, K. J. (2012). Five spaces of cultural criminology. *British Journal of Criminology, 52*(3), 441–462.

Hayward, K. J., & Maas, M. M. (2021). Artificial intelligence and crime: A primer for criminologists. *Crime Media Culture, 17*(2), 209–233.

Lynch, M. J. (2015). The classlessness state of criminology and why criminology without class is rather meaningless. *Crime, Law and Social Change, 63*, 65–90.

Matthews, R. (2014a). Cultural realism? *Crime Media Culture, 10*(3), 203–214.

Mooney, J. (2022). Left Realism: "Taking crime seriously." In H. N. Pontell (ed.) *Oxford encyclopedia of criminology and criminal justice.* https://doi.org/10.1093/acrefore/978019 0264079.013.671

Powell, A., Stratton, G., & Cameron, R. (2018). *Digital criminology: Crime and justice in digital society.* New York: Routledge.

Steinmetz, K. F., Schaefer, B. P., & Green, E. L. W. (2017). Anything but boring: A cultural criminological exploration of boredom. *Theoretical Criminology, 21*(3), 342–360.

Winlow, S., & Hall, S. (2019). Shock and awe: On progressive minimalism and retreatism, and the new ultra-realism. *Critical Criminology, 27*, 21–36.

Wisecrack. (2019). The Office: How nonsense conquered the workplace—Wisecrack Edition. YouTube. Retrieved October 28, 2022 at www.youtube.com/watch?v=VHDZwAQ7Plk

Yar, M. (2018). Toward a cultural criminology of the internet. In K. F. Steinmetz & M. R. Nobles (eds.) *Technocrime and criminological theory* (pp. 116–132). New York: Routledge.

Young, J. (1998). Breaking windows: Situating the new criminology. In P. Walton & J. Young (eds.) *The new criminology revisited* (pp. 14–46). New York: Palgrave.

Young, J. (2013). Introduction to the 40th anniversary edition. In I. Taylor, P. Palton, & J. Young (authors.) *The new criminology: For a social theory of deviance—40th anniversary edition* (pp. xi–li). New York: Routledge.

# INDEX

*Note*: Endnotes are indicated by the page number followed by 'n' and the endnote number e.g., 20n1 refers to endnote 1 on page 20.

Printed in the United States
by Baker & Taylor Publisher Services